the series on school reform

Patricia A. Wasley
Bank Street College of Education

Ann Lieberman
NCREST

Joseph P. McDonald
New York University

SERIES EDITORS

This series also incorporates earlier titles in the Professional Development and Practice Series

D0594853

Taking Charge of Curriculum

TEACHER NETWORKS AND CURRICULUM IMPLEMENTATION

Jacob E. Adams, Jr.

FOREWORD BY ANN LIEBERMAN

Teachers College, Columbia University
New York and London

\

LB2806.15
.A35
2000

Published by Teachers College Press, 1234 Amsterdam Avenue, New York, NY 10027

Library of Congress Cataloging-in-Publication Data

Adams, Jacob E.
    Taking charge of curriculum : teacher networks and curriculum implementation / Jacob E. Adams, Jr. ; foreword by Ann Lieberman.
        p.   cm. — (The series on school reform)
    Includes bibliographical references and index.
    ISBN 0-8077-3949-9 (cloth : alk. paper) — ISBN 0-8077-3948-0 (pbk. : alk. paper)
        1. Curriculum planning—United States.   2. Curriculum change—United States.
    3. Teachers—Social networks—United States.   I. Title.   II. Series.
    LB2806.15 .A35   2000
    375'.001'0973—dc21   00-021191

ISBN 0-8077-3948-0 (paper)
ISBN 0-8077-3949-9 (cloth)

Printed on acid-free paper
Manufactured in the United States of America

07   06   05   04   03   02   01   00   8   7   6   5   4   3   2   1

For Leslie Witherspoon Adams
who gracefully traveled this road with me

Contents

Foreword

ALTHOUGH THERE ARE MANY books and studies on the subject of school reform, we still know very little about how to organize, support, and implement new curricular reforms in classrooms. As states across the country issue all kinds of mandates to improve schools by changing classroom practice to raise student achievement, the mandates themselves often serve to hide the complexities of classroom practice that must be understood before new content can be successfully introduced and new teaching strategies can actually be implemented in the classroom. The problems of translating policies into workable practices, organizing opportunities for teachers to make the necessary adaptations in their classroom contexts, and the necessity for and organization of long-term support at the district level all become part of the implementation puzzle. These problems are exacerbated when the curricular innovations involve strategies such as "problem solving" and "project-oriented" and "cooperative" learning, which require teachers to change the way they enact their role. Since these strategies call for students to participate more fully in the development of content, more is asked of teachers than to be solely the deliverers of content.

This understanding is central to the story intelligently told by Jacob Adams in his description of California's attempt to introduce a radical change in the teaching of mathematics—a change supported by the National Council of the Teachers of Mathematics, as well as by the state's department of education. No ordinary study, it is a fascinating story of twelve teachers whose experiences, made known to us through Adams's careful scrutiny, demonstrate how teachers' practices help mold policy and, even more important, what it takes to provide for and facilitate teacher learning within a professional network.

We learn again that implementation is a process that must have time to play itself out. We learn how teacher knowledge grows over time, as teachers try out new strategies, adapt them to their classrooms, and eventually make them part of their everyday practice. We also learn why networks appear to provide the kind of support, flexibility, multiple sources of information, and development of collegiality that are important to the successful implementation of new curricula.

This important book engages us in many of the crucial educational issues of our day. Readers will find themselves asking, What is the relationship between policy and practice, and how does it get played out over time? How do teacher professional networks provide important alternatives to traditional staff development strategies? What are the connections among state, district, school, and teachers' classrooms, and what forms do they take when curriculum implementation is the goal?

This is a thoughtful and accessible book for those who seek to understand how policies—for better or worse—are shaped by the practices of teachers. Issues of implementation will continue to be inescapable and to dominate the process of school improvement. How well we come to understand these issues will in great measure determine the success—or failure—of future curricular and school reforms.

Ann Lieberman

Acknowledgments

THIS STUDY NEVER WOULD have progressed without cooperation from the numerous state and organization officials, school district administrators, principals, department chairs, and teachers whose voices and experiences grounded this research in the educational policies and practices of the time. These busy individuals accommodated my requests for interviews and information by sharing resources, welcoming me into classrooms and network meetings, forfeiting prep periods and lunch breaks, arriving early or leaving late. Their stories animate this research; their candor imbues the narrative with ever more interest and usefulness. I readily, happily acknowledge my debt of gratitude to them all.

Colleagues, too, assisted along the way, criticizing arguments and drafts, structuring work environments conducive to analysis and writing, affirming the research, even introducing me to the notion of networks and their unexplored potential. In this regard, my thanks go to William Clune, David Cordray, Michael Kirst, Milbrey McLaughlin, Allan Odden, Marshall Smith, and three anonymous reviewers at Teachers College Press.

Special appreciation is due Joseph Murphy, who first saw the utility in publishing this research as a book and whose encouragement was instrumental in bringing the project to fruition.

While I gratefully acknowledge the contributions of these individuals to this work, I also assume responsibility for the final product.

Introduction

EDUCATIONAL REFORMS THAT REACH into classrooms require that teachers change their beliefs, knowledge, or practices. Without such a direct effect on teachers, classroom reforms are unlikely to influence what is taught or how it is taught. At the classroom level, therefore, assuming the validity of any particular change, the crux of educational reform involves teacher learning and adaptation.

Developments in mathematics education during the 1980s and 1990s illustrate how teacher learning and adaptation are fundamental to curriculum reform. During this period, teachers witnessed the advent of constructivist learning theory, pathbreaking professional standards, and new curriculum frameworks. In combination, these developments essentially recreated the mathematics classroom. Pushing aside common attributes of traditional classrooms such as their basic skills focus, scripted curriculum, reliance on textbooks, testing, individual work, and didactic teaching, constructivist norms instead shift instruction toward large concepts, students' interests and questions, primary sources, manipulatives, performance assessments, group work, and coaching. The philosophical shift embodied in these changes affects core assumptions about learning and teaching. Namely, that transmission of many facts does not constitute knowledge; and that knowledge results instead when students assimilate new facts, experiences, or ideas into what they already understand. Learning, therefore, requires engagement on the part of students, asking questions, posing and solving problems. Good teaching shepherds rather than dictates students' interests, helping students make connections, draw conclusions, find meaning. In the lingo of the times, students must be "active learners" with teachers behaving in "interactive ways," facilitating students' explorations, mediating their learning opportunities (see Brooks & Brooks, 1993). Implementing these educational reforms requires teachers to acquire new knowledge about subject matter, change materials, reorganize classrooms, adopt new instructional roles, even change their relationships with students, none of which can occur without substantial learning and adaptation.

How do teachers adapt to such change? How do they learn what is implied by the changes, what is expected, or what to do? School systems and teacher organizations share responsibility for developing teacher competencies. Both entities rely primarily on "staff development." The purpose of staff development is to ensure that teachers have the subject-matter knowledge and instructional skills required to teach the content of a state's curriculum framework (Smith & O'Day, 1991). However, professional training often falls short of this objective. Observers routinely characterize staff development practices as "unconnected to classroom life, . . . often a mélange of abstract ideas that pays little attention to the ongoing support of continuous learning and changed practices" (Lieberman, 1995, p. 592). In other words, staff development often fails to foster the professional capacities needed to support emerging educational reforms and improved practice. Given the limited utility of typical professional development activities, what kinds of experiences help teachers negotiate the shifts in expectations, knowledge, and practice that arise from consequential school reform?

This book examines a professional structure of growing interest and potential importance to teachers' learning and practice: the teacher professional network. The research explores the role of a network in helping teachers implement a novel and challenging high school mathematics curriculum. Implementation practices and beliefs among network teachers are contrasted with the experiences of nonnetwork teachers who also were engaged in implementing this curriculum. The volume thus provides a classroom-level perspective on curriculum policy, curriculum implementation, and ways different professional support strategies facilitate teachers' learning and practice.

In examining the structure and operation of network and nonnetwork implementation strategies, the book also compares their influence on two key factors that govern teachers' learning and implementation efforts: motivation and capacity. The research demonstrates how the network enabled teachers to better manage the context in which they work, garnering time, information, and other resources within a structure that enhanced collaboration and personal efficacy, allowing a professionally negotiated, hence common, vision of practice.

Finally, drawing lessons from the implementation experiences of these network teachers, the book explains the potential of teacher networks to enhance teachers' collaboration and skills, to negotiate more uniform implementation results, and to build linkages between policy and practice. Discussion and analysis are drawn from case studies of Math A implementation in 12 California classrooms (in three school districts) representing network, support-group, and traditional staff development implementation strategies. The book begins with the demands of policy on practice. It ends with a practice-based model for professional development and educational policy implementation. At base here is the issue of support for teachers' learning, implementation, and school improvement.

The three parts of the book introduce readers to teacher networks and the challenge of curriculum implementation; examine up close, often in teachers' own words, curriculum implementation in California classrooms; and explain implementation differences between network and other classrooms.

Chapter 1 reviews the conceptual basis of teacher networks. It examines teachers' implementation needs and the shortcomings of traditional professional development activities to serve these needs. The chapter defines teacher networks and predicts their implementation utility in terms of structuring collaboration that helps teachers interpret new curriculum and by providing a context that builds professional capacity.

Chapter 2 discusses evolving mathematics policy and early implementation challenges. The analysis covers criticisms of U.S. mathematics education and California's move to address recognized shortcomings through a new state mathematics framework. A new course, Math A, is introduced, which challenges teachers' thinking and practice. Early implementation is symbolic, incremental, or bargained, demonstrating how Math A can mean different things in different places, even across classrooms within a single district. The resulting state question asks how to achieve more uniform policy outcomes that reflect the state's challenging curriculum goals. The local question involves how usefully to adapt policy prescriptions to local contexts, goals, and needs. The chapter concludes with analysts' suggestions that teacher networks hold promise for mediating the relationship between policy and practice.

The task of converting Math A policy to practice falls to classroom teachers. Chapter 3 portrays the classroom-level implementation experiences of 12 teachers: four in the network, four relying on a periodic support group, and four utilizing typical staff development supports. The narrative recounts their experiences with Math A and knowledge of the curriculum. It examines teachers' adaptations of state curriculum materials, their organization of Math A instruction, their changing role in the classroom, and their emerging commitment to Math A practice. The chapter contrasts patterns of Math A implementation across network, support-group, and staff development classrooms.

In Chapter 4 readers see how the motivation of classroom teachers to implement Math A undergirds the transformation of policy into practice. I examine a range of factors that influence teachers' responses to Math A, including conflict or alignment between personal and policy goals;

teachers' evaluations of Math A in practice; reactions of parents and other professionals; and supports or constraints proffered by districts, schools, and academic departments. The network's advantage becomes apparent through its organization of external resources and reinforcing activities.

As motivation establishes a foundation for implementation, capacity provides the wherewithal to erect the structure. Accordingly, Chapter 5 examines the structure and operation of the network, staff development, and support-group implementation strategies used by teachers in this study, assessing the strengths and weaknesses of each in regard to building teachers' capacities that foster implementation. The analysis merges attention to the network's structural components—common preparation period, cross-school meetings, intensive summer training, a "linker" (a person who bridges network and external resources), and informal interactions—with its functional dimensions, including promoting collaboration, focusing teachers' interactions around academic content and pedagogy, creating reciprocal relationships, and facilitating frequent interactions and professional interdependencies.

The final chapter uses the comparisons of network and nonnetwork classrooms to define the implementation potential of teacher networks. The chapter explores the central role of teachers' learning in implementation, learning that is required by implementation's novel demands, broad scope of change, ongoing process, constructed knowledge, need for motivation, and dependence on classroom teachers. The network's contribution to implementation is defined in five propositions regarding the role of teacher networks in facilitating teachers' professional development and classroom change. The chapter closes with policy implications focusing on the utility of teacher networks for policy implementation, curriculum development, and teachers' professional development.

PART I

Teacher Networks, Math Policy, and the Implementation Challenge

CHAPTER 1

Educational Change and Teacher Networks

> What teachers do and the institutional context within which they do it sets
> primary conditions for the limits and possibilities of reform.
> —Richard F. Elmore and Milbrey Wallin McLaughlin, *Steady Work*

BEGINNING IN THE EARLY 1980s and continuing unabated into the twenty-first century, U.S. policy makers have routinely sought improvements in America's schools. With widespread public support, state legislatures and courts nationwide have mandated changes in educational finance, governance, and curriculum that span the gamut of elementary and secondary school operations.

During this reform period, policy initiatives have appeared in discrete phases. Early on, reformers attempted to raise academic standards simply by intensifying educational practices already in place, such as lengthening school days and increasing graduation requirements. Subsequent reforms restructured school organization and governance in order to empower teachers to work more effectively with students. By the mid-1990s, school improvement strategies shifted again, crafting goals and incentives for better student achievement through performance-based accountability systems (Murphy & Adams, 1998). As these policies evolved, reform innovations pushed closer toward the core processes of schooling: teaching and learning.

Mathematics reforms of the 1980s and 1990s represent the most far-reaching and complicated of the policy and professional innovations to result from this period of intense educational scrutiny and transformation. Shifting from behavioral to constructivist learning theory, changing teachers' role from expert to guide, and transforming curriculum from facts and skills to concepts and projects, mathematics reforms posed substantial challenges for math teachers, recasting their professional roles, work environments, and relationships with students (see Fennema & Nelson, 1997; National Council of Teachers of Mathematics, 1989, 1991; National Research Council, 1989). While many policy makers and educators facilitated this transition, targeting what Lynn Beck and Joseph Murphy (1996) termed "the learning imperative," the track record of educational policy tempered informed observers' expectations. That history indicates that "improvements" of this kind seldom develop the practical effect that transforms educational practice or student learning. More often than not, reforms targeted at classrooms have failed to change what is taught or how it is taught. In Larry Cuban's (1993) words, "the overall mortality rate for classroom reforms is high" (p. 4). In fact, educational reforms frequently fall short of their objectives, especially when changes are attempted across levels of government (Cuban, 1993; Elmore & McLaughlin, 1988; Fullan, 1992; McLaughlin, 1998; Sarason, 1990). When policies fail, they are likely to do so during implementation. Why? As one analyst concluded, the overarching lesson from empirical research on policy implementation is that "it is incredibly hard to make something happen" (McLaughlin, 1987).

THE UNCERTAINTY OF EDUCATIONAL CHANGE

Policy implementation implies change; it requires that individuals learn and do something new. Thirty years of research on educational change and policy implementation testifies that meaningful change is no small feat. Michael Fullan (1992) captured the problem, writing that

> the crux of change involves the development of meaning in relation to a new idea, programme, reform or set of activities. But it is *individuals* who have to develop new meaning. . . . [Therefore,] successful school improvement . . . depends on an understanding of the problem of change at the level of practice and the development of corresponding strategies for bringing about beneficial reforms. (pp. 26–27)

What can reformers and others understand about the problem of educational change? Research has demonstrated at least eight important lessons. For instance, change is complex, uncertain, and ambiguous. It evolves over time, requiring participants to learn from experience, and its outcomes are hard to predict (David, 1993; Firestone & Corbett, 1988; Fullan & Miles, 1992; Hall & Hord, 1987).

Change is multidimensional. In the case of curriculum implementation, teachers simultaneously must manage alterations in materials, teaching strategies, and classroom organization. Their practice must reflect new learning theories, instructional roles, and relationships with students. They must expand their knowledge of subject matter (Fullan, 1991; Fullan & Pomfret, 1977; Snyder, Bolin, & Zumwalt, 1992).

Change is messy and trying. Early implementation particularly can be rough, with teachers running through cycles of trial and error, complaining about the difficulty of day-to-day coping, sacrificing other core activities, and feeling frustrated by unsuccessful attempts to make something work (Huberman & Miles, 1984). In the wake of Kentucky's nationally prominent systemic school reform, Kentucky teachers explained the frustrations of large-scale change in terms of "flying the airplane while trying to rebuild it" (see Adams, 1997).

Change is stymied by multiple barriers. In their investigation of early attempts at systemic school reform, Jane David and Paul Goren (1993) identified five such barriers: lack of clear direction, weak incentives to change, a regulatory and compliance mentality, limited learning opportunities, and poor communications. In regard to learning opportunities, teachers' change efforts suffered from little content knowledge, infrequent collaboration, no time to practice, and poor professional development. Barriers such as these impeded reform progress.

Change is shaped by local context. Characteristics of communities, districts, schools, departments, and students condition the success or failure of change efforts. Moreover, with local context so prominent in change processes, adaptations of policy are bound to occur, and thus variation in outputs across localities should be anticipated (Jones, 1997; McLaughlin, 1987).

Within local contexts, change depends primarily on the responses of classroom teachers. As they are the conduit of reform, teachers must change before reform develops any practical effect. The stages of concern that teachers experience (from basic awareness to exploring effects) and the different levels of use they exhibit (from simple awareness to full use and evaluation) further reinforce the personal nature of change: Success depends on each individual making his or her own meaning in response to change (Fullan, 1991; Hall & Hord, 1987).

For individuals, change is a function of motivation and capacity; that is, teachers change to the extent that they are motivated to change and have the capacity to change. Implementation reduces to a combination of pressure and support, creating individual-level incentives that focus attention and direct effort, and ensuring the capacity needed to carry out new roles and responsibilities (David, 1993; Elmore & McLaughlin, 1988; Fullan, 1992; McLaughlin, 1987). At base, the nature of individual-level responses determines the extent of policy implementation.

Because individual-level capacity undergirds change efforts, change progresses or falters on the basis of ongoing assistance to implementers. With learning preeminent, assistance becomes the sine qua non of change. In Michael Huberman's and Matthew Miles's (1984) experience, "large-scale, change-bearing innovations lived or died by the amount and quality of assistance that their users received once the change process was underway" (p. 273).

In sum, the landscape of educational change leads one to conclude that, at the level of practice, the problem of change is as complicated and uncertain as it can be. When the innovation that policy makers prescribe fundamentally alters curriculum and instruction, change encroaches upon the subjects and materials teachers ply and the means they use to succeed.

What changes in curriculum change? Implementation of new curriculum is a classroom phenomenon driven by teacher learning. Decker Walker (1990) captured the centrality of the classroom in curricular matters, admonishing readers that "until curriculum comes to life in a classroom, it remains only a plan, and unless it reaches the students there, it makes no difference in what they learn" (p. 225). Yet, classrooms are crowded, complex, norm-driven social settings. How is one to make sense of the variety of roles, activities, and influences that bear upon teachers as they "deliver" a curriculum, particularly a new curriculum, to the students in their charge? How is one to organize and make sense of information compiled through research, or to link new constructs, such as teacher professional networks, to this setting? And how is one to affect the attitudes and capacities of teachers that determine their classroom behavior?

Following theoretical trends in mathematics education, one useful way to conceptualize classroom-level curriculum implementation is to adopt the perspective of curriculum as a social construction (Fosnot, 1996; Goodson, 1990). In short, this perspective holds that curriculum is negotiated at the multiple levels of policy and practice. For central governments, like states, curriculum policy making is a political activity dependent on broad community values and carried out by multiple actors (Kirst & Walker, 1971; Walker, 1990). Once codified in state policy, curriculum nevertheless remains fluid as it travels from state to district to school to department to classroom and across classrooms. For teachers, using curriculum is a professional activity dependent on time, motivation, materials, capacity, and expectations, and carried out in concert with 30 adolescents (Walker, 1990). Thus, the curriculum that students confront is finally "constructed" from facilitating and constraining factors found in and around classrooms. Within these multiple policy levels, expertise resides with professionals, although control is shared between policy makers and teachers. The former establish conditions of practice as the latter work within the confines of those conditions to craft learning opportunities for students.

Readers have already seen that curriculum implementation encompasses changes in materials, classroom organization, roles and behaviors, subject knowledge, and expectations. Like other educational changes, curriculum implementation is a dynamic process that is neither automatic nor certain (Snyder, Bolin, & Zumwalt, 1992). It is driven by the needs of teachers to develop new content knowledge and skills and characterized by the mutual adaptation that signals active problem solving in the midst of change. If, as Milbrey McLaughlin argued, what matters most to policy implementation is local capacity and will, and if policy cannot mandate these things that matter most, then implementation must rely on other mechanisms to address teachers' needs to learn, practice, and evaluate the potential of change.

TEACHER NEEDS AND IMPLEMENTATION

Organizationally and professionally, individual teachers have the ability and opportunity to shape policy during implementation. One reasonably can argue that individuals then must be the target of interventions designed to facilitate change in classrooms, that institutions cannot change until the individuals within them change (Elmore & McLaughlin, 1988; McLaughlin & Oberman, 1996). By extension, implementation research also must focus on these individuals.

Factors Supporting Teacher Change

If change depends on teachers, then what do teachers depend on to change? Lampert (1988) summarized conditions under which classroom change most likely will occur. For example, teachers tend to change their practice

> when they can observe new practices being used in actual classroom situations . . . when they can try them out and get feedback on their attempts . . . when they can discuss new techniques with peers . . . and when they can smoothly integrate the new behavior or new technology into their existing classroom routines. (p. 158)

Change is likely to occur also when teachers' concerns about practice are addressed (Hall & Loucks, 1978), when teachers collaborate in identifying problems and finding solutions (McLaughlin & Marsh, 1978), and when collaboration is adequate to produce shared understanding and investment. Change is likely when teachers have a sense of efficacy about their work (Berman & McLaughlin, 1978), when the focus is curriculum and instruction, when time is sufficient to ensure gains in knowledge and skill, and when "norms of collegiality" prevail (Little, 1984). In the latter case, teachers frequently talk about their work, observe one another, and plan and evaluate curricula together with administrators (Lampert, 1988). Unfortunately, these conditions do not characterize many schools (Little, 1990a). As Little (1990b) concluded, "felt interdependencies in teaching are few. . . . Teacher collaboration is largely 'voluntaristic' and generally peripheral to the main work of the organization" (p. 520).

Reliance on Inadequate Professional Development

Because learning is central to educational change, and because professional development comprises the typical format through which teachers are expected to learn, professional development becomes a pivotal component in curriculum implementation and school change. Yet typical professional development offerings fall short of this responsibility. "Simply put, most forms of in-service training are not designed to provide the ongoing, interactive, cumulative learning necessary to develop new conceptions, skills, and behavior" (Fullan, 1991, p. 85). A gap exists between what we know about promoting classroom-level change and what we do to facilitate it. Evidence of this gap appears in four illustrative assessments of teachers' professional development practices.

Corcoran (1990), for example, reported that teachers do not view their professional development opportunities as particularly useful. In recounting results of a National Education Association survey, Corcoran found that teachers regard personal experience and contact with other teachers as their most effective sources of additional knowledge. In contrast, inservice training ranked last; only 12% of teacher respondents considered this training to be effective.

Little's (1990a) analysis of the conditions of professional development in secondary schools suggested reasons why inservice offerings received low marks from teachers. She found that teachers' motivations and opportunities for professional development are linked to fundamental conditions of teaching in secondary schools, including multiple and sometimes conflicting goals, teacher–student relationships, the nature and consequences of teacher interactions, and the significance of departmental structures and subject-matter affiliation. However, these conditions are more likely to erode teacher motivation than to bolster it and are more likely to constrain teachers' opportunities to learn than to enrich them. This complexity in teachers' working conditions requires a greater range of support than the intellectual content found in typical inservice training.

Moreover, most staff development is organized outside the school day and is independent of specific teaching assignments; learning, thus, is hindered by work load, time, and teaching responsibilities; and staff development offerings typically are either content- or pedagogy-free and thus offer small benefit. Little (1990a) concluded:

> At best, only a small proportion of secondary teachers encounter a form of professional development that places a premium on the close study of subject matter, is respectful of the teacher's own knowledge and circumstances, and relies on teachers as colleagues. At the same time, the organization of the salaried workday militates against studied reflection of practice, mutual support among colleagues, or the exercise of leadership by those who have arguably earned the right to do so. (pp. 215–216)

In the same manner, Smith and O'Day (1991) discussed teacher inservice opportunities as severely limited in scope and duration. They argued that "only rarely are [school or district inservice experiences] of sufficient depth and scope to give teachers the experience necessary to make major changes in their approach to instruction" (p. 242). Problems include content that bears little relationship to school curricula and/or lack of depth and time. Conventional professional development programs, they concluded, "show few positive and lasting results" (p. 242).

In contrast, Smith and O'Day pointed to National Science Foundation summer institutes, the (San Francisco) Bay Area Writing Project, and teachers' centers as examples of inservice experiences that positively influence teacher knowledge and pedagogy. Unlike most staff development offerings, these experiences often are focused on content that is relevant to teachers' work assignments and are of sufficient length to be powerful interventions.

McLaughlin (1991), similarly, linked the efficacy of professional development experiences to ongoing assistance, collegial structures, concrete training with follow-through, administrative support, norms of professional growth, nurturing structures of communication, and a central role for teachers. This view of inservice professional development highlights the

> conditional, mutually reinforcing, and contextual nature of factors that support professional development. It underscores the embedded nature of the education system and how policies at one level—state, district, or school—can enable (or constrain) the efforts of actors at the next. (McLaughlin, 1991, p. 79)

Both these positive and negative assessments lead to the same conclusion: ensuring that teachers have the subject knowledge and instructional skills required to teach the content of a state's curriculum framework involves ongoing contact among teachers, a greater range of support for teachers, links to teaching assignments, time during the school day, a mix of content and pedagogy, depth, sensitivity to teaching contexts, and a central or controlling role for teachers.

In terms of the curriculum implementation problem addressed in this book, these characteristics of teachers' professional development foster the individual-level motivation and capacity needed to enhance implementation. Unfortunately, such opportunities are rare (National Commission on Teaching and America's Future, 1996), and limited learning opportunities for teachers militate against policy implementation and positive school change (David & Goren, 1993).

LINKING POLICY AND PRACTICE THROUGH TEACHER NETWORKS

According to a California state official, in 1991—6 years beyond adoption of the state mathematics framework that underlies the research in this book—the biggest implementation problems included basic issues such as lack of course knowledge and understanding among practitioners, lack of district commitments to attempt implementation, lack of district support for teacher release time and staff development training, and inappropriate assignment of students to the course. The state viewed these problems as typical of any curriculum change. This view assumes that greater familiarity with a new curriculum alone may lead to deeper implementation. As the state official noted:

> It is not hard to sell the idea that you want to do something that will make the kids more mathematically powerful and make them be able to contribute in our society. It's not a hard idea to sell, especially for those kids who are high risk and dropouts. I mean, who would not want to do that?

Good ideas notwithstanding, curriculum implementation has to be viewed as problematic. Policy has a poor record of changing practice. The failure of policy generically to effect change came long ago to be regarded almost as common wisdom (Ingram & Mann, 1980; Wildavsky, 1979).

On the other hand, researchers have come to understand that policy can effect change (Fuhrman, Clune, & Elmore, 1988; Kirst & Jung, 1980; Odden, 1991; Peterson, Rabe, & Wong, 1986, for example). The efficacy of policy as change agent derives, in part, from characteristics of the policy itself and of the process that shaped it, such as clarity of purpose, scope of change, level of conflict, specification of appropriate causal theory, and symbolic versus material intent (Fullan, 1991; Winter, 1990). It depends also on local capacity and will. On balance, policy can change practice, but change is difficult and complicated, neither automatic nor fully predictable. Change depends on both the art and craft of policy making (Wildavsky, 1979) and on the response of local implementers (Berman & McLaughlin, 1978).

Even at the local level, however, educators respond to and affect reform initiatives differently. The political incentives and concerns of school boards and superintendents differ from the administrative concerns of principals, which differ again from the practical concerns of teachers (Elmore & McLaughlin, 1988). Policy and administration establish the conditions under which teachers work but cannot control teachers' behavior. Curriculum implementation responsibility devolves to individual teachers, what McLaughlin (1990a) called the smallest unit.

Although analysts have come to recognize the importance of individual teachers to policy implementation, our models of implementation do not yet fully reflect the concrete realities of classroom practice. Early implementation analyses, for example, assumed relatively direct connections between policy inputs, local responses, and outcomes. This "missing input" model of education policy ignored attributes of the local policy system in predicting implementation outcomes (McLaughlin, 1990a). Subsequently, policy research shifted to address important local factors (Berman & McLaughlin, 1978; Fullan, 1991, for example). Policies came to be defined as individuals throughout the system interpreted and acted on them (McLaughlin, 1987). Change depended finally on the individual at the end of the line, the so-called "street-level bureaucrat" (Weatherley & Lipsky, 1977), and these individuals were embedded in a local policy system. Bargaining and adaptation became a dominant model of implementation (Ingram, 1977). Implementation perspective shifted to individual motivation and capacity (McLaughlin, 1987, 1990a).

Still, our conception of what fosters individual motivation and capacity is too narrow. Milbrey McLaughlin and Allan Odden, in separate analyses, suggested that an "embedded structure" of major importance to teachers may not be the policy system but rather teacher professional networks (McLaughlin, 1990a; Odden, 1991). Odden argued, in fact, that networks not only connect teachers to each other but also enable teachers to shape state policy and to structure related supports and technology before their formal adoption. He asserted that, subsequently, these teachers play key roles in school districts as policy implementers.

If this is the case, then examining the operation of teacher professional networks within the context of local policy structures may expand our model of policy implementation and our understanding of possible connections between policy and practice. Where before we saw only a complex local system mediate between state policy and practice, now, through professional networks, we may see a direct connection between state policy and practice that operates independently of the local policy system yet influences the local system's response to state initiatives. In other words, teacher networks may enhance educational policy implementation by grounding it in professional norms and practice. To the extent this occurs, professional networks would promote systemic school reform by coordinating control over the components of instructional guidance: curriculum, pedagogy, teacher professional development, and assessment.

Accordingly, this book explores whether and how a teacher professional network affected the classroom implementation of a novel mathematics curriculum, Math A, in California. The analysis here defines and examines the implementation impact of these networks. This perspective is consistent with the view of implementation as driven by individual motivation and capacity. At this point, however, teacher professional networks are relatively unexamined, as is their influence on policy implementation. Understanding the operation of teacher networks would be interesting in itself. Asserting their influence on implementation expands our model of the educational policy process.

WHAT WE KNOW ABOUT TEACHER NETWORKS

Teacher networks are a form of professional community. Characteristics of professional communities include a commitment to serving clients through the application of specialized knowledge, shared norms and values regarding practice, collaborative learning, coordinated practice, deprivatized practice (for the purpose of observing and critiquing others' work and for socializing junior members), and collective control over important decisions affecting their service, including who may practice and the boundaries of that practice (Cooper, 1988; Louis, Marks, & Kruse, 1996; Secada & Adajian, 1997). Professional communities thus provide a context within which members come to "understand their practices, professional growth, and development" (Secada & Adajian, 1997, p. 193).

Teachers' professional community can be distinguished from other such communities insofar as its technical knowledge and norms of behavior focus on teaching and student learning. Thus, a professional community of teachers will exhibit coordinated efforts to improve student learning, reflective dialogue about curriculum and instruction, collective control over a school's curriculum, collaboration that promotes common understandings of practice, and peer coaching, team teaching, and class-room observations to develop individuals' specific practice (Louis, Marks, & Kruse, 1996; Secada & Adajian, 1997).

This basic conception teachers' professional community suits an exploration of teacher networks, enabling one to place network interactions within a larger context of professional discourse and service to students. Logically, the stronger and broader one's professional community, the more support one will find for improving practice, including, when useful, assimilating new theories, materials, and behaviors into practice. However, as Lieberman and Grolnick (1998) observed, "teachers have not yet developed a tradition of sharing their own expertise among themselves. Networks play a major role in providing opportunities for teachers to validate both teacher knowledge and teacher inquiry" (p. 723). Teacher networks are a form of professional community that structures teacher collaboration around immediate and general issues of practice. The second and third parts of this book examine the operations and contributions of one such teacher network. Before that specific examination occurs, however, it would be useful to sketch a conceptual model of networks in general and teacher networks specifically. Thus equipped, readers may be able to better assess the operations and contributions of the network they will soon meet.

The Network Concept

Conceptually, a network is a set of points or nodes connected by lines. The lines serve as communication channels, conveying messages, services, or sentiments, with exchanges intended to further the network's purpose. Not all pairs of nodes need to be connected directly, and nodes and connections can change over time. Network structures vary in terms of the density of their connections. A typical structure is one in which some actors are more extensively connected among themselves than are others (Knoke & Kuklinski, 1982).

Networks are built upon informal exchanges and reciprocal relationships. The informality places network activities outside or alongside formal arrangements for making transactions; the reciprocity contrasts with one-way, superior–subordinate, expert–learner communications (Huberman, 1982). These two basic traits enable characteristic network functions. For example, networks provide a common language, serve as alternatives to established systems, show relationships between individuals and organizations, provide members with a shared purpose and commitment, link micro and macro social structures, provide a mixture of information sharing and support, mobilize and exchange resources, restrict or facilitate access, and build cohesion in systems (Huberman, 1982; Scherer, 1981).

The work of networks is facilitated by the trust engendered among its members (Cohen, 1993; Hering, 1983; Peterson, 1977; Scherer, 1981). Trust encourages, even allows, reflection and risk taking; it is a component of influence because it "enhances credibility and gives legitimacy to persons, actions or perspectives" (Scherer, 1981, p. 3).

Several design features have been associated with effective networks. These features include an explicit purpose, fluid and responsive composition, and informal organization (with linkages built among those one knows, respects, and trusts; or among those perceived as influential, knowledgeable, and supportive). They also include cooperative and self-managing members, distributed leadership, links with external constituencies, activities designed to build expertise, and empowerment of those with task expertise (Cohen, 1993).

In practice, networks comprise persons, groups, or organizations (the nodes) that exchange valued commodities, such as information, labor, knowledge, opinion, influence, power, and affect. Networks may be formally constituted or informal, transorganizational or internal to a single organization, visible to all members or so dispersed that the extent of participation is not wholly understood by any one member. Networks may operate with one center, many centers, or no center (Freeman, 1989; Miles, 1978).

Furthermore, a network is defined not simply because of an association among individuals but by the types of relations that characterize their linkage. That is, individuals associate in different ways. The context of their association determines the character of the network they represent at any moment, drawing distinctions between, for example, social, kinship, collegial, authority, or communications networks (Knoke & Kuklinski, 1982; Paulson, 1985).

In this regard, teachers' professional relationships rest upon their orientation toward their work (Little, 1990b). What is this work? It entails managing groups, establishing routines, maintaining records, dealing with individual needs and responses, evaluating student abilities, and promoting learning (Feiman-Nemser & Floden, 1985)—in other words, the fundamentals of classroom interactions. However, teachers have not developed a tradition of sharing expertise among themselves (Lieberman & Grolnick, 1998). Instead, individualism, presentism, conservatism, and egalitarianism predominantly characterize teachers' orientations toward this work (Little, 1990b). The phrase "teachers have peers but no colleagues" captures the prevailing norm of noninteraction. Clearly, norms of noninteraction or noninterference inhibit shared problem solving (Feiman-Nemser & Floden, 1985).

In fact, teacher professional relations cover a range of interactions. Little (1990b) differentiated professional ties among teachers based on the relatively weak or strong influence these professional ties exerted on teachers' practice or commitments. Her typology extends from the relatively weak interaction of "storytelling and scanning for ideas" to the relatively strong interaction of "joint work." Joint work, or collaboration, anticipates truly collective action. Little (1990b) described this work as "shared responsibility for the work of teaching (interdependence), collective conceptions of autonomy, support for teachers' initiative and leadership with regard to professional practice, and group affiliations grounded in professional work" (p. 519). In such a situation, the intellectual, social, and emotional demands of teaching supply the motivation to collaborate (Little, 1990b).

Teacher Networks Defined

With the foregoing characteristics of networks as foundation, a definition can be tendered. A teacher professional network consists of the linkages and voluntary, reciprocal interactions among teachers, their colleagues, and professional referents that are instrumental in shaping teachers' beliefs, knowledge, and practice. These linkages may extend only within schools or they may span schools, districts, levels of government, and professional organizations. This definition distinguishes teachers' professional networks from their social or friendship networks. In short, teacher professional networks enable teachers to share or acquire the professional expertise that strengthens service to students.

Nascent Knowledge of Teacher Networks

Research on teacher networks is relatively new, appearing prominently only in the 1990s. In general terms, networks positively affect teachers' motivation and capacity (Johnson, 1990; Lieberman & Grolnick, 1996, 1998; Lieberman & McLaughlin, 1992; Little, 1990b; Rosenholtz, 1989, for example). Therefore, teacher professional networks may succeed in promoting teachers' learning and classroom change where typical staff development supports have failed.

Lieberman and McLaughlin (1992) characterized networks as powerful and problematic, situating networks' potential in their focused activity, varied opportunities for collegiality and professional growth, affirmation of teacher knowledge, and leadership development. Similarly, Lieberman and Grolnick (1996) described networks as "a way of engaging school-based educators in directing their own learning, allowing them to sidestep the limitations of institutional roles, hierarchies and geographic locations, and encouraging them to work together with many different kinds of people" (p. 4). Their study of 16 teacher networks identified themes and tensions associated with network formation and development, defining networks' contributions in terms of shared knowledge, flexible organization, location of adult learning in challenging involvement and problem solving, leadership development, and authentic professional community built around shared work.

Examples of network influence foreshadow their larger potential. Crandall, Bauchner, Loucks, and Schmidt (1982), for example, documented how a school-based network, keyed to an external facilitator, succeeded in working jointly to carry out school improvement projects and to implement innovations with "reasonable fidelity." The Bay Area Math Project fostered change by building a supportive community of mathematics educators, linking teachers through summer institutes, follow-up events, mini-grants, reunion weeks, and connections to other math-based professional organizations (Giganti, 1991). The Foxfire Teachers Outreach Network and the Puget Sound Educational Consortium encouraged and organized teachers' learning through shared activities and action research projects (Lieberman & McLaughlin, 1992). The Ford Foundation-sponsored Urban Mathematics Collaboratives fostered subject-matter networks that reduced teacher isolation and nurtured a greater sense of professionalism among participants (Wisconsin Center for Education Research, 1992). The Southern Maine Partnership linked university professors and school practitioners through "dine and discuss" events that grew into regional support groups for school restructuring efforts (Lieberman & Grolnick, 1996).

In short, researchers and practitioners are recognizing the influence of networks on teachers and teaching. Researchers now must broaden this nascent knowledge, chronicling ways in which networks operate and examining the relationship between network operations and aspects of teachers' professional development, professional community, and practice. Curriculum implementation presents an interesting focus for network studies because of its central place in teachers' craft and because of potential conflicts and congruence between state and local perspectives on curriculum implementation.

WHY NETWORKS MAY BE IMPORTANT

Conceptually, networks should influence curriculum implementation by structuring communications that help teachers interpret curriculum policy and by providing a context that builds professional capacity.

Communication and Collaboration

Networks are nested within a convergence model of communication (Rogers & Kincaid, 1981). Convergence views communication between individuals as a process of change in which information is shared in order to achieve a common purpose, like mutual understanding or collective action. That is, the interpretations and experiences of the individuals communicating must converge in order to promote mutual understanding. This model contrasts with linear or transmission theories of communication. It assumes that language is vague and that a "message"—statement or policy directive, for instance—may require further signals or experience to delimit its meaning. The imprecision of language and variety of experience, together, create the possibility for alternative meanings or "mixed signals." In network terms, participants act as reference points for one another. Their relationships affect each individual's perceptions, beliefs, and actions (Knoke & Kuklinski, 1982; Peterson, 1977). As a result, when persons come into repeated contact with one another, they come to share orientations (Eulau & Siegel, 1981).

In this sense, network theory is similar to group theory. As long ago as 1951, Truman asserted that group experiences and associations are the primary means by which individuals know, interpret, and react to their social context. Group experiences produce uniform behaviors and attitudes in individuals, which then cause these individuals to be accepted by the group. Frequency of interactions gives groups their "molding and guiding powers."

In this sense, also, network theory is similar to a candidate theory of implementation proposed by Goggin, Bowman, Lester, and O'Toole (1990). Their communications model of intergovernmental policy implementation rests on the assumption that implementers must interpret a barrage of policy messages. Their interpretations depend on the form and content of the message, legitimacy and reputation of the sender, and inducements and constraints in the system. A single implementation message, therefore, may be interpreted differently in different locations. Interpretation (or meaning making), then, becomes a function of local context (see McLaughlin & Talbert, 1990), and the most important characteristic of context with regard to teacher change is that it is interactively constructed (Jones, 1997). "There is ample evidence to show that individuals' learning is facilitated by others, that meaning is often socially constructed, that tools serve as mediators, and that social systems as organic entities can engage in learning as much as individuals do" (Salomon & Perkins, 1998, p. 16). To the extent that networks promote communication, they overcome teachers' isolation and individual work to clarify meaning and enhance practice.

Isolation is a fundamental social reality of teaching (Bird & Little, 1986; Johnson, 1990; Lieberman & Miller, 1991; Little, 1990b; Lortie, 1975; Rosenholtz, 1989). In the absence of professional dialogue, teachers have little opportunity to develop common goals and means to attain them (Rosenholtz & Kyle, 1984). Worse still, isolation erodes teachers' sense of efficacy, success, and self-worth (Bird & Little, 1986; McLaughlin, Pfeifer, Swanson-Owens, & Yee, 1986; Rosenholtz, 1989), factors strongly related to successful implementation.

Collaboration addresses teachers' personal needs (social interaction, reassurance), pedagogical needs (advice, subject-matter expertise), and organizational needs (coordinating students' learning, maintaining standards, initiating and sustaining change) (Johnson, 1990; see also Nias, 1998). And although it requires substantial effort to achieve, collaboration has been shown to result in "widespread implementation of new practices, renewed professional commitment among experienced teachers, enduring habits of professional development in participating schools, and changes in the routine organization of school life" (Little, 1984, p. 85). Particularly in reference to curriculum changes, Odden and Busch (1998) reported how teachers created and improved curriculum units over time as a result of collaboration around instructional program issues. More generally, McLaughlin and Yee (1988) concluded that colleagues "provide both the stimulation central to opportunity and the feedback and comment that enhance individual capacity and power" (p. 35). Echoing this sentiment, Nias (1998) argued that "collegial talk" is such an essential aspect of professional learning that it cannot be left to chance. Collegial talk possesses a motivating character all its own.

> Teachers' main motivation and reward for involvement with one another will be found in the work of teaching. This is not to say that teachers do not have other motives for seeking one another out, but to argue that they are unlikely to sustain a pattern of significant out-of-classroom involvement in the absence of interdependent work-related interests. To the extent that teachers find themselves truly dependent on one another to manage the tasks and reap the rewards of teaching, joint participation will be worth the investment of time and other resources. To the extent that teachers' success and satisfaction can be achieved independently, the motivations to participate are weakened. (Little, 1990b, p. 523)

Against this backdrop, networks can be said to harness the potential of productive, professional interdependence.

Context and Professional Discretion

Teachers are important to implementation, and their implementation role encompasses more than the simple, mechanical adherence to curriculum policy prescriptions. In fact, the contexts and tasks of instruction suggest a central role for teachers in shaping the curriculum that students experience.

The implementation context includes substantial leeway for teachers to exercise professional judgments regarding the classroom configuration of curriculum. The ambiguity stemming from the policy adoption process itself, as a result of bargaining and compromise (Elmore, 1978; Ingram, 1977), conveys upon implementers the discretion to interpret and shape policy further as it is translated into practice (Baier, March, & Sætren, 1988). Teachers' "street-level" accommodations and coping mechanisms (Lipsky, 1980) may significantly alter the curriculum that students experience. As teachers routinize procedures, modify goals, ration services, assert priorities, and limit or control clientele, they define the practical effect of curriculum policy. In fact, loose implementation linkages across levels of government and between governmental decrees and classroom activities enable implementers to operate in what one analyst described as "idiosyncratic, frustratingly unpredictable, if not downright resistant ways" (McLaughlin, 1987, p. 172).

The contexts of teaching similarly afford teachers opportunities to shape policy variously in the course of their daily work. These contexts include subject matter, department and school organization and culture, professional associations, community education values, and policy (McLaughlin & Talbert, 1990). They influence the nature and quality of practice by affecting teachers' dispositions toward their work: their motivation, conception of task, enthusiasm over subject matter, and sense of efficacy (McLaughlin & Talbert, 1990).

The tasks of instruction, too, rely on teachers' capacities and spontaneous judgments. When new curriculum fundamentally alters teachers' subject knowledge, beliefs about student learning, activities, and instructional strategies, implementation becomes a process of reconstructing practice.

> At a minimum teachers must revise their plans to include the changes in content, purpose, or form, and revise their class activities to realize these changes in plans. They may also need to reconsider their conception of the subject, the student, teaching, education, or society and to reconcile new ideas and values with familiar ones. They may need to learn new teaching skills and strategies. The more difficult and extensive the changes demanded of teachers, the more difficult it will be to implement that curriculum change in the classroom. (Walker, 1990, p. 251)

Furthermore, curriculum policy is merely a point of departure. In large measure, students and teachers implicitly negotiate what content is covered and how it is transformed in its presentation (Sizer, 1984).

Teacher–student interaction is a two-way process in which each influences the other (Brophy & Evertson, 1981). Students "influence the pacing, the standards of mastery, the emphasis, and even the coverage of all their courses. By giving or withholding their cooperation, students can, in effect, bargain with teachers over the terms of their work in the classroom" (Walker, 1990, p. 238).

This teacher–student bargaining surfaced as a theme in Metz's (1993) research in eight midwestern schools. A majority of teachers she interviewed confirmed that they changed what or how they taught in order to get students to cooperate. Teachers lessened their demands for academic work, time on task, or conformity in return for students' cooperation. In addition, teachers look primarily to students, rather than their colleagues, for feedback (Lieberman & Miller, 1991). Schools go so far as to "frame their common enterprise" differently in relation to the students they serve. Hence, student characteristics—skills, family expectations, academic goals, motivations, and the like—significantly define a school's goals and affect the context of teaching (McLaughlin, 1993). This attribute of classroom life led McLaughlin (1998) to declare that students constitute the context of greatest significance for teachers. Given that the diversity of student abilities, idiosyncratic nature of their motivations, and variety of strategies needed to facilitate student learning cannot be preprogrammed in policy, teachers must adjust content and pedagogy in response to students' reactions, motivations, and abilities. In short, the wise exercise of discretion requires a foundation of professional capacity.

Networks, then, may develop teacher professional competencies that foster implementation. They do this by providing ongoing opportunities for teachers to enhance their understanding of an innovation, experiment with its technology, and receive feedback from peers and other trusted sources. These opportunities parallel those central to the development of a teacher's career. McLaughlin and Yee (1988) described a teacher's "level of opportunity" as "the chance to develop basic competence; the availability of stimulation, challenge, and feedback about performance; and the support for efforts to try new things and acquire new skills" (p. 26). These opportunities extend beyond staff development programs to include conferences, mentoring relationships, joint work, and observation of other teachers' classrooms, namely, the domain of teacher networks.

Bridging Policy and Practice

There is another reason why teacher networks may be important. From the perspective of policy system operations, teacher networks may bridge the gap between policy and practice. Researchers routinely conclude that many educational reforms aimed at classroom practice fall short of developers' expectations or public ambitions (Elmore & McLaughlin, 1988; Hanushek, 1994; Sarason, 1990, for example). Reforms falter, in part, because they fail to develop a practical effect in classrooms. Teachers reject them or are incapable of implementing them. Conversely, policy makers seldom provide needed classroom supports in their education prescriptions. Operating at opposite ends of states' responsibilities to provide efficient systems of education, policy and practice prove to be terribly misaligned.

In effect, policy and practice operate independently. Policy emanates from public demands and results in the authoritative allocation of values. It is a statement of goals (what society sets out to accomplish) and theory (regarding the relationship between a perceived problem and its proposed solution) as much as a program for action. In contrast, practice originates in the professional decisions of teachers, which are oriented to facilitating student learning (Darling-Hammond, 1985). The difference is substantial. The nature of problems, resources, and legitimacy is fundamentally different for policy and practice. Policy serves constituents and balances interests. Practice serves students (its clients) and brokers learning opportunities. Current models of policy implementation acknowledge the loose coupling of policy and practice, yet assume that they interact through the local policy system. When this interaction fails, both informed policy making and supported practice suffer. The investigation in this book looks beyond the formal policy system for professional channels able to carry and sustain innovation, that is, able to motivate teachers to change and to facilitate their capacity to change, assuming, of course, the validity of a particular innovation. At the level of policy system operations, therefore, teacher professional networks may bridge the gap between policy and practice, creating connections and information exchanges that serve both domains.

STUDYING NETWORKS AND CURRICULUM IMPLEMENTATION

How does one integrate professional networks into the constellation of school system factors that already influence policy and practice? Conceptually, with the addition of networks, one can view teachers as embedded within two systems: a local policy system, composed of district and school organizations, and a professional one. The professional system, operating as a teacher network, provides an alternative source of perceptions, beliefs, and actions for its members. Operationally, a range of network and policy system attributes can be identified that foster or impede implementation, or, alternatively, that facilitate or constrain practice.

Network Attributes

One of the primary provisions underlying professional collaboration is the existence of shared agreements among the collaborators: about the promise of a program, its roles and relationships, and its implementation (Little, 1984). The agreements are reached through the convergence of individuals' ideas and experiences.

> The uniqueness of an individual's personal network is responsible for the uniqueness of his meanings. In other words, the codes and concepts available to interpret information are based on each individual's past experiences which may be similar, but never identical, to another individual's. As an individual's pattern of interaction with others becomes similar (overlapping) to those of another individual's, so do their codes and concepts for interpreting and understanding reality. (Rogers & Kincaid, 1981, p. 45)

The focus of network analysis, therefore, shifts research from organizational or policy system structures and procedures to informal processes (Peterson, 1977). Key attributes of these informal processes include:

- how one gains *access* to the network, or the way nodes are connected (Lave & March, 1975; Peterson, 1977)
- the *content* that focuses network interactions, or the kind of material transmitted (Ford & Ford, 1987; Miles, 1978; Peterson, 1977)
- the *character of relationships* within a network, establishing reciprocity as the basis for trust and collaboration, with all parties acting as knowledgeable contributors (Little, 1984)
- the *frequency of interaction* (Huberman, 1982; Little, 1984; Little et al., 1987; Truman, 1951)
- the *strength* of the network, that is, the extent to which any network member has multiple types of relations with other actors in the network (Burt, 1982)

These relational measures capture properties of a social system that cannot be measured by simply aggregating the attributes of individuals (Knoke & Kuklinski, 1982), or by looking only at characteristics of a local policy system. In effect, the operational characteristics of networks provide researchers with a new window through which to view local change processes.

Determining Teachers' Implementation Behavior

The literature on education change (Fullan, 1991; Fullan & Miles, 1992, for example) asserts that school-level change involves learning, in the sense of finding new meaning. It results more from evolution than rational planning (due to the complexity of simultaneous demands placed upon a local school system). It is problem-laden (requiring constant problem solving) and resource-hungry (in terms of time, dollars, energy, and the like). It requires ongoing management attention and cooperative strategies (monitoring, informing, and problem solving; cross-role teams of teachers, department heads, administrators, and others; legitimacy; and system-wide cooperation). Change is also systemic, focusing on the interrelationships of school system components and on the system's culture (cf. Smith & O'Day, 1991). Finally, change is implemented locally, carried out by teachers, principals, parents, and students.

Notice how the characteristics of successful local change closely resemble the tasks and strategies of effective professional development: Learning, problem solving, ongoing effort, cooperation, coordination, and attention to context promote innovation for local school systems and for the individuals within them. Within this environment teachers are key actors in shaping policy outputs. They construct practice from facilitating and constraining factors found in and around their classrooms, including professional (network) and policy system attributes.

To conceptualize how teachers construct practice and promote (or do not promote) curriculum implementation, analysts need a systems view of individual-level implementation behavior. In this regard, Donald Ford's living systems theory (Ford & Ford, 1987) provides a useful template for understanding individual-level implementation behavior. The theory's applicability is evident in its use of the important implementation factors of will and skill (McLaughlin, 1987) and its utility in explaining, in Martin Ford's (1992) phrase, person-in-context functioning.

In this systems view of human competence development, (implementation) behavior becomes the product of an individual teacher's motivation, skill (or capacity), and environment (or context). Transactions between individuals and their environments stand at the core of the theory.

> People must establish priorities among their various goals and develop ways of relating their intentions to environmental constraints and demands across time and contexts. A person's behavior must be understood as a continually flowing stream of events that varies within boundaries both in terms of its organization and its relationships to a varying context. (Ford & Ford, 1987, p. 3)

Thus (implementation) behavior is constructed from a teacher's informational-behavioral transactions with his or her environment.

> Information is collected, sifted, organized, reorganized, used, and retained to organize, regulate, and control ongoing [implementation] behavior patterns. . . . Humans also use their information-based self-construction capabilities to construct, elaborate, maintain, operate, and revise a repertoire of behavior patterns for future use. (Ford & Ford, 1987, p. 11)

Specifically, motivation animates individuals' attention and activity. Capacity establishes the extent to which an individual can attend to, collect, and evaluate information; solve problems; formulate and adapt plans; and communicate. The environment offers resources and opportunities—material, information, social-emotional support, and opportunities to practice—but also demands and constraints. In the study of teacher networks, the network becomes part of a teacher's "environment" or working context. The study then explores whether and how a network enhances teachers' motivation and capacity to implement change.

Application of this conceptual lens to implementation research organizes the analysis of implementation around teacher motivation, capacity, and environmental transactions (context in action). *Motivation* refers to an individual's goals and evaluations of self and environment. *Capacity* is defined in terms of generic skills, such as problem solving, planning, and communicating, and in terms of specific skills required by a particular change. With curriculum changes, for example, the term *specific skills* refers to the subject-matter knowledge and teaching skills required by the curriculum. Motivation and capacity compose attributes internal to individual teachers, separated from (although surely influenced by) the environment. Student variables (achievement level, maturity, family background, and level of cooperation) and policy prescriptions compose part of the classroom environment that constrains or facilitates implementation. Policy system and network factors constitute environmental influences outside classrooms.

Figure 1.1 portrays this analytic framework. It views curriculum implementation as a function of individual teachers' motivations and capacities, which, in turn, are influenced by student reactions, policy prescriptions, local policy system factors, and network participation.

With this analytic framework as research template, several questions emerge that must be answered in the process of assessing the network's effect on Math A implementation. For instance, how does any particular network operate? Is curriculum implementation, and therefore practice, different in network and nonnetwork classrooms? What are teachers'

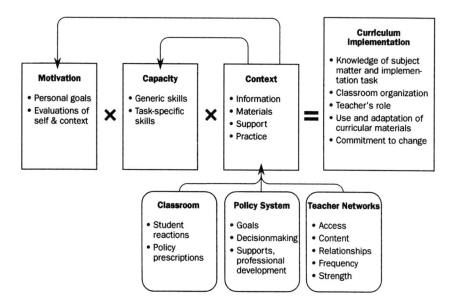

Figure 1.1. Analytic framework: Implementation as the product of motivation, capacity, and context. Arrows indicate input to and feedback from context.

instructional goals, and do these differ from curriculum policy goals? How do teachers assess curriculum, given their experience with it in the classroom? What implementation resources and opportunities, or demands and constraints, do teachers find in their environments that affect their implementation practices? Such questions explore whether and how teacher professional networks foster individual teachers' motivation and capacity to implement curriculum. They also lead researchers into classrooms, where they can see how teachers mediate the demands of policy on practice and how teacher networks may enhance policy, practice, and professional development.

CHAPTER 2

The Challenge of Implementing a State Mathematics Curriculum

> There is now a national consensus on the nature of instructional programs in mathematics that can achieve the goal of mathematical power for all students. Throughout the 1980s the vision was refined and many individual teachers began to shift what they do in their own classrooms. . . . To date, however, no large scale change is occurring in California schools or anywhere in the nation. . . . The understanding of what mathematics instruction must become is now clear enough to warrant decisive action throughout the state.
> —A 1985 California State Department of Education document

DURING THE 1980s, a spate of national, state, and professional commissions criticized the quality of mathematics education in U.S. high schools. The National Commission on Excellence in Education (1983), for example, cited declining Scholastic Aptitude (now Achievement) Test scores and increasing enrollment in remedial mathematics college courses. According to the commission's analysis, many 17-year-olds lacked the higher-order intellectual skills needed to solve mathematical problems requiring several steps. The National Science Board Commission on Precollege Education in Mathematics, Science, and Technology (National Science Board, 1983) stated flatly that schools were failing to provide children with "the intellectual tools needed for the 21st century" (p. v).

Results from the mathematics component of the National Assessment of Educational Progress (NAEP) corroborated these findings. NAEP assessments through 1990 indicated a low percentage of students attaining moderately high levels of math proficiency and a small and unchanging percentage of students learning advanced material (Mullis, Dossey, Foertsch, Jones, & Gentile, 1991). For instance, the math performance of 17-year-olds declined between 1973 and 1982. Between 1982 and 1990 performance among this age group recovered to approximately its 1973 level. In addition, only 56% of 17-year-olds in 1990 demonstrated proficiency in moderately complex procedures and reasoning (such as computing with decimals, fractions, and percentages; recognizing geometric figures; and solving simple equations). Only 6–7% demonstrated proficiency in multiple-step problem solving and algebra.

As analysts noted, NAEP findings through 1990 indicated that "a challenge still exists in reaching targets discussed in conjunction with reforms in school mathematics" (Mullis et al., 1991, p. 5). Other observers had earlier concluded that "although most students are successfully learning a number of mathematical skills, they exhibit serious gaps in their knowledge and are learning a number of concepts and skills at a superficial level" (Carpenter et al., 1988, p. 40).

Criticism from these reports was remarkably consistent. In short, mathematics education in U.S. high schools at the time often lacked rigorous academic content, focused on low-level skills, failed to match a vision of how mathematics training might fit into the emerging technological labor market, and produced poor achievement among its clientele.

Political and professional responses to shortcomings in U.S. mathematics education and related criticisms of public schooling[1] dominated state policy making throughout the 1980s. Observers characterized these policy responses variously. Joseph Murphy (1990), for example, highlighted how states evolved different *targets of reform,* which he described as (1) repairing components of the educational system, (2) restructuring the system, and (3) reconceptualizing education as part of a comprehensive children's services delivery system. Lorraine McDonnell and Richard Elmore (1987) stressed the *strategies and instruments of state educational reform,* such as mandates, inducements, capacity-building transfers of money, and system-changing transfers of authority. Reflecting on changes in mathematics education during this period, Thomas Romberg (1989) described three *levels of reform:* (1) a legislative-administrative approach, (2) a fix-add approach, and (3) a systemic approach. Each succeeding level encompassed and moved beyond its predecessor.

Level 1 reforms represented a change in goals—increasing graduation requirements and student performance expectations, for example—but did not challenge existing ideas about knowledge, work of students or teachers, technology, or professionalism. Elsewhere, Michael Kirst (1988) described such changes as an intensification strategy.

Level 2 reforms identified specific components of the system that needed to be fixed or added, such as curriculum frameworks, texts, tests, inservice training, and methods of credentialing. Reformers viewed change as incremental and the fix-add components as starting points. Most school mathematics reforms of the 1980s fell into this category (Romberg, 1989).

In contrast, Level 3 reforms sought to conform the entire mathematics education system to a comprehensive vision of a reformed school mathematics program, such as the visions contained in the widely cited reports, *Everybody Counts: A Report to the Nation on the Future of Mathematics Education* (National Research Council, 1989) and *Curriculum and Evaluation Standards for School Mathematics* (National Council of Teachers of Mathematics, 1989). These notions of reform emphasized mathematical literacy, problem solving, reasoning and communicating, valuing mathematics, and becoming confident in one's ability to handle mathematics (Romberg, 1988). Learning would take place within exploratory, investigative learning environments where teachers and students would make full use of calculator and computer technology (Romberg, 1989). At this level, the process of change would constitute a professional development strategy. Systemic reforms such as these would empower teachers and other educators through their professional organizations to improve mathematics education (Romberg, 1989).

Similarly, Smith and O'Day (1991) argued that a state-driven, systemic reform strategy, encompassing both the vision of Romberg's Level 3 and the system-wide focus of Level 2, is necessary both to generalize successful local improvements and to structure the changes in content and pedagogy implied by an emphasis on higher-order thinking skills. Systemic school reform requires a common vision of reform; a coherent system of instructional guidance, meaning coordination among state curriculum frameworks, school curriculum, and teacher training and certification; and state assessments redesigned to test the skills and competencies included in the new curriculum frameworks.

STATE MATH POLICY AS SYSTEMIC SCHOOL REFORM

After 1983, California's overall mathematics improvement strategy evolved to reflect Smith & O'Day's notion of systemic reform. Initially, legislators mandated statewide graduation requirements,[2] including 2 years of mathematics, and launched a school-level accountability program, including state and local targets for performance on "quality indicators." Policy makers tinkered with components of the existing education system—length of the school day and year, amount of homework, "tougher" discipline policies—in an attempt to ratchet up system expectations and to improve performance. They launched experiments with "mentor teachers" and new teacher certification mechanisms in order to improve the quality and to enhance the motivation of the state's teacher corps.

Subsequently, the State Board of Education initiated a multiple-year curriculum reform process, developing model curriculum standards, revising state curriculum frameworks, adopting new standards for texts, revamping state achievement tests, strengthening teacher preparation and development, and enhancing school-site and district leadership (Honig, 1988). Reformers viewed curriculum changes as a long-term effort to gain leverage over content and instruction, the central features of learning (Honig, 1985, 1988). Alignment among these elements promised to generate substantial pressure on districts and schools to comply with state standards and, thus, to reflect a vision of what students should know and be able to do (Honig, 1988).

Math A: New Policy, New Course

In the mid-1980s, California introduced a new high school course called "Math A." It originated in the 1985 California mathematics framework (California State Department of Education, 1985), the first in a series of new state curriculum frameworks promulgated in the aftermath of the state's omnibus education reform legislation, Senate Bill 813.[3]

Math A was designed as the first step in a course sequence for entering freshmen who were not ready for a college preparatory program but who were ready to learn content beyond the K–8 curriculum (California State Department of Education, 1985). In effect, Math A reconceptualized the content and pedagogy of mathematics education. It attempted to move students away from memorization and paper-and-pencil computations toward an emphasis on problem solving, reasoning, and communicating (California State Department of Education, n.d.). It integrated standard topics such as measurement, geometry, and algebra, and encompassed novel topics such as logic and probability.

Characteristics of Math A instruction included "active lessons," where teachers circulate among groups working on projects, and "cohesive units," where a cluster of ideas appears repeatedly in different ways. A "high-intensity curriculum" taught a few ideas in-depth rather than many ideas superficially; work was student generated via projects and open-ended investigations; and assessments varied, including reports, projects, journals, presentations, outlines of lessons, and summary paragraphs. In addition, Math A utilized cooperative learning, algebraic tiles and other manipulatives, calculators, reading and writing, and situational lessons (Stanley, 1989). Teachers were to rely less on direct instruction and more on coaching, leading discussions, and exploring alternative solutions (Cohen & Peterson, 1990).

The state intended Math A as a pathway into college-prep algebra. In practice, school districts used Math A variously to replace remediation math, general math, and pre-algebra, and even to eliminate tracking; for example, requiring all freshmen to take Math A as they entered high school, regardless of their future career or academic plans.

In short, Math A demanded considerable change in the way teachers conceived and presented mathematics content to students. It reflected the integrative, problem-solving approaches contained in prominent national reports (for example, National Council of Teachers of Mathematics, 1989; National Research Council, 1989; National Science Board, 1983). It codified in state curriculum policy professional assessments regarding the way technological changes and information uses altered both mathematics and its applications. As Romberg (1988) concluded:

> Knowledge was seen as objective, teaching as transmission and control, and learning as absorption. . . . Today our society needs individuals who can continue to learn and adapt to changing circumstances and produce new knowledge. Knowledge [in this new context] is seen as constructive, teaching as guiding, and learning as occurring through active participation. (p. 9)

Math A reflected much of what Smith and O'Day (1991) regarded as systemic reform. The policy expressed a coherent direction for change and targeted central aspects of instruction: curriculum, pedagogy, and assessment. However, teacher preservice and inservice training, the final component in Smith and O'Day's instructional guidance system, fell beyond the reach of early Math A policy statements. That is, neither the state curriculum framework (California State Department of Education, 1985), nor a widely circulated and detailed description of Math A content and philosophy (Stanley, 1989), nor the Math A materials themselves (California State Department of Education, 1991) included more than a cursory discussion of the professional development implications of the new course.[4] The framework recommended "well-planned, extended [professional development] programs . . . in which teachers have the opportunity to see new techniques demonstrated in classrooms, try out new methods with their own students, and reflect on changes in the curriculum" (California State Department of Education, 1985, p. 6). The framework also recommended coaching for teachers and support over time, to build teachers' confidence and to integrate content and methodology, but it cautioned that "most in-service programs will have to be substantially overhauled for these criteria to be met" (California State Department of Education, 1985, p. 6).

Thus, while California curriculum framework writers attempted to provide uniform guidance regarding Math A content, they relegated professional development to more or less coordinated efforts by the state, counties, school districts, and universities. Absent a strong professional development component, the state lacked the policy system coordination believed necessary for Math A implementation. As the research in this book suggests, the teaching profession itself, rather than state and local policy mechanisms, may be better positioned to play this professional development role.

Math A and Constructivism

Attributes of Math A support a constructivist conceptualization of its implementation. For example, Math A constitutes a professional model of what math should look like in high school classrooms. At its root, Math A injected a question into schools and classrooms about what mathematics should be, how it should serve students, and how it should be taught. A constructivist perspective best captures the diversity of professional responses to these fundamental policy questions.[5]

In addition, state officials initially expected Math A teachers to develop their own materials and to define Math A in practice. In fact, in the late 1980s teams of teachers developed 15 Math A units that the California Department of Education disseminated in 1991 and used to train Math A teachers. Still, materials were not uniform at that time—there was no Math A textbook,[6] for example—and variability prevailed. This variability, however, was problematic. To the extent that locally produced or revised materials reflected the spirit of the framework regarding Math A, they contributed to policy and professional knowledge about Math A's classroom potential. To the extent that variations included ersatz textbooks and classroom drill and practice, practitioners and others learned little.

The policy language of Math A, too, was vague and open to multiple interpretations. As Cohen and Peterson (1990) suggested about the mathematics reform movement within which Math A nested:

> The current reform movement in mathematics instruction has collected quite a variety of vogue-ish ideas and practices: from manipulatives to cooperative learning, from calculators to problem solving, from an emphasis on student talk to the addition of probability and estimation. These disparate pieces seem to lend themselves to being picked up in random bits and then enacted in variously interpreted permutations of each bit. The leading ideas of this movement do not yet cohere in an integrated conception of mathematics teaching and learning, rooted in a distinctive epistemology and framing a distinctive practice. This quality of the movement's leading ideas . . . in-

creases the likelihood that each teacher will apprehend and enact the ideas in his or her own terms. (p. 159)

By the early 1990s, enough time had elapsed and work had been produced that Math A designers could describe innovation components, but, again, variation prevailed as discrete teachers, departments, and districts continued to define policy in practice.

One would expect this variable or "adaptive" implementation of Math A, at least initially, because of the nature of the policy itself. Math A's broad changes, uncertain technology, and debate over goals and means, along with the loosely coupled nature of the education system, created an implementation situation in which policy was likely to be (even should have been) modified, revised, or otherwise adapted to better match local contexts (Berman, 1980).[7] A balance needed to be struck, however, as the state seemed to recognize, between policy outputs that reflected the state's challenging goals and those outputs that usefully adapted policy to local contexts. Erring too far in one direction would encourage nonimplementation; erring too far in the other would lessen the state's legitimate political function and ability to define and advance statewide curriculum reform.

Furthermore, adaptations or variations in policy may be necessary to gain students' cooperation, to match curriculum with students' motivations and abilities, and to better fit the interests and backgrounds of teachers; in short, to promote better practice. Diversity in professional responses to the policy creates natural experiments in practice that clarify and extend the practical meaning of Math A for students, teachers, and school systems. With fundamental questions entering the system (via Math A) regarding the shape of mathematics, how it should serve students, and how it should be taught, wide debate anchored in different practices broadens knowledge regarding Math A's potential, role in professional development, design shortcomings, and instructional utility.

STATE POLICY AS CLASSROOM CHANGE AGENT

Math A represented a departure from the curriculum and instructional practices typically found in California classrooms. A State Department of Education official described the differences, explaining:

Math A represents the most substantial change in mathematics curriculum in any of the K–12 grades. It's a replacement for ninth grade general math. It's a complete replacement. There's no similarity whatsoever between the Math A course and the general math course it's replacing. So that is a truly radical replacement.

In the sense that state policy substituted one curriculum for another, the policy was ambitious. Its ambition derived from a vision of what mathematics education should encompass given society's increasing reliance on technology. The so-called "new basic skills" of the twenty-first century include reading, writing, and arithmetic but also communication, complex problem-solving skills, and scientific and technological literacy (Murnane & Levy, 1996; National Science Board, 1983).

Can traditional secondary school mathematics foster these new skills and higher proficiencies? A consensus developed during the 1980s that traditional high school math curricula failed to provide all students with sufficient mathematical "power" (Smith, 1991), defined as the ability to discern mathematical relationships, reason logically, and use mathematical techniques effectively. Mathematically powerful students exhibit curiosity, risk taking, and perseverance; they extract information from data and deal successfully with problems (California State Department of Education, 1985). In short, the goal of mathematical power for all students required a different curriculum.

In 1985, however, this emerging vision and its operational meaning for California classrooms spurred debate. The math framework adopted that year reflected a compromise between two groups (D. Stanley, personal communication, April 11, 1990). On one hand, defenders of the status quo supported a traditional sequence of high school mathematics courses (algebra, geometry, and the like), which emphasized discrete topics, abstract concepts, and symbol manipulation. On the other hand, a new cadre of reformers promoted an alternative conception of high school mathematics. This alternative was organized around major mathematical ideas and applications; it integrated content from different strands of mathematics. These strands included number, measurement, geometry, patterns and functions, statistics and probability, logic, and algebra. The framework's authors noted this shift in perspective, writing:

> The 1985 framework recognizes changes in the use of mathematics. Although the underlying principles of mathematics are constant, the optimum structure for the presentation and use of mathematics has been shifting in response to the rapidly expanding importance of technology in solving problems. (California State Department of Education, 1985, p. 2)

Accordingly, five major themes appeared throughout the framework: problem solving, calculator technology, computational skills, estimation and mental arithmetic, and computers.

The 1985 framework also urged different instructional strategies to support this new course content and structure on the grounds that "delivery of instruction is inseparable from curricular content" (California State Department of Education, 1985, p. 12). The framework heralded a shift toward dynamic instructional processes, such as teaching for understanding,[8] continual reinforcement and extension of math concepts, problem solving, situational lessons, concrete materials, flexibility in instruction, cooperative learning, and attention to questioning (California State Department of Education, 1985).

The compromise of the 1985 framework included both this emerging philosophy of mathematics education and the traditional sequence of college preparatory courses, with one exception: Math A. Math A reflected the content, structure, and delivery of the reformers' vision. As one participant in the process noted, Math A acted as reform's wedge into the high school curriculum (D. Stanley, personal communication, April 11, 1990). The wedge opened the state's math curriculum to reform ideas because ninth-grade general mathematics boasted no supporters. As one state official remarked, ninth-grade general math is "the only math course in California that would have no opposition to replacement. . . . Nobody's toes were stepped on."[9]

Subsequently, professional opinion coalesced around this reform vision of math content and pedagogy (for example, National Council of Teachers of Mathematics, 1989; National Research Council, 1989, 1990). A 1990 draft of the next California mathematics framework,[10] for example, followed the "direction, coherence, and momentum" of these national mathematics reforms (Curriculum Development and Supplemental Materials Commission [CDSMC], 1990, p. 1.1).

The newer California framework called for "new, empowering mathematics programs" (CDSMC, 1990, p. 4.1) that followed in structure and content the standards established by the National Council of Teachers of Mathematics (1989). In language and philosophy, the newer California framework extended the course charted by the state in 1985. Essential characteristics of mathematics programs, for example, were defined as active students, large mathematical ideas, assessment integrated into instruction, teachers as facilitators rather than imparters of knowledge, deep understanding versus superficial skills, cooperative learning, manipulatives, and writing (CDSMC, 1990, pp. 4.4–4.8). This proposed framework moved beyond its predecessor, however, in that it abandoned traditional, discrete high school math courses, like algebra and geometry. Traditional courses were viewed as "obsolete and inadequate for the task at hand" (CDSMC, 1990, p. 7.4). In their place the framework substituted a 3-year, common course sequence for all students, composed of Course 1, Course

2, and Course 3. Every student would take this sequence but sample it at greater or lesser depth depending on proficiency and interest.[11] This strategy implied substantial changes in materials and teaching techniques, much like the demands associated with Math A.

Math A in the newer framework acted as a bridging course between eighth-grade mathematics and the preferred entry point in the high school math sequence, Course 1. This is the same position Math A occupied in the 1985 framework, spanning the gap between eighth-grade math and Algebra 1. In fact, authors of the newer framework remarked that "continued expansion of Math A, with corresponding reductions in remedial or 'general mathematics' courses, may provide the best preparation for teaching the common course sequence" (CDSMC, 1990, p. 7.12). Actually, Math A always exemplified the state's vision of mathematics education. As one state official suggested, "Take out the word 'Math A' [from the course background paper] and you have a philosophy paper of what we really want kids to do." In effect, California was reconstituting its entire high school mathematics curriculum to reflect and extend components that first appeared in the state's 1985 design of Math A. The wedge of Math A threatened to open all mathematics education in the state to profound reform.

At the same time, the demand for improved mathematics achievement continued to receive focused attention in national school reform efforts (U.S. Department of Education, 1991), and the reform vision contained in national reports and state frameworks (CDSMC, 1990; National Council of Teachers of Mathematics, 1989; National Research Council, 1989) began to shape the interpretation if not the content of national assessments of mathematics achievement (Bourque & Garrison, 1991; Mullis, Dossey, Owen, & Phillips, 1991). Nevertheless, in mid-1991 a California Department of Education official noted that "no large scale change is occurring in California schools or anywhere in the nation" (Smith, 1991, p. 1). This comment draws attention to the responses of school districts and teachers to state mathematics reforms.

DISTRICT RESPONSE AND CLASSROOM PRACTICE

How did districts, schools, and teachers respond to the introduction of Math A? In the late 1980s, there was no clear or direct answer. An initial survey indicated that implementation was low (George, 1987). But early in the process, between 1985 and 1988, the state lacked a plan to promote Math A. According to a state official, implementation was left to districts, and districts acted or not on the basis of their own interests and capacities, experimenting and developing materials as they proceeded. In effect, districts carried on in different directions, while the state made no concerted effort to facilitate or harness this energy or to disseminate promising practices. The State Department of Education did hire a single "missionary" to travel among the districts and "talk up Math A." But there was little more to Math A at this time than a philosophy paper and a few good ideas.

After 1988, the state composed a strategy to develop Math A instructional materials, disseminate them statewide, and train teachers in their use. Still, as of 1991, there were no systematic indicators of Math A's usage or, importantly, of its character or content in California classrooms. Instead, state officials described indicators of increasing activity: number of local agencies training teachers, number of Math A inservice days logged per year, number of conference presentations or discussions regarding Math A, number of districts instituting "pilot" projects or moving toward district-wide adoptions. Similarly, anecdotal evidence accumulated of Math A's acceptance and efficacy: the central valley veteran teacher who regained a lost sense of excitement and commitment through Math A, the southern California gang member who stayed in school because of Math A, and so forth. Such images do indicate in a fashion that Math A was "catching on," as state officials asserted, but they demonstrated little about how districts perceived and used Math A, just as they revealed little about classroom practices.

District 1: Symbolic Adoption

The three districts in this book, for example, approached Math A in quite different ways. District 1's initial response can be characterized as symbolic. In 1985, shortly after the state framework appeared, the district approved a course called Math A and adopted a best-available textbook (there were no state-sanctioned Math A instructional materials available at the time). The district regarded Math A as a beginning course for ninth graders who were not ready for algebra. Implementation, however, was left to teachers' interests and initiative. A district official described this strategy as a "soft-sell" in which the district would initiate no change process but would support experiments by individual teachers or departments.

In fact, the textbook adopted by the district was little different from a standard pre-algebra text. One network teacher described this text as "baby algebra." As a result, Math A in the district fell short of state policy expectations, failing to reflect the intent or spirit of the mathematics framework. The district's early response to Math A amounted only to symbolic compliance with the state framework insofar as the district implemented a policy shell that included the Math A title but none of course's intended substance.

Subsequently, however, math departments in three District 1 schools embarked collaboratively on an effort to implement Math A in a manner consistent with state policy. Their motivation was professional: to improve service to students. Their scheme utilized the expertise and contacts of staff from a local university, and they garnered financial support from a national foundation. The district fully supported this enterprise (financially and structurally), and district officials, teachers, and observers alike hailed the result. Furthermore, by drawing math teachers from other schools into the training sessions associated with this effort, the district hoped to seed other departments with this "new" Math A. District officials expected implementation advances to occur through lower-level linkages among practitioners, a bottom-up strategy that assumed that teacher initiation and support for Math A must precede a district mandate for implementation. These linkages among practitioners became the teacher network that constitutes the central focus of this book.

District 2: Incremental Change

Officials in District 2 responded to the implementation challenge cautiously and incrementally. District commitment to Math A was high, moving toward district-wide adoption, but the pace of change was slow, allowing other districts to work through problems associated with experimental or draft curricula and novel teaching methods. This incremental approach assumed district-level pacing of implementation to ensure quality and coherence and a minimum of confusion and frustration during district-wide adoption. A lead Math A teacher in the district praised this caution, asserting that too much change too fast would lead to more problems than successes.

Implementation in District 2 began with collaboration among district, county, and university staff, and with participation in California Math Project mini-projects, or local pilots exploring classroom applications of Math A. The district hosted inservice workshops for math teachers interested in experimenting with Math A. With state-produced Math A units finally available, the district designated 1990–91 as a pilot implementation year; Math A was introduced into 10 schools. A district-wide pilot, in which each eligible school would offer at least one Math A section, was planned for 1991–92. District-wide implementation would wait another year and benefit from the results of the pilots. Math A here, as in District 1, served as a link between eighth-grade mathematics and college-prep algebra, although the process of implementation was more top-down.

District 3: Political Bargaining

Implementation in District 3 represents a case of political bargaining. It reflected an aggressive but contested top-down response involving conflict among different district interests. On one hand, the school board included Math A as a graduation requirement in its first year of implementation, 1990–91. The administration supported this move as an appropriate response to state policy, which it interpreted to mean that all students should experience Math A and a subsequent college-preparatory sequence. The district also made a large financial commitment to Math A implementation, purchasing manipulatives (up to $2,500 per teacher); cabinets to keep them in; calculators; and flat-topped, movable desks to accommodate tiles, cubes, or other materials and to facilitate small student work groups. The district paid for summer training for Math A teachers, Saturday workshops during the school year to refine and expand course materials, and conference time. It provided each Math A teacher with $300 to cover the cost of incidentals, like the brown trout used in a unit on ratios.

Simultaneously, however, the district math council (composed of all department chairs) objected to the graduation requirement, felt that all students would not benefit from Math A, and desired more course options to meet the district's 3-year math requirement. The conflict involved a math council desire to win a 3-year math graduation requirement, a superintendent who supported Math A and allegedly proposed to "cram it down [the math council's] throat," department chairs who viewed Math A as undercutting a successful consumer math program, and others who saw Math A's instructional strategies as beneficial to all courses in the long run but who viewed the current course as a purposeless collection of promising ideas.

This intradistrict wrangling spawned a debate over the place of Math A in the district's curriculum. Administrators preferred to use Math A as an entry-level course in ninth grade, thus aligning it with the state framework. Math council members preferred to reserve Math A for eleventh graders (where it resided in the curriculum at the time I conducted interviews). Placing Math A later in the sequence served several purposes. It prevented students who fell under the Math A graduation requirement from taking the course during the district's pilot year. It also provided an option for students who attempted algebra but failed. Council members argued that students who were unsuccessful in algebra would have no place to turn if Math A was not available. Furthermore, the council placed little trust in Math A's ability to prepare students for college-preparatory courses. As one department chair recounted the issue:

[The principal] thinks that a student would take Math A and then go directly . . . into a college-prep algebra course, that Math A would somehow take care of all of the weaknesses that the student would bring from the junior high level—whether it's arithmetic or the inability to be comfortable with mathematics and so forth— and take care of all those problems and make them ready for col- lege-prep algebra. I haven't found anybody yet who feels that the course is that kind of panacea, who actually deals with it.

In short, by the end of 1990–91, the fate of Math A in District 3 was problematic. Within the context of high district commitment to implemen- tation, administrators and department chairs debated the course's value and place in the curriculum, while teachers labored to understand and improve state-produced Math A units and to elaborate and debate their instructional utility.

IMPLEMENTATION CHALLENGES

Within these districts Math A practice varied from one classroom to the next. In three District 2 classrooms, for example, I observed practice that directly reflected state content and goals, adaptations that reflected the spirit of Math A but ranged beyond the state-produced materials, and practice antithetical to state goals, in which the teacher reverted to drill and practice on basic skills. (I discuss these differences in detail in Chap- ter 3.)

The implementation vignettes presented in this chapter demonstrate how state attention to Math A implementation catalyzed local imple- mentation efforts. Implementation efforts gained depth and speed only after the state introduced Math A curricular materials and organized professional development workshops. This state effort spurred and fo- cused local activity. Prior to this, the major district-wide implementation activity in these districts had been the adoption of an ersatz Math A textbook by District 1.

In illustrating variation in district response and classroom practice, the vignettes also introduce some of the complexities of implementation. For example, the difference between teacher- and district-driven change efforts in Districts 1 and 2 represents classic and competing top-down and bottom-up implementation strategies. The symbolic, incremental, and politically bargained nature of these districts' responses to state policy reveals how the essential character of implementation can differ across settings. District 1's shift from symbolic district action to substantive department-level action shows too how implementation processes can evolve. Smaller issues emerged also, such as the utility of pilot projects or other implementation experiments, resource availability (district versus extramural funding), and the relationship between administrator control and practitioner commitment.

In addition, these brief implementation portraits depict how local responses to state policy strongly influence the practical effect that policy has. For example, District 1's adoption of a best-available textbook indicates how inadequate materials can undermine policy intent, and even implementers' motivation. District 3's experience in debating Math A's place in its mathematics sequence demonstrates not just how implementers must work to understand the relationship between old and new policies (algebra and Math A), but also how policy goals can be transformed through local bargaining (Math A as transition to algebra or culmination course).

One can see, too, how conflicts arise during implementation, such as when groups use new policies (Math A) to replace older ones (consumer math); and how stakeholders use new policies to leverage existing local conflicts, such as when the math council in District 3 used Math A to win a 3-year math graduation requirement.

These brief portraits of implementation responses in Districts 1, 2, and 3 demonstrate fundamentally that Math A can mean different things in different places, even across classrooms within a single district. Moreover, different classroom practices can range from consistent with to antithetical to state policy intentions. The state-level question arising from these practices involves how to achieve more uniform policy outcomes that reflect the state's challenging goals, goals that ask more of teachers and students than ever before. The local-level question involves how to usefully adapt policy prescriptions to local contexts, goals, and needs. The answer to both questions may arise from a closer examination of the implementation process.

PART II

Curriculum Implementation in the Classroom

CHAPTER 3

Town Halls, Solo Performers, and Clearinghouses: Implementation Results in Network and Other Classrooms

> They said it couldn't be done. . . . But if you've got the horses out in the field, and you've got the commitment, and you've got some logic behind you, . . . it can be done. . . . It's very easy to implement if you've got the support model to do it.
>
> —A California State Department of Education official

TEACHERS' IMPLEMENTATION EXPERIENCES BEGIN with the demands of policy on practice. In the case of Math A, these demands were substantial. Math A reconceptualized the content and pedagogy of high school mathematics. Like conventional pre-algebra, Math A was intended to bridge general and college-preparatory mathematics. Beyond this shared goal, however, Math A and pre-algebra were fundamentally dissimilar. Math A built upon exploration and application of mathematical concepts rather than explication and skill mastery, math themes rather than discrete topics, cohesive units rather than the ubiquitous two-page spread, cooperative learning and group work rather than lecture and individual seatwork. Math A asked teachers to facilitate students' learning rather than to transmit knowledge. It expected students to be active learners rather than passive receptacles. It utilized concrete models and hands-on manipulatives rather than abstract algorithms and paper-and-pencil exercises. In that Math A's scope of change was so broad, the demands of policy on practice were substantial. In that the changes targeted content and instruction, the demands were significant. In that the changes allocated student and teacher resources differently, the demands were material. Because Math A reached into classrooms in substantial, significant, and material ways, its implementation in a manner consistent with state policy depended on classroom teachers. In the case of Math A, policy would gain meaning only in practice.

TEACHERS' EXPERIENCE WITH MATH A

All the teachers in this study were piloting Math A, so all were operating at a similar, early stage of implementation. Early implementation meant that the course was new to the districts and to the teachers, all of whom had less than 2 years of classroom experience with Math A. From both personal and organizational perspectives, teachers confronted novel philosophy, materials, and instructional strategies.

In all three districts, the implementation pilot meant, too, that Math A materials were still being developed and tested. During the academic year in which this study was conducted, for example, Math A lacked a textbook specifically designed to reflect state policy prescriptions and the "spirit of Math A," as the teachers phrased it. Math A materials were being developed simultaneously with the course's implementation. As one support-group teacher described the process:

> This whole thing is in the pilot stages, and things were not complete. And we had to begin, so we just started with what we had available. And we added some material; we deleted some material that we felt was too repetitive or not appropriate. And we're continually trying to upgrade the curriculum so that what's being presented to students lends to the meaning of the unit and also that the problems and so forth that we go over, we understand what we're getting at and what the answers are.

A network teacher reinforced the "in progress" status of the Math A pilots, explaining, "We have no book because the units are still being piloted, and they're not written in their final form." However, teachers lacked a Math A textbook also because the state conceived of Math A, in part, as a professional development strategy. Early on, the state intended that teachers collaborate in order to develop appropriate instructional materials.

Early implementation also meant that districts offered Math A only in a limited number of schools and taught by a small number of teachers. As a result, four teachers in this study (three in the staff development district and one in the support-group district) stood alone as the only Math A teachers in their buildings. One Math A teacher in District 3 said of his lone peers, "We have seen, . . . especially early on, [that] those teachers felt a little isolated." Such isolation constrains teachers' capacity to sustain innovation.

In the staff development and support-group districts, implementation pilots also meant that district policy makers had not settled on the place of Math A in the high school curriculum, that is, whether it would serve as a bridge to algebra or whether it would be available to students who had failed algebra. Nevertheless, these districts were committed to the eventual district-wide implementation of Math A. District 1 already had adopted Math A district-wide, even if the shape of the adopted course failed to reflect the state's framework or intent and its final constitution devolved to building-level initiatives.

OPPORTUNITIES CREATED BY IMPLEMENTATION PILOTS

The importance of these pilots to teachers emerged in four ways. First, the pilots freed teachers from district expectations and constraints regarding the amount and type of material that had to be covered during the course of an academic year. A staff development teacher described this situation as follows:

> Every other math course has a district guide that says how many chapters you will cover. It has warm ups; it has tests. We have proficiencies that have to be met—supposed to be met, et cetera. Very structured, tight, very closely [linked] to the textbook.

Drawing the contrast to Math A, another support-group teacher claimed, "I'm basically free to do what I want to do," while another similarly noted that Math A "is a pilot project, so we have no guidelines. It was just kind of doing [your] own thing."

Two teachers indicated in their remarks how this freedom had a positive effect on practice within the pilot. On one hand, it engaged teachers more in the process of instruction. A staff development teacher argued that, with tight district control over the pace of instruction, "it's very easy to become lazy and say, 'Okay, today we're doing section 3 of Chapter 6; your homework is . . . ' and give a 10- or 20-minute lecture. Give them problems to do." But, he argued, that type of programmed instruction failed to reach all students, and particularly it failed to capture Math A students: "For some kids, [programmed instruction is] great. For these Math A kids, it turns them off and you've lost them. That way hasn't worked. So why should I expect it to work this year? That's why I don't do it." Not doing this, of course, meant that he had to devise alternative ways of presenting material and engaging students. As he acknowledged, "I kind of design my own way of going about that."

On the other hand, this freedom from district expectations and constraints allowed students' academic needs to set the pace of instruction. One support-group teacher explained, "We have no time line. I can do what I want when I want. I have no curriculum to follow. And if [students] got stuck on something, we could spend more time on it because I was under no pressure to be to page 289 by such and such a date." Similarly, her staff development counterpart recounted how

> sometimes we get on a neat lesson and I'd spend 10 days on this one lesson. And [the unit] would say, "This will take a period and a half." And we'd spend 10 periods.

In contrast, his peer across town viewed pacing as her biggest problem. A balance needed to be struck, she implied, between slowing the pace to foster understanding and losing control of the class.

> Sometimes I feel that it's no point in rushing them. It would be better just to go over it and over it, you know, with sort of different points of view to get them to learn material. . . . But then again, if I let them take 10 days to do one assignment, they'll sit around and talk.

The pilots also were important to teachers insofar as they fostered a sense of experimentation. For example, Math A was described by two network teachers as "a 3-year experiment, okay, a pilot," and, similarly, as "all trial and error." Experimentation enabled Math A teachers to "iron out the kinks" and to accumulate and share experience. As support-group teachers put it, "So we find out what was working for them, what wasn't working," and, "We would spend the day going over the new units, particularly those who had done them before—piloted them previously." This experimentation, along with the risk-taking behavior teachers describe ("You can see my face print all over the floor on things that I've flopped on"), formed a context essential to defining the practical effect of Math A, as these characteristics enabled teachers to test, revise, and improve these "works in progress." A network teacher expressed a corollary belief that because teachers had been using the Math A units for only 2 years (in the network case), it was too early to evaluate Math A's potential. In other words, thorough street-level implementation would take time (cf. Kirst & Jung, 1980).

In addition, these "works in progress" created frustrations for teachers but also opportunities to exercise leadership and expertise. This sentiment was clearest among network teachers. As one teacher reflected,

Math A based on the state-produced materials, with its unfamiliar content and instructional strategies, was evolving as it was being implemented. In this case, policy was shaping practice, and practice was shaping policy. Network teachers saw Math A as "a process of evolving . . . [in which] evolution will allow it to become better." The keys to this evolution were (1) that "it's being tested in the classroom," and (2) that evolution is a matter of teacher collaboration.

Finally, teachers' experience with Math A often began prior to their participation in a formal pilot. According to the network department chair, for a year before the pilot got underway, teachers received materials from the future network coordinator. These teachers "would just use [the Math A materials] helter-skelter in their regular class." This haphazard exposure to Math A curriculum materials created an opportunity for teachers to explore Math A materials in advance of their formal introduction. The effect of this early exploration was that teachers began to see that there was a different way of looking at mathematics. Also prior to undertaking the pilot, the future network coordinator taught a course in Math A where she used drafts of the state-produced materials. Again, she shared the materials, informally, with interested math teachers. This kind of early exposure may have piqued teachers' interest in the course and laid the groundwork for their assent to the pilot. This sentiment was conveyed directly by a District 2 math resource teacher who remarked that the teachers who volunteered to pilot Math A had access to draft materials ahead of the pilot, which raised their interest and willingness to attempt this unusual course.

Math A pilots across these districts provided a common context for teachers' implementation efforts, but this context reveals little about the shape of Math A in network, staff development, and support-group classrooms. The study adds networks to conceptions of teachers' professional context and explores whether and how a network enhances teachers' motivation and capacity to implement Math A. To make this assessment, however, readers first must know whether any differences existed in teachers' experiences with Math A implementation.

Within their common enterprise, teachers' Math A practice can be differentiated in terms of teachers' knowledge of Math A; the content or materials they used in class; and their organization of instruction, role in the classroom, and commitment to Math A. On these dimensions, Math A differs from conventional mathematics courses in its reliance on teacher-developed materials, manipulatives, group instruction, and a restructured professional role for teachers as facilitators of learning rather than transmitters of knowledge. The extent to which these core concepts appear in the comments of these teachers provides a first indication of policy confronting practice, for, presumably, a teacher must know what to implement before he or she goes about its practice.

TEACHERS' KNOWLEDGE OF MATH A

Teachers across these network, staff development, and support-group classrooms were generally knowledgeable about Math A's role, structure, and methodology.

The greatest difference among these teachers and cases in terms of teachers' conceptions of Math A involved the role of Math A, or its place in the high school curriculum. All four network teachers identified and used Math A as a transition course to algebra, which coincided with the state's intent. In the network district, Math A was

> basically a class for students who are not quite ready for the traditional algebra classes at the high school level. So primarily it's for ninth-grade students who still are weak in some basic skills, and they would not succeed if we put them directly in an Algebra 1 class.

Other network teachers and their department chair widely expressed this sentiment, indicating that the place of Math A in District 1's curriculum was clear and that teachers viewed this placement as appropriate. The district office reinforced this message. As a teacher explained, "We're always under the goal that these kids next—a good majority of them—will be in algebra or some algebra-type course."

In contrast, none of the support-group teachers identified Math A as a transition course, and none were using it this way. At the time I conducted interviews, district officials and teachers were contesting the place of Math A in the district's curriculum, with administrators pressing for Math A to be used as a bridge to algebra, while department chairs preferred that it serve students who had failed algebra; and during the pilot, Math A classes enrolled mostly sophomores and juniors.

Math A in the staff development district served both purposes, and teachers were divided regarding its best use. Teachers 1 and 2, for example, instructed mostly juniors who had failed algebra. Teacher 1 also disagreed with the state's intended use of Math A as a bridge ("If a kid fails algebra, where is he going to go? In other words, if you put him in Math A [in ninth grade], then he goes up to algebra his sophomore year and fails, he has no place to go"). Teachers 3 and 4, on the other hand, instructed freshmen and intended for them to advance into algebra. Interestingly, Teacher 1 in the staff development district and Teacher 3 in the support-group district, both of whom instructed mostly juniors who had failed algebra, characterized Math A, respectively, as a "leper colony" and a "dumping ground," conceptions of the course that the state had hoped to avoid (Stanley, 1989). These examples demonstrate as much about the embeddedness of education system components—about how actions at one level establish the context and facilitate or constrain action at another—as they do about implementation differences among these cases.

In terms of teachers' conceptions of Math A, the greatest similarity across these teachers and cases related to characteristics of instruction, namely, cooperative learning and the use of manipulatives. Each of these notions appeared in the comments of nine teachers, three in each case. In terms of the state's intent regarding cooperative learning, students' understanding required opportunities for them "to express their own thoughts, to compare alternative approaches, to share insights that may be incompletely formulated, and in general to discuss ideas they do not yet know well" (Stanley, 1989, p. 3). In a practical sense, the student groups that manifested this desire changed the organization of instruction. As a network teacher explained, "So in a traditional class it's more [of an] individual orientation; the Math A program that we work on is based on working in groups." In a more theoretical sense, another network teacher noted, "Groups help students learn in the math program."

Likewise, Math A to these teachers meant manipulatives, the hands-on materials that students could operate. Teachers' frequent use of manipulatives represented a different approach to presenting mathematics to students, and this new approach was prominent across the cases in teachers' conceptions of Math A. A network teacher described this new approach, saying, "It's not just so abstract. It is more—they can see it. It is more tangible, I will say." With the "tangible" math manipulatives in mind, this network teacher's support-group counterpart characterized the difference between pre-algebra and Math A as the difference between "the old page-a-day-and-no-time-to-play syndrome versus play-and-play-and-learn-on-the-way." This difference denoted how Math A teaches mathematics through hands-on experiences, not just by paper-and-pencil computations. A network teacher related how play-and-play operated in practice.

> Usually we are using some sort of manipulative with each unit. It could be cubes, for building structures that they have to get the surface area and the volume of; it could be tiles for getting area. We'll do drawings of things that you have to get area of; we'll

make posters of different principles; it could be a string. So there's always some sort of hands-on stuff.

Teachers in District 3 benefited from large district purchases of manipulatives, storage cabinets, and discretionary money to purchase incidentals, like the M&Ms required by one Math A exercise. Others made do with fewer resources and even incorporated the search for a manipulative into a problem-solving situation for students. For example, one staff development teacher explained:

> We never use tape measures. But when [students] had to measure the circumference of their heads, for instance, they said, "Now all we have got is these yard sticks. Now how're we going to do this?" So they pondered and argued, and they said, "If we had some string." So they came up with the idea of string. So then I gave them pieces of string. They now know that there's not a single way to do something. . . . Some of [the Math A units] start off: have tape measures, have yardsticks, have everything. You don't need all that fancy, expensive stuff, in my opinion. Like why use tape measures when a string and a ruler will do just as well. . . . I think the valuable thing is making [students] figure out how to measure something that is round with something that is rigid and straight.

Teachers' descriptions of Math A also illustrated the prominence of three additional characteristics, which appeared in 7 of 12 instances across these cases. First, teachers conveyed how instruction focused on math themes rather than discrete skills and computations. For example, "We're not just teaching strict computational kinds of things or sections of curriculum. It is more of a holistic approach where the curriculum itself is integrated so that kids can see the interrelationships in mathematics."

Second, teachers recounted active lessons in which students constructed their knowledge of mathematics from explorations, games, models, and the like. As a network teacher concluded, students became more active and interested in the mathematics they encountered.

> Pre-algebra courses basically are designed to just crunch out numbers and formulas and teach you how to perform on those things. You could spend a month on fractions and just be doing worksheets and worksheets of fractions. Whereas [in Math A] we'll do probability and have probability problems and probability applications and probability games. All of these require the use of frac-

tions, so they'll have to use fractions and learn some more about them, but they'll also be a lot more interested actually in the way we're doing it.

Finally, teachers across these cases described how Math A utilized various problem situations to engage students in mathematics. In terms of the state's intent, Math A should help students deal effectively with new and unusual problem situations outside their classrooms. It should integrate problem solving into the way students approach all mathematics, and it should incorporate problem solving into every lesson (Stanley, 1989). One staff development teacher characterized Math A directly in these terms: "Math A is problem solving—sums it all up." Six other teachers (two in each case) also identified this characteristic as integral to their Math A practice.

In short, teachers across these cases demonstrated a general knowledge of the role and characteristics of Math A. Their greatest similarities involved those attributes of the course that demanded significant changes in instructional strategies, and therefore in daily practice. Their greatest differences related to the role of Math A in the high school curriculum, a decision embedded in contexts beyond their classrooms.

These data illustrate two additional points related to teachers' knowledge of Math A. The first point, that knowledge evolves over time, reinforces the notion that implementation is a process rather than an event. A second observation, that multiple sources of information are available within a network, in part distinguishes resources available to network teachers in this study from their staff development and support-group peers.

Knowledge Evolved

Teachers' knowledge of Math A evolved, which required time and information. As the network coordinator explained:

> When Math A first came out in the 1985 framework, at that time I don't think we understood clearly the philosophy at the state level, and we looked at the series of topics as just that. . . . But the whole idea of using manipulatives, of small-group cooperative learning, teachers taking a different role, that was not emphasized at all. So there were a number of years in which we used a textbook and we had a course called Math A. And it was more like a pre-algebra course; that's basically what it was. As we became more aware, and as we attended more conferences at the state level, many

teachers in the district became more knowledgeable of the philosophy of what Math A was about, and so we wanted to try something that, in fact, implemented those ideas . . . not only in terms of topics covered, but in terms of methodology and strategies.

In this case, knowledge of Math A evolved to a point where teachers expressed a willingness to undertake its implementation. Knowledge of Math A continued to evolve as network teachers gained experience with the course in their classrooms. Comments of the network coordinator also demonstrate the distinction in levels of implementation. Initial implementation of Math A involved a course title change and textbook adoption but had little practical effect in classrooms. As she noted, "It was more like pre-algebra." The practical effect awaited changes in "topics, methodology, and strategies."

Departmental Reinforcement of Math A Concepts

Unlike their staff development and support-group counterparts, network teachers had department chairs who were knowledgeable about Math A policy, taught Math A classes, and reinforced core policy concepts among their teaching staffs. All four network teachers cited their department chairs as key resources in their attempts to implement Math A. Only two nonnetwork teachers (one in each nonnetwork case) indicated that their chairs were supportive, but neither of these was closely involved in the implementation process.

For example, the network coordinator (who also was a department chair) articulated and advocated Math A characteristics. She communicated these ideas to network teachers and kept tabs on their development. As she said, "I think the vision of what they are trying to achieve is clear each time we have a monthly inservice, and I can see that their vision has clarified."

What ideas composed this vision? To begin, the fundamental goal of Math A, in this chair's view, was to prepare more students for success in college-preparatory mathematics. Math A addressed this goal, she argued, by training students to be "powerful" in mathematics, meaning that students can think, conjecture, justify, and solve problems. Next, Math A differed from conventional mathematics in both its theory and pedagogy, specifically, in its belief that students construct math knowledge; in its organization around in-depth math (rather than discrete, sequential topics); in its conceptualization of teachers as facilitators of student learning; and in its reliance on group learning, manipulatives, and concrete models, all of which were ideas embedded in the framework.

The department chair in a second network high school was similarly informed and articulate. In his view, Math A was distinguished by its emphasis on mathematics in context. By this he meant that

> numbers are not in isolation. If you are dealing with probability, for example, you want to bring in some experimental-type things that the kids can look at—take a look at samples, try things out, look at the theoretical probability against the empirical evidence. Then [students] have gone through the experiential mode. . . . And we also want some hands-on application . . . so [students] understand that there is meaning to it. So we teach more for understanding and teach in-depth as opposed to just covering topics. . . . The skills are within the activities themselves.

In both instances, the chairs reinforced key characteristics of Math A that were reflected in the framework and refined in their own classrooms. Teachers drew on these departmental resources to inform their own practice. One network teacher commented:

> Then we have [the chair] who is the department head and one of the major forces in the Math A curriculum and [who] is also very active at the Sacramento level. So we are very fortunate to have her input and her contact with Sacramento and many other districts. So she is abreast of all this information.

Similarly, while the pace of learning may have differed among individuals in the network, the four classroom teachers, math resource teacher, and two department chairs and others associated with the network together represented a substantial knowledge base regarding the theory, purposes, and pedagogy of Math A. This resource was shared among themselves and with nonnetwork Math A teachers in the district, and this knowledge base supported implementation. Teachers' instructional materials, on the other hand, began to shape Math A's practical effect in their classrooms.

MATH A CONTENT

All 12 teachers used the state-produced Math A units as their core instructional material. This happened by design. The implementation pilots called for this material. The interesting implementation result involved what these teachers did with the state units during their implementation.

Eleven of the 12 teachers adapted the state material as they attempted to shape a practical effect for Math A in their classrooms. The one exception was Teacher 3 in the staff development district, who explained, "Usually I'm not creative. I'll use what they hand me." For the others, however, their growing experience with Math A led to a sense of freedom and flexibility to adapt Math A materials. Thus, adaptations followed as teachers grasped the practical meaning of policy in practice.

State-Produced Materials

State-produced Math A units had been developed by teacher writing committees beginning in 1987, with revisions continuing through the term of this study in 1991. Topics included surveys and data analysis, spatial visualization, fencing and packing (perimeter and area), large numbers, what are my chances? (probability), graphical interpretations, balancing (linear equations), growth and decay (measurement, estimation, data organization, and like), sequences and sums, motion, rectiles, and math in nature. Teachers in this study indicated that they covered approximately eight or nine of these units in a year.

As I mentioned earlier, during the 1990–91 academic year, Math A lacked a textbook designed to reflect state policy prescriptions and the "spirit of Math A." The materials comprised loose-leaf units considered to be still in progress. One result of handling these materials in progress was to create for teachers a materials management problem, of sorts. In part, this resulted from how the units were conveyed to teachers: "Dittos. It's groups of dittos," exclaimed a network teacher. "That's all it is. [For] each unit, we get a set of dittos. One is the teachers' set, and one is the students' set."

At one point, I visited a Math A teacher in her classroom. In the course of our conversation, I asked her to show me a sample of her Math A material. She rose from her desk, faced the chalkboard, and stretched her arms out full length as if she was about to take off. "There," she said, gesturing with her head. "There are my Math A materials." Below the chalkboard, piled two deep, and running the length of the room, were 12 or 14 boxes of loose papers—dittos, in fact. Part of her frustration with Math A resulted from the effort required to handle, sort through, keep track of, and reproduce such a mountain of paper. A staff development teacher echoed the other teacher's frustration, explaining problems associated with not having a text.

> It's a problem that I really don't know what I'm going to do next week. You have to wait and see how today goes to see what

you're doing later. . . . Plus, you see all the mess in the room? You have to have all this stuff. There're all the papers for this next unit that's coming up, and you have to get them organized somehow and not lose them.

If the loose-leaf nature of Math A was frustrating at times, an inadequate textbook, according to teachers, was worse. The network district's early adoption of what it judged to be the best-available text fell short of policy expectations for Math A in that the text failed to reflect the intent or spirit of the framework. Network teachers uniformly disparaged it. As one teacher described it, the book was too varied. "It's a pre-algebra book. In that textbook you will cover from addition and subtraction of whole numbers and decimal numbers all the way to an introduction of trigonometry. So the students were getting a lot for a 1-year course." Another teacher connected the book's development to its reception by teachers. As he described the problem:

> The state made its guidelines for what [it] wanted in the Math A curriculum. So this company threw together a book based upon the objectives. So they answered every single objective that was required. . . . And it was the only book on the market, so, therefore, we adopted it. But it's a terrible book. . . . It's boring.

Another teacher summarily dismissed the book, saying, "It's like baby algebra. It's sort of routine."

A Math A textbook, based on the state-produced units, was in progress in 1991. Four of the 12 teachers across these cases (one network, two staff development, one support group) who addressed the issue viewed this development with apprehension. As one teacher suggested, "I'm leery about a textbook. You do a textbook and suddenly I'm concerned that you might not be in groups. It might be easy not to have groups." In other words, the textbook as a teaching tool seemed too rigid to facilitate the type of classroom interaction characteristic of the unit-based Math A.

As one might expect, the state-produced Math A units more closely resembled Math A policy goals. This was evident in several respects. First, the units explored mathematical concepts through applications-based exercises. For example, in describing their transformation from the former textbook-driven Math A to the current state unit-driven curriculum, the network coordinator said:

> So we decided to look at alternative approaches where we can have hands-on, experiential-type math activities that will go be-

yond the pre-algebra concepts. Here we're talking about sequence and series; we talk about probability and statistics, and having the youngsters collect data, analyze the data, and so forth; and if they don't know their multiplication facts, we give them calculators to facilitate problem solving, and we also have a skill-building maintenance program within it.

Second, the units utilized manipulatives. A network teacher summarized the difference between Math A and other math classes, saying, "There is a lot more activity going on in the classroom . . . [Math A classes are] doing cooperative types of activities or hands-on types of activities." Another network teacher suggested that the use of manipulatives formed a theme that carried through the Math A curriculum: "We work with models. We have manipulatives that they touch. Those things carry through."

Third, the Math A units led to different types of assessments. On one hand, teachers continued to give more traditional individual student assessments, for example, asking students to multiply two fractions. On the other hand, a newer type of assessment was used, which one network teacher described as a "one-problem test." In this instance, students were presented, for example, with a probability game. The question was: Is the game fair or unfair? Part of a student's answer included the steps utilized to arrive at a conclusion. In order to decide if the game was fair or not, students used a tool that they learned, such as a tree diagram, to demonstrate all possible outcomes and to explain how they got an answer. In so doing, students were required to build an argument rather than simply offering a numeric answer. Similarly, a support teacher described a mix of traditional quizzes and problem-based assessments.

In sum, teachers' core materials, like the nonroutine instructional strategies they described earlier, shaped Math A's practical effect in these classrooms.

Adaptations of State-Produced Materials

Using the state Math A materials, however, did not mean that teachers progressed through the units sequentially starting with page one. In fact, for 11 of the 12 teachers across these cases, adaptations of the state curriculum material formed a routine part of their Math A implementation. And although network, staff development, and support-group teachers described these adaptations and their motivation for undertaking them in similar ways, the pattern of results differed across cases. In fact, the manner in which these adaptations were undertaken in each case, and their results in practice, suggested three patterns or models of implementation results.

A Town Hall Model. Implementation in the network was analogous to a town hall meeting. Teachers met together and negotiated curriculum changes within the framework of the network; and the network linked classroom teachers within schools, across schools, and to others "in the town," such as department chairs and a math resource teacher. All four network teachers indicated that their adaptations of the state material resulted from teachers' interactions, for example, "We talk about it as a group" and "On a work level we've gotten so many ideas from each other. . . . And so we do a constant sharing of ideas and seeing what works and what doesn't work and what to try out." Another network teacher indicated the level of detail these discussions reached within teachers' common preparation periods.

> We go through the lesson. We say, "How did it go? What happened? How did yesterday go—the day before go? Did it work well? What was wrong? What helped? And what are we going to teach tomorrow? What's the concept of the ideas? And what do we want to get across?" And we look ahead. Do we need to give a test? Do we need to make up tests? What can we use for homework? And we talk about some problems we have and how we can handle it. And we get our material ready, the manipulatives, ready.

Adaptations here were linked to the state units and based on teachers' shared experiences. As a result, practice was similar from classroom to classroom.

A Solo Performer Model. In contrast, implementation in the staff development district assumed more of an idiosyncratic character. Three of the four teachers adapted the units—one did not—and each teacher operated separately from the others. As one noted, "I'm out on my own. Strictly on my own." He also observed that "every school that you're going to go to . . . some do it a little different." Another staff development teacher echoed this sentiment, indicating that Math A in the district was "different for different schools."

The within-case disparity among teachers' Math A practice was greatest in the staff development district. Teacher 1, for example, abandoned the state units. According to him, "The state has, oh, they have their little packets—the units—and that's fine. I tried them in here." In their place, he substituted a curriculum of his own device.

> I took from career math, I took from general math, I took from pre-algebra, all of these, and then I put them together in my computer. I spent the last 2 years plugging them all in. Now this is strictly 180 degrees different from what the state wants because, like I said, they don't want the kids to do rote. [I do it] because these kids, they need the basic foundations.

In this instance, the teacher's instructional model was the Saxon math curriculum (which the school had used extensively), which he described by saying, "You go over something and then you keep reviewing it all the way through the year." He believed that this approach was best for his students. He also understood the difference between "Math A" in his and other classrooms. Comparing his class with another teacher's, he said:

> I've seen his class, and I know how he runs his class, and it's great. It really works for his kids. This happens to work for my kids. I mean, he's seen my class, and he's cringed. And he says, "That's what we're supposed to be getting away from."

Teacher 2 in the staff development district adapted the materials but within the context of the state units and the spirit of Math A. Although she supplemented the state material "a lot," her adaptations were undertaken because "sometimes [a unit] doesn't give [students] the best background. Sometimes you need time fillers, other things to do." Basically, though, Math A in her class closely followed the state units.

Teacher 3 also based his practice on the state units, but his adaptations ranged farther from this base than those of Teacher 2. As he noted, "I kind of feel an obligation to do the units." But he also described his approach to them, namely, "[I] pick and choose out of them what I think are good and what the kids can use. . . . [Also] I steal any and every idea I can get. Whoever I see doing something neat, I spike the idea and bring it into the classroom." These ideas included writing sessions and basic skills reinforcement in a computer lab and numerous problem situations. "I do a lot," he explained,

> That's not part of Math A so-called, if you want to say those units are Math A. . . . I think that other stuff is needed. I think the Math A is good, but I'm not sure [students] would be totally prepared.

In other words, I'm not throwing out all the traditional. I still think these kids need skills.

As he described his choices regarding what to include or omit, his decision rule centered around a personal conception of student success: "I want these kids to be successful; I want them to learn to think, to be able to solve problems on their own." This perspective clearly falls within the spirit of Math A.

Finally, Teacher 4 in this district used the units as they were written, using what they gave her, as she explained. In short, teachers' adaptations in the staff development district were undertaken individually and practice varied more broadly here than in the other cases. One teacher abandoned the state units; another tinkered with them; a third teacher explored the boundaries of the units, using computer labs and problem situations to engage students and to emphasize problem solving; and a fourth teacher employed the units in their unfinished form.

A Clearinghouse Model. Implementation among teachers in the support-group district functioned like a clearinghouse; changes were undertaken by individual teachers but reviewed by a curriculum revision committee and disseminated to all Math A teachers. In this process there was a clear sense among support-group teachers that adaptations were appropriate. As one teacher explained:

> I don't buy into all of [the state material]. In fact, I feel very comfortable with just being able to be free to do what I want to do and not have to line up with the framework or anything else. In fact, in our district our philosophy here was let's take what's good from the framework and what will be good for our kids and let's put it into effect. You see, that's our philosophy.

Adaptations by support-group teachers were pervasive. One teacher commented that all the district's 17 Math A teachers "have done some modifications of those units." Teacher 1 described how he "created a lot of new things that I wanted to try or I thought might work or I'd like to see if it would work. And a lot of it wasn't thought of prior, but it just came as we went along in the unit." Still, adaptations came from a sense of what was challenging for students.

Teacher 2 noted that "people are generating more individual activities that don't appear in the packets, that they think would work well for them." Teachers 2 and 3 employed a (privately bound) Math A "textbook" that had been developed in another district; they used this text to supplement the basic state Math A units.

Adaptations became a standard component in this district's implementation effort. The district, for example, established a "revision" committee to coordinate the modifications of Math A materials. As teachers modified their units, they sent the changes to a teacher-coordinator who, in turn, distributed them to the revision committee. At the same time, however, that revisions were underway, teachers maintained their connection to the core units. Teacher 1, for example, expressed general satisfaction with the state-produced material. As he reflected, "I would have to say, though, that I have been very pleased with the overall progress of the booklets the state has written."

In short, adaptations were extensive in this case as they were in the others. The process of adaptation here, however, was formalized to the extent that actions of individual teachers were compiled, reviewed, and disseminated. And although teachers acted alone, the basis of their practice—the revised curriculum materials—became more alike over time as revisions across teachers were merged and disseminated. As Teacher 1 explained:

> So the packets that we will have for next year will be substantially
> different. They will have a flavor of the state, but they will also
> have the local flavor. And the teacher will have more to draw
> from because we put in—a lot of the material is supplementary.

As it happened, Math A would be the district's first example of a course that was taught with similar materials and methods across the district's 10 high schools.

The Nature of Teachers' Content Adaptations

One network teacher casually suggested that curriculum adaptations were just part of a teacher's job: "We've said that we're going to use the materials from the state. . . . And I'm sure people will vary them as they see fit." Moreover, network teachers knew that adaptations of the state Math A units were encouraged. As the network department chair noted:

> Our project itself has never just used these units as they are writ-
> ten. . . . We do not ask [teachers] to follow the pilot literally, and
> that I think is the difference. In fact, we encourage them, keeping
> within the spirit of what Math A is about, we encourage them to
> experiment and try different things.

Nonnetwork teachers similarly adapted state Math A materials as a routine part of their implementation. What kind of adaptations did teachers undertake? Teachers' comments indicated four types of adaptations.

Filling Gaps in Existing Material. Teacher adaptations filled gaps in existing material. On this count, six teachers (three in the network district, two in the staff development district, and one in the support-group district) observed that Math A lacked sufficient work on basic skills development. The issue was as simple as supply and demand: "We include a lot of the basic skills because our kids here . . . need reinforcement in their basic skills, and those aren't included in the [Math A] units." Network teachers at one high school addressed this omission by introducing short units on basic skills reinforcement between regular Math A units. Said one:

> [We] throw in—in between some of the [Math A] units—maybe 1 or 2 weeks of going back to reviewing adding, subtracting, multiplying, and dividing fractions; adding, subtracting, multiplying, and dividing decimals. And like at the end of this year, we're going—the last 3 weeks—to go back to solving algebraic equations, unknowns, and variables because they won't get it.

Another acknowledged that they were "looking for ways to implement a week or two here or there" of instruction in basic skills. One teacher remarked that this basic skills instruction "wouldn't be as exciting as [students'] regular units, but . . . there are some skills that are really important. . . . And it would be better if there was a little more work in some of those areas."

A support-group teacher similarly explained how he filled this gap in basic skills for his students.

> I keep a textbook [*Career Mathematics for Industry and Trades*] over there along with my [Math A] notebooks, and occasionally we'll do some repetitions in fraction problems or some simple linear equations or things like that, just to reinforce some of the math that is limited in the packets. Because the packets, they'll do things, but there isn't a great [deal] of background and there isn't a great deal of repetition. So sometimes you'll have to add them a little bit.

He added this kind of material because he believed that his students needed the reinforcement.

All teachers who adapted the state units included some basic skills material. But this type of modification raises a question about the extent to which "reinforcement" misses the spirit of Math A. The risk is that "reinforcement" detracts from rather than supports the Math A curriculum. The tension here is between conventional basic skills development, like that found in other math courses, and skills development as a by-product of work on larger mathematical ideas, like probability, which Math A promoted. It is not that Math A units omitted lessons in basic skills, but that they approached skills development in a different way. A staff development teacher characterized this difference by describing Math A as "sort of a back-door approach to learning your basics." A network teacher similarly indicated that Math A was "more concerned with showing [students] applications for these skills and helping them improve those skills through applications and improving their thinking skills."

The tension was not unnoticed by teachers in this study. In part, tension arose from a conflict in policy goals: the state goal that promoted Math A as a bridge to algebra but with untried technology, and local goals related to course sequencing and its implied progression in skills development. A staff development teacher detailed the dilemma as follows:

> I can teach what the state wants. That's no problem to do. Fine. Then a kid comes out of [my class] and he's got a B in my Math A. He has done B work in Math A. Now he's going to go into your algebra class and you ask him for fractions, you ask him to find a simple one unknown, and he can't do it. So you as an algebra teacher say, "Hey, I don't care what you teach in your Math A, but you're not giving these kids the background and the building blocks that they need to survive in my class."

It was unclear whether the dilemma would be addressed best by adding traditional material to the state units or by bolstering teachers' capacities to deal with basic skills development through novel means.

Expanding Coverage of Existing Topics. Teacher adaptations also expanded coverage of topics that were addressed in insufficient depth. In the first instance, above, adaptations added topics that had been omitted; here, adaptations provided expanded coverage of existing topics. One network teacher commented, "We also add material of our own. We find the state units to be incomplete in covering stuff. . . . So often we'll make a new worksheet, or add a new lesson to clarify an idea, or to fill in a gap between two lessons." Similarly, another network teacher remarked:

We look through the [Math A] material. If it's not enough or we don't think it's strong enough, we supplement and we find other dittos, other materials . . . to help us. Because some of the stuff we don't think is strong enough, or there's not enough homework, and, like, a lot of times [the Math A materials include] a test to give at the end of the unit, and we need to give two or three tests in between.

Her network partner also voiced a concern about inadequate assessment and homework.

Fine-Tuning State-Produced Material. Teacher adaptations fine-tuned the state-produced materials. Another way of looking at this is that adaptations worked the kinks out of pilot materials. This was clearly how the teachers viewed their efforts, in part. And in this category, a range of issues arose. A network teacher began the list:

For example, we may have to retype or reword the exercises to suit our class period. Sometimes there's too much for one class period, or too little. Or maybe it's not adequate for group work, so maybe we have to change it so it's more adequate for people working together instead of making it like an individual worksheet.

Sometimes the material assumed too much on the students' part, or moved too quickly, or was too complex. Lessons expected to take 2 days, took 4; or those expected to take 1 day, took 2. Another network teacher noted that Math A lessons "seem to take a little longer than whoever wrote them planned." A staff development teacher similarly added more background material.

On this dimension, there was, not surprisingly, an experimental quality to the teachers' implementation efforts. One network teacher confessed that "we are having the students be guinea pigs. We try the units and say, 'Well, this doesn't work, so we have to make some changes.'" However, the experimental quality of the pilots engaged teachers more deeply in their instruction.

Teachers also acknowledged improvements in the quality of the state materials over time. This comment from a network teacher was exemplary: "Some units are written better than others, actually. At the start of the year, the units were a lot more difficult to work with. The last two are better."

Addressing Departmental Goals. Teacher adaptations addressed specific departmental goals. This adaptation applied more to the network case because Math A there was more integrated into the constellation of course offerings at network schools. For example, one network department wanted to assign homework every day, and of a different nature than the homework students' received in eighth grade. At another network school, the department required students to write "a lot," so Math A students were required to keep a notebook, which became part of their assessment.

Bases of Teachers' Content Adaptations

If filling gaps, expanding coverage, fine-tuning materials, and addressing departmental goals constituted types of adaptations, upon what basis were the adaptations undertaken? Teachers' comments suggested five reasons. Adaptations were based, first, on teachers' judgments regarding what their particular students needed, that is, what worked best for students. The desire to make Math A work for their kids was "the biggest factor" motivating teacher adaptations: "You just look and see what the students are going to do," said a network teacher. "Sometimes you look ahead and think what they're going to be able to do. A lot of times you go into class and you find out what they are going to do. It isn't based on just one class."

Teachers learned what their students could do and would do through exchanges in the classroom, and teachers interpreted new Math A materials in light of this experience. As one network teacher suggested:

> We get the units in advance, and I know what my kids can do and what they cannot do. And then what we do is sit as a group and say, "I think this unit doesn't reflect the reality of the kinds of kids that we have in the class." So we don't have to do it. We have that flexibility.

This flexibility was echoed by the teacher's department chair.

> Some of us involved in the [Math A] project sometimes look at the [Math A] material and say, "Well, gee, it's frustrating for my youngsters. We are not moving as I thought we were supposed to. Let's look at alternative materials.". . . If you find something that's better for that unit, use it. You are free to do that.

Network teachers already had abandoned one ersatz Math A curriculum because they felt that it inadequately addressed students' needs. As a department chair noted, "We used that [pre-algebra textbook] for a year or two and we found that, gee, it was not enough. . . . [For example,] just touching the surface [of topics] without going in-depth, we found that that was not working for the youngsters."

Regarding these adaptations, it is important to note that all these Math A teachers confronted similar students: All exhibited poor math skills and risked school failure. Most Math A students were poor, and many were recent immigrants (see Appendix, Table A.3). Thus, teachers in this study faced similar challenges in adapting curriculum materials to match their students' abilities.

Across these cases, the decision rule espoused by teachers regarding their adaptations reflected the value: make it challenging for students. Recall what a support-group teacher said earlier: "We're continually trying to upgrade the curriculum so that what's being presented to students lends to the meaning of the unit." This challenge mitigated against the dumbing down of the curriculum. A professional development challenge within this implementation process, then, entailed enhancing teachers' abilities to adapt the materials within the spirit of the framework and the format of Math A.

Second, adaptations were grounded in teachers' expertise. As the network coordinator explained, "When [teachers] are working in teams and when they are, in fact, becoming masters of what they are to do in the classroom, [then] if they come up with a supplementary lesson or if they think of a way of enhancing an idea . . . we allow them to." For network and nonnetwork teachers alike, however, as one teacher explained, "some teachers are better in manipulatives; some teachers are better in making problems; some teachers are better in classroom management," and teachers naturally follow their strengths. According to a network teacher, one benefit of the network was that each teacher's strength was put on a common table for others to draw from.

Third, adaptations arose from teacher characteristics, their experiences in the classroom but also their own personalities and creativity. To an extent, therefore, initial adaptations were idiosyncratic.

Fourth, adaptations grew out of teachers' familiarity with Math A ideas, strategies, and materials. As a network teacher described the process, "Now that we've used these units a couple of years, we're a little bit more flexible. If we feel we have to change certain things or vary it for our classes, we decide on that." In other words, with experience came familiarity, understanding, and adaptations.

Fifth, adaptations accommodated complementary instructional strategies. For example, a network high school and a staff development teacher incorporated a math lab into their Math A curricula. In the first instance, students came into the lab 3 days a week, every other week. There they encountered activities that supplemented classroom lessons: a computer activity, a hands-on application of concepts learned in the classroom, and a Math A activity.

In sum, the Math A curriculum presented to students comprised an amalgam of state and local expectations, material, and activities. In these cases of Math A, implementation molded policy and practice.

ORGANIZATION OF INSTRUCTION

The state's vision of Math A classrooms included full use of cooperative learning. One of the course's fundamental characteristics, in fact, involved reorganizing classrooms to facilitate group work among students. Working in groups (of two to four students) would enable students to adopt a more active stance toward the material they were learning (Stanley, 1989), and, in this setting, students would become responsible to each other, in part, for learning.

Accordingly, all 12 teachers in this study attempted to incorporate group work into their practice. As the earlier discussion indicated, this characteristic of the course stood out in teachers' conceptions of Math A. But teachers also used groups at varying rates and with different assessments of their own success. All network teachers, one staff development teacher, and two support-group teachers used groups (of two to four students) constantly. One of their peers in the staff development and support-group cases, respectively, mixed group and whole-class instruction. The remaining two staff development teachers and one support-group teacher found these groups to be quite problematic.

Network teachers used groups more often and may have been more comfortable with their operation than their counterparts in the other cases. Teachers' use of groups and admitted effort or expertise also varied more widely in the nonnetwork cases.

It was evident from all teachers' comments, however, that they viewed these groups as among their biggest implementation challenges. As one network teacher explained, "I have to learn. The teacher has to learn how to work with groups and teach the students how to work in groups." Her staff development counterpart conveyed her own lack of proficiency at managing groups: "I'm not real good at organizing group work and getting it to really work the way a real good person would." A support-group teacher also indicated how her organization of instruction was related to her ability to maintain control over the students. She said, "[Students] do pair work every day. And as far as my class, getting more than two of them together is chaos. It's social time. [But] I can get them to work two together." Thus, group-based instruction opened new territory for teachers and students alike, and the learning needs of both were high.

Still, for those teachers who possessed or developed some proficiency in working with groups, their comments illustrated the potential of this instructional strategy for facilitating students' learning. First, for example, a goal of Math A in network classrooms was that students tackle problems as a group, and, as a network teacher observed, groups established a structure in which students could use each other as a resource in learning mathematics.

> As a goal, right, it would be to attack a problem as a group, to work on it together. Sure you'll have the stronger kid who'll pick it up quicker and the weaker kids will look to the stronger kids, but . . . the idea is that they'll be using each other as a resource.

Second, he argued, groups facilitated student interaction, which created situations where students could turn to each other for help if they chose to.

> The desks are always arranged in groups, but that doesn't mean that every single day we do an ideal cooperative learning assignment. We don't. Many times we may give [students] a traditional assignment. But the fact that they are sitting together in groups allows them to converse, talk mathematics with a partner. If they get a problem that they can't do, they can ask someone for help. So that's what we are trying to do, realizing they can use each other as a resource in problem solving.

Another network teacher described an extension of this notion.

> Even when the students are not necessarily working on a group project, where they're working individually, the fact that they're sitting in a group does make them think more like a group. It will help promote their relationships with each other so that when they have to do a project together, there is a better chance that they can work together. So it does help put a mind set for the students that this is a group. And that it's okay to talk together and work on something together. And that that's expected.

Third, proximity may facilitate interaction, but groups also resocialized students regarding appropriate classroom behavior. After all, from first grade through eighth, students were taught not to talk during class. Math A delivered the opposite message. A staff development teacher described the transition, saying:

> In the beginning it was really tough to tell these kids in particular that it's okay to talk in class. It's okay to get out of your seat and walk around. They couldn't believe it: "This guy is not real. That's not school. He's supposed to yell at me if I talk. Therefore, we play a game, you know. I try to talk, pass notes, and he tries to catch me. Hell, now he encourages me to talk."

He went on to explain the advantage of suffering through this resocialization process.

> Because the student who is helping [another student] kind of couches it in their language or their way of thinking or in their developmental stage in the reasoning process, which obviously isn't mine. So what I think is perfectly obvious, to them isn't.

Relearning classroom behavior took time and presented unfamiliar social challenges. As one network teacher's understated comment suggested, group cohesion did not develop automatically.

> Some students don't want to work together, and you have to encourage them. And some of them [say], "I don't want to be with *these* others." But once they get together, most of the time I've seen that they enjoy it. But they have to get used to it.

As this comment implied, group work evolved over time. "This doesn't happen automatically in September," cautioned a network teacher, "but eventually as the year progresses, [students] will ask their friends [for help]."

Fourth, like students, teachers were experimenting and learning how to handle groups. Teachers talked of developing strategies for using groups productively in instruction. For example, teachers worked with different sized groups, combining students in twos, threes, or fours, although the preferred size seemed to be four. Also, teachers linked the process of forming groups to their eventual success. According to a network teacher, part of this issue involved control; part, balance.

> Groups have been successful if I do the planning of the groups. If the kids group themselves it becomes a place where they visit, show photographs, and they want to get together in groups. But when I let them do that, it just fails. . . . [Instead,] I grouped in four most of the time. I allowed them to choose one person, and then I randomly threw the groups together. So just let randomness take place. Other times I looked to see who is in which group, and if they were A students, I tried to put C and D students in the group so that there was always strength and weakness in each group.

One network teacher also mentioned that groups were rotated, monthly in one class, to give students an opportunity to work with everyone and to become comfortable with everyone. Occasionally, desks were moved back into rows for tests or other assessments "to see what [students] can do on their own."

Finally, teachers clearly expended much effort to make these groups productive. What kept them at it, in part, was a belief that there were lessons embedded in group work that extended beyond the Math A classroom. One network teacher described the issue as follows:

> I think also the students are learning how to work with other people around. I guess [in] high schools, we are not teaching that way. I mean, the kids will go outside in the marketplace and they have to work with somebody. They will never be alone. That's something; they didn't have that training before. But now we are trying to incorporate that.

Like other attributes of Math A, group work was designed in part to facilitate students' understanding of a world beyond the classroom.

THE TEACHER'S ROLE

If group work posed a major challenge to teachers in this study, then relearning their place in the classroom presented a second. Another implementation result was that 10 of the 12 teachers across these cases recognized and attempted to accommodate a new role expected of them in Math A, but the transformation was difficult. Three of the four network and support-group teachers, respectively, and one staff development teacher recognized and articulated their new role. The fourth network teacher recognized the role change but was struggling to express it in practice. Similarly, a staff development teacher and one of her support-group counterparts indicated that their roles had changed only somewhat ("not as different as they'd like it to be"), and two staff development teachers failed to associate a new instructional role with their Math A practice.

The network coordinator characterized this re-visioned teacher's role as a "facilitator of learning":

> The teacher is no longer the imparter of knowledge. The teacher is not there to demonstrate a rule, have kids copy that demonstration, and then practice that rule many times until they memorize how to do this. The teacher instead is a facilitator of the students' knowledge. The teacher creates an environment that's meaningful for the student and in that environment, hopefully, continually asks the right questions so eventually the student can formulate and, in fact, state a new concept. Now at some point in time the teacher does tell. The teacher has the obligation to tie loose ends together, to synthesize, or [to] help the student articulate. So the teacher doesn't take a vacation during this time. But the role has changed drastically, and the role is to be one of a questioner, a prober, helping a student see the idea instead of explaining one more time how you do this and hope the student can follow that process and remember it.

Similar sentiments were evident in the remarks of classroom teachers. For example, one network teacher said of Math A:

> I think my role is being redefined by this type of class. If I had never had this type of class, then my role would be different in that I would be less in participation with the students. I would be less forcing them to try to come up with the idea themselves and giving them materials to do that. It would be more of: "Here's how this idea works, here's how we get this idea, now I want you to put it into use, and here're the problems in the book to do so." The Math A is so much student active and has [students] writing and creating and trying to discover the ideas.

Likewise, a support-group teacher placed this new role at the heart of his definition of Math A. He described Math A as "a different approach to presenting mathematics where the teacher is the facilitator and the student is a learner by doing, principally. That's the whole spirit of Math A."

Relearning how to behave in the class, however, was as difficult for teachers as it was for students. As a department chair reported, teachers experienced different levels of success in adapting to this new role. One remark by a network teacher illustrated teachers' struggles to accommodate this new role, acknowledging the model but grappling with its implementation.

> As a [Math A] teacher, I'm supposed to be, okay, give some instruction but facilitate more and allow [students] to discover some ideas. When they work together, I want them to work out the answer and to help each other. And if they need help, I go and support them and help them. But they still haven't gotten used to it. Some I've noticed, they still want the answer from the teacher. They need it reinforced. But I think they're smart enough, or if they got used to it, they could help each other and work it out. That's the ideal way.

In situations where teachers were able to facilitate rather than tell, where discovery played a larger part, classroom dialogue assumed a more dynamic character. A network teacher described his ambition in this regard, saying, "I want the youngsters to be actively engaged in what they are doing, sharing, talking with each other, solving problems, you know, giving results, giving rationale, why they did things the way they did it and that type of stuff." This reinforced another goal of Math A proponents, namely, that students be more excited about math. The group organization, hands-on activities, and greater interaction were designed to work in combination to engage students. When it worked, one teacher asserted, the result was "productive noise."

These data also suggested a link between the organization of a classroom—rows and individuals versus tables and groups—and a teacher's role in classroom instruction. In this case, the group organization provided teachers with time needed to facilitate rather than tell. Two network teachers in different schools described this effect in virtually identical ways. The first commented:

> The idea is that they'll be using each other as a resource, whereas previously they would always ask the teacher, "Can you help me? Can you help me? Can you help me?" And it was real difficult for the teacher to run around to help 20 to 25 [students], or whatever the class size, and give each kid an adequate time of help. Now when they're in groups, you know if you walk over to the group and explain it and everyone is paying attention, there are four kids paying attention. So it reduces the teacher's time in explanation,

and then the kids can repeat it. If one kid understands it, then you can say, "Explain it to your partner," right there as you see that someone else is struggling. And that works great.

The second said:

You have 37 kids in your class, then for sure you would not be able to reach everybody, and you wouldn't have time to sit individually with each one of them and help them. So if you have [students] whom you pair, or four people, one in the group will be able to understand what is happening and that person will then help you to make sure that the rest of the group is working.

In both instances, group organization enabled the teacher, first, to reach more students than otherwise would be possible and, second, to transfer some of the responsibility for addressing a problem back to the group. Teachers then focused on helping the group find a solution.

TEACHERS' COMMITMENT

Probably the primary way to assess teacher commitment to Math A is to understand teachers' assessments of Math A in practice. This question is addressed in Chapter 4. Teachers' comments regarding their motivation to continue teaching Math A, however, began to illuminate their commitment to the course after only a year or two of experience with it in their classrooms. Commitment was higher among network teachers than among their counterparts in other cases. Three of the four network teachers evidenced high commitment to Math A and interest in continuing to teach it. The fourth teacher also indicated a measure of commitment, but clearly at a lower level. Interestingly, the only two teachers across these cases who did not readily volunteer to teach Math A were Teachers 3 and 4 in the network. Their hesitancy, however, subsided as their Math A experience increased.

Teachers outside the network demonstrated more varied commitments to the course. Commitment among the staff development teachers ranged from high to low, with the low ranking resulting from Teacher 1's decision to abandon the state units in favor of a basic skills curriculum. Commitment among support-group teachers, in contrast, was apparent across the teachers, two ranking high and two ranking medium.

In all these cases, commitment, or the lack of it, arose from teachers' experience with Math A in their classrooms. It was a resultant rather than an input. Teachers' actual expressions of commitment were more idiosyncratic; together, however, they demonstrated a variety of ways that commitment can emerge.

For example, one network teacher remarked that, with Math A, he had encountered a better way to teach. "I personally as a teacher would never go back to teaching as I taught previously in the traditional form. I feel [that Math A] is a much more exciting course, much more relevant for all types [of students]."

Other teachers indicated their satisfaction with the state-produced (and locally adapted) Math A materials. On one hand, this showed up in the network district as a refusal to revert to the original, ersatz, textbook-based Math A.

> I don't want to have to go to this book again, that's for sure. If we don't have the [state Math A] materials, I don't want to teach Math A again . . . I mean the units that we've been working on. It would be such a disappointment, and I don't think I could hide my frustration from the kids.

On the other hand, when asked for the most important things she could do to ensure the successful implementation of a course like Math A, a second network teacher determined "to continue with the state-produced Math A materials." Another teacher summarized his satisfaction with the way the course had developed by demonstrating a preference for Math A over his other assignment: "I'd rather have Math A classes than advanced algebra classes."

One network teacher expressed his commitment to one of the strategies or components of Math A, in this case, the group organization of instruction.

> For me to teach in a classroom now that would just have desks in a row is just almost—I won't say impossible—impractical. But I mean it's something that if I had the choice I wouldn't do it. I like the desks where kids can talk to each other and work together and that type of thing.

Two other network teachers suggested that they would carry on with Math A even if the district withdrew its support. "I would still teach the [Math A] stuff," asserted one of the teachers. "Now that I've done it for a year, I have my materials. I have my own lesson plans that I've written, notes and everything. I would just keep going."

A fifth way that commitment was expressed involved the transportation of Math A concepts and strategies into other parts of the schools' curriculum.

An alternative way of expressing commitment was to suggest that other parts of the system must change in order to accommodate the material and style of Math A. In this example, the network teacher was talking about assessments:

> Many people ask me, "Are your test scores better?" The standardized CTBS tests that the kids take from the [state]. I don't know if they would be. . . . In my opinion, that means the tests have to change. The tests are written in the old form.

In one instance, commitment was high because the staff development teacher saw Math A's positive effect on students.

> I think Math A is the only way to go. We've got to have Math A. [Why?] I think to get these kids some survival skills. . . . Math A can alleviate the need [for pictures of hamburgers on cash registers, for example]. It teaches them to think, to reason, to understand.

Finally, in the network case, the work invested in Math A by teachers—the training, learning, experimenting, failing, adapting—clearly created a sense of ownership of this curriculum, which itself generated a hard-earned commitment not likely to be awarded to new endeavors. One teacher expressed it this way: "If we've been using it and testing it for years, letting things work, and then we say. 'This doesn't work, this does,' there's some sense of ownership there."

In short, teachers' reasons for expressing commitment varied across the cases, but together they indicated that the practical effect of Math A in these classrooms was positive.

SUMMARY: PATTERNS OF IMPLEMENTATION

Implementation results revealed similarities across these network, staff development, and support-group cases. For example, all teachers were piloting Math A and using the state-produced Math A units as their basic instructional materials. All teachers also were generally knowledgeable about the central components of Math A—its role, structure, and pedagogy. In addition, 11 of the 12 teachers routinely adapted the state materials, and all of the adaptations were undertaken on the basis of student need. The types of adaptations teachers engaged in also were similar across the cases: filling gaps in existing material, expanding coverage of existing topics, fine-tuning in-process state Math A units, and, in the network case, addressing departmental goals. In short, all of these similarities deal with the structure of Math A and teachers' knowledge of course concepts.

In contrast, implementation results differed on issues dealing with the practice of Math A. For example, the teachers differed across the cases in their means of adapting Math A materials. Network teachers practiced a town hall model, where adaptations were negotiated among classroom teachers and practice was similar across the four classrooms. Staff development teachers, in contrast, practiced an individualist model, where adaptations were undertaken (or not) by teachers separately and practice varied widely, from exploring the boundaries of state policy and intent to abandoning the state units altogether. Support-group teachers adapted their materials in yet a third way, adopting a clearinghouse model, where curricular adaptations were undertaken individually but subsequently cycled through a curriculum revision committee and then disseminated to all teachers. Adaptations were mainly consistent with state policy, and variations in practice were assumed to narrow over time as teachers' materials became more similar.

Variations in practice also occurred within these cases. When this occurred—regarding teachers' organization of instruction, role, and commitment—the general pattern of implementation results indicated that practice among network teachers varied more narrowly than among their staff development or support-group counterparts, and practice in the network more closely approximated the state's image of Math A. Dissimilarly, practice among staff development teachers varied more widely than among teachers in the other cases, and practice here diverged more often from the state's prototype. In each instance, practice among support-group teachers hewed a middle course between the other two cases.

The conceptual framework of this study asserts that implementation results are a function of teachers' motivations, capacities, and interactions with their environment. Their environments particularly offer supports or impediments that facilitate or constrain teachers' implementation behavior. Thus, an exploration of teachers' motivational foundations, their goals and evaluations of relevant contexts, may illuminate differences in the implementation results described here and further elaborate the implementation potential of teacher professional networks.

PART III

Explaining Implementation Differences

CHAPTER 4

Comparing Teachers' Motivations

> I want to be a better teacher because of Math A. I'm not saying I am. I have a motivation . . . I'm thinking it all the time. What can I do to make this activity better? What can I do to bring the mathematics into focus more? What can I do to get more kids involved in this activity? Can I use this activity with another class that's doing statistics? . . . So I have a pretty high motivation to continue on. It's been a good challenge.
>
> —A support group teacher

> I felt like I was hit by a Mack truck every day.
>
> —Another support group teacher

IMPLEMENTATION RESEARCH HAS COME to focus on the motivation and capacity of individual implementers (for example, Goggin, Bowman, Lester, & O'Toole, 1990; McLaughlin, 1987, 1990a). In this study specifically, motivation refers to the direction, persistence, and vigor of Math A teachers' implementation behavior (Ford & Ford, 1987). Two factors shape this behavior. Motivation arises, first, from teachers' personal goals. Goals simply express the desired outcomes that focus and animate one's activities. Motivation arises also from teachers' evaluations of their own capabilities to accomplish implementation tasks and of the degree of support teachers expect or experience as they attempt implementation. Accordingly, teachers' motivations to implement Math A derive from answers to three questions: Will implementing this policy help me to accomplish my (teaching) goals? Am I capable of implementing it? Am I likely to encounter encouragement or disdain by trying?

Capacity, the complement to motivation, refers to the skills one needs to pursue implementation (Ford & Ford, 1987). The capacity to "deliver the goods," so to speak, entails generic skills, like planning, problem solving, and communicating; it also involves skills specific to the implementation task. In the case of Math A, specific implementation skills include utilizing cooperative learning, integrating manipulatives into instruction, and facilitating students' explorations of mathematical concepts.

In effect, motivation without capacity leads to inept implementation. Capacity without motivation, however, leads nowhere. Motivation, thus, establishes a foundation upon which implementation efforts build.

The motivation of classroom teachers to implement Math A, therefore, undergirds the transformation of policy into practice. In this regard, a range of factors potentially influence teachers' responses to Math A. Teachers' implementation contexts may include conflict or alignment between personal and policy goals or among teachers' various evaluations of Math A in practice. Implementation contexts also may include reactions of parents, other math teachers, and professional organizations; supports or constraints proffered by districts, schools, and academic departments; the availability of resources outside a district; and reinforcing activities closer to one's classroom. At base in the implementation of Math A, however, lie teachers' goals regarding their practice; that is, what teachers fundamentally hope to accomplish with the students in their charge.

TEACHERS' PERSONAL GOALS

Math A policy goals fell into two categories. First, the policy contained an outcomes goal regarding students' success in the math sequence. As a network department chair explained, "The fundamental goal of Math A would be to prepare more students for success in the college-preparatory program." Her assessment coincided with the state mathematics framework, which positioned Math A between eighth grade arithmetic and college-preparatory algebra. Another outcomes goal, however, sought to enhance students' enjoyment of mathematics and to foster confidence in its pursuit. Second, Math A included a number of process goals related to how students learn mathematics. These process goals included group instruction, active students, mathematical explorations, manipulatives, math themes, and teachers as facilitators of student knowledge.

In contrast to the state goals, teachers across these cases expressed personal goals regarding Math A in more immediate and sometimes beseeching terms. A comparison of teacher and policy goals reveals that network teachers incorporated the state's goals regarding Math A outcomes into their own constructions of desired outcomes, whereas teachers in other cases, with one exception, did not. As a network department chair explained, "The teachers at [this high school], we want to see the numbers of students who are participating in the college-preparatory sequence increase. That's really important to us." Specifically, three of four network teachers expressed their goals, in part, in terms of preparing their students for algebra. The fourth network teacher acknowledged that he also was working to prepare students for algebra, but he chose to cast his personal goals in other terms. Outside the network, only one of eight teachers described his goals similarly, focusing on his students' preparation for algebra.

The commitment of network teachers to this outcomes goal arose from two circumstances. On one hand, network teachers viewed their use of Math A in terms of addressing specific department-level needs. That is, network teachers were concerned that African-American and Latino students were not succeeding in college-preparatory math classes and that somehow teachers needed to foster greater student success. Addressing this problem meant helping incoming freshmen to better adjust to the demands of high school. A network department chair explained, "I've always wanted to start some kind of course [to help these students], and I've tried many and failed many, many times." Math A, in this instance, addressed both goals, supporting minority students and helping students adjust to high school.

On the other hand, network teachers' goals were nested within similar local policy system goals. In the network case, unlike its staff development and support-group counterparts, district goals defined Math A as a transition course between eighth grade arithmetic and Algebra 1. Teachers and district officials both attributed a similar mission to Math A, namely, to place more students in algebra.

In contrast, district officials in the staff development case did not forcefully state district goals for Math A. As one staff development teacher interpreted his district's intent, "I'm basically free to do what I want to do. And the district sort of has that approach, too: Do what is best for you." Schools and teachers in this case interpreted Math A goals differently. For Teachers 1 and 2, Math A served juniors and seniors who had failed algebra. In this situation, the locally constructed purpose of Math A was different from the role ascribed to it in the network case. Here officials viewed Math A as a means to maintain student interest in mathematics or to provide credits needed for graduation rather than to assist students along in the math sequence. Interestingly, these staff development teachers also were the ones who described Math A as "a leper colony" and "a dumping ground." As one of them declared, "I pick up all the strays. . . . Most of these kids have been kicked out of somebody else's class."

Conversely, Teacher 3 in the staff development district was strongly committed to Math A as preparation for algebra: "My intention is that every one of these kids will go into algebra next year—not pre-algebra or anything else. Into algebra." Teacher 4, however, viewed this transition more as a theoretical possibility than a likelihood.

In the support-group case, district goals were contested. Administrators preferred to align Math A locally with the state framework; department chairs urged that the course be available to upperclass students who had failed algebra. One support-group teacher noted that the role of Math A in the district was "up in the air," with mixed messages coming from district officials about whether the course was important, whether it still would be offered in 5 years, and, if so, what it would be like at that time. As she viewed the situation, "There are a couple of people on the math council [composed of department chairs] that don't think a lot of Math A, and they're fighting it; and then there are others who feel that it has its good points." Like two of her staff development peers, however, she taught sophomores and juniors primarily, most of whom were not bound for algebra. She too characterized Math A as "a dumping ground." In support of this notion, she described the variety of paths her students might take after completing Math A and defined the course's potential against these circumstances.

> Some of them will take consumer math. Some will take basic algebra. I've got juniors, which means they can quit taking math. I have sophomores, which means they've completed their 2-year requirement, which means they can quit taking math. Most of them said they're going to take more math. For some of the kids, it has given them a little boost because they have finally done well in a math class and they finally have understood something, something difficult.

These support-group teachers, who did not use Math A as a transition course into algebra, focused on the (policy) goal of having students enjoy and appreciate mathematics, rather than preparing them for future courses.

Two of the four network teachers and one of the eight nonnetwork teachers also incorporated Math A's process goals into their own conceptions of desired outcomes. These network and support-group teachers alike focused on the benefits to students of cooperative learning and group work. In this regard, one network teacher described a broad view of the advantages offered by Math A's particular instructional processes. In explaining his goals, he said:

> Personally, I think the groups are a very important goal. . . . I think that the group work is something that they can take with them when they forget about math. I think that doing a lot of writing in their math class and explaining how they got things—that process

improves their thinking skills quite a bit. It makes them understand it more, it requires more understanding on their part. And that is a skill which when you forget about the math, they are learning more about how to express their thoughts and how to organize their thoughts on paper.

Apart from policy and pedagogy, teachers across these cases fundamentally wanted their students to succeed. Teachers stated this message clearly and consistently. As one network teacher put it, his goal was to "make more of these kids successful." His staff development counterpart expressed this sentiment similarly, even urgently, saying, "I want these kids to be successful, to learn how to think, to be able to solve problems on their own." The alternative he envisioned involved young adults perennially punching pictures of Big Macs on cash registers that required no independent thought on the part of their operators.

Specifically, 10 of the 12 teachers in this study expressed their teaching goals in terms of facilitating students' success. Definitions of this success included pursuing algebra (four teachers), learning to work cooperatively with others (three teachers), graduating from high school (two teachers), gaining confidence (two teachers), improving thinking skills (four teachers), developing skills applicable beyond the classroom setting (two teachers), pursuing some endeavor beyond high school (one teacher), understanding that many answers can be "right" (one teacher), realizing that failure carries no stigma but is only part of the learning process (one teacher), and developing a "good" level of competence (one teacher).[1]

On one dimension, preparing students to succeed included mundane tasks. As one network teacher described her efforts:

Mainly [my goal] is to instill some discipline into how [students] study: how to do your homework, how to be organized, how to get ready for each math class. And in the end, I want them to learn to do that for every class [and] learn how to use those same skills: taking notes, keeping class work, keeping your homework organized, and to study for a test.

On another dimension, this preparation presented clear challenges. A network department chair put it this way:

I have to deal with the socialization that the Math A youngster wants to come in with, the sense that school is a place to be, but academics [are] not foremost. It's more of a social gathering type thing, and those energies that are playing among the ninth graders

coming to high school without a sense of purpose, you have to
also deal with that energy. You have to take that, harness it, and
redirect it.

Two exceptions to this theme relating teachers' goals and students'
success arose among the staff development teachers. In these instances,
teachers cast their personal goals in terms of ensuring that students produce assigned work (Teacher 1) and having students enjoy math (Teacher
2). In the latter case, the teacher aligned her goals, in part, with Math A
policy goals and with three support-group teachers who also viewed
students' enjoyment of mathematics as central to their learning. In the
former instance, Teacher 1's expression of goals, in unimaginative terms,
contrasted with his motivation to substantially alter the Math A curriculum. Recall that he abandoned the state Math A units. He did so, as he
explained, because "there are certain things that I feel that these kids
need." In this way, he did indicate a desire to foster students' success,
although his means diverged from other teachers in the study.

On the whole, teachers' goals evidenced an immediate and personal
quality. For them, desired outcomes related to individuals, behaviors,
and family circumstances. Teachers dealt with policy and its up-close
consequences. A network department chair suggested, "There's an inequity in the way we're teaching [certain students]." This personal quality
of teachers' goals distinguished classroom expectations from more distant
and abstract policy intentions.

As a result, teachers stated goals simply. A support-group teacher
commented, for example, "I think probably the main goal, believe it or
not, is to enjoy math. . . . And that to me is the key." A network teacher
explained:

> My first goal is that I want [students] to graduate from high
> school. I don't want them to drop out of school. And so a lot of
> my energy goes first into the social atmosphere of the classroom to
> make sure there's good attendance, to make sure kids come to
> class regularly.

Another said: "My overall goal is to have them understand that they
could pursue something more than just high school, and that they should
be prepared—mathematically, let's say, and socially—how to interact
with all the people."

Desiring his students to succeed but also working amidst high student
absenteeism, a network teacher defined his goals in terms that he could
address. He said, "I really have to work harder now, especially this year,

to just make my classroom almost a requirement to reach whoever is in the room." His self-imposed standard linked his sense of success or failure with the domain he controlled: his classroom. He could not address the problems associated with getting students to his class, but once they were there, whoever they were, he redoubled his efforts to teach them mathematics. As he related, "In some classes there are only 50% of the students that show up. But of that 50%, at least 90% are learning."

Cast in these terms, teachers in each case desired a curriculum that was itself motivating and efficacious. A network teacher observed that "we're looking for curriculum that is fresh for high school kids." The advent of Math A enabled faculty in the network case to drop a course, fundamental math, that they believed did not work. Dropping the course related to the network's purpose in using Math A. Thus, the freshness of the Math A curriculum in the network case yielded a twofold benefit: replacing an unsatisfactory curriculum and motivating low-level math students. A staff development teacher similarly described the power of Math A to motivate and hold students' attention, explaining:

> I actually have a couple [of students] who come to class and do their Math A and then they take off for the rest of the day.... Or [others will] come in for the first two or three periods of the day [through Math A] and then they're gone. Or I had one little girl, Lydia, she comes in [to Math A] after lunch; she usually cuts the mornings.

In fact, teachers viewed motivating students to engage mathematics and to enjoy it as central both to their instructional challenge and to students' understanding. One support-group teacher represented this challenge, saying:

> If you can motivate a student, I think that's probably the single most difficult task that a teacher has with most of his students. It's not can he communicate the information, or whatever, but can he motivate the student to open up and focus on this, "Oh, let's get into this."

His peer across town framed the importance of motivation to students' learning, commenting, "I think that if [students] are enjoying [mathematics], they are probably getting something out of it, too. I don't know how you grade that or test it, but I think that in the long run that will make whatever the future holds for [them] a little more palatable." In other words, teachers linked students' motivation and learning in the same way that the overall argument in this book connects teachers' motivation and implementation behavior.

In summary, Math A teachers across these cases expressed their personal goals primarily in terms of fostering students' success. In the network case, unlike the others, teachers' goals also coincided with state policy goals regarding the intended outcomes of Math A, namely, that students subsequently enroll in college-preparatory algebra. This factor, along with the network teachers' use of Math A to better serve a segment of their student population, to assist students in the transition to high school, and to replace an older curriculum that did not work, enabled network teachers to attribute a common purpose or mission to Math A that escaped staff development and support-group teachers. In turn, this common purpose also helped network teachers to avoid the designation of Math A as a dumping ground. Furthermore, the alignment of teacher, district, and state goals in the network case mitigated conflicts regarding desired outcomes that might constrain teachers' motivation, assessment of Math A, and implementation behavior, as happened in the support group case. As the discussion below demonstrates, this common purpose and alignment of policy and professional expectations also may explain modest differences in teachers' evaluations of Math A in practice.

TEACHERS' EVALUATIONS OF MATH A IN PRACTICE

Beyond personal goals, teachers in this study confronted a range of factors influencing their motivation to implement Math A. Primary among these influences stand teachers' assessments of Math A, assessments shaped by their experiences with Math A in the classroom. Central to these assessments, particularly in light of teachers' goals regarding the success of their students, were the reactions of Math A students to this new and different curriculum.

Teachers' General Assessments of Math A

More than any other factor, teachers' classroom experiences with Math A figured prominently in their discussions of Math A and affected their overall assessments of the course. On this dimension, with one exception, teachers across these cases evaluated Math A in generally positive terms.

Eleven of the 12 teachers evaluated their experiences with Math A favorably. Eleven teachers, that is, affirmed Math A's potential, based on positive outcomes they observed with their students. Specifically, three of the four network teachers, one of four staff development teachers, and two of four support-group teachers awarded Math A high overall marks, reporting their assessments in enthusiastic terms. For example, a staff development teacher asserted that "Math A is the only way to go. We've got to have Math A." Why? "To get these kids some skills, survival skills, if you want to use a trite term." A network teacher summarized his position, saying, "The strategies are effective." By this he meant both the content of Math A and its instructional strategies. As he explained, "The problems are richer, they're better written, and also working in groups has reduced the individual [student's] anxiety." He concluded, "It's a much more exciting course, much more relevant for all types [of students]."

Five other teachers also reviewed Math A positively, although not as enthusiastically as those teachers described above. The reservations expressed by one network teacher and two staff development and support-group teachers, respectively, centered variously around the appropriate place of Math A in the high school curriculum, expressed as a concern regarding the "dumping ground" character they attributed to Math A when the course served primarily a hodgepodge of juniors and seniors; the efficacy of Math A's approach for a broad selection of students; the scope of the mathematics, specifically that the math might be inadequate to assist students into a college-track program; and the utility of the "100% hands-on" approach. Reservations notwithstanding, one staff development teacher described Math A as "a good experience for kids," and the support-group teachers in this category dubbed Math A "a viable approach" in which students were "actually probably learning more than they have."

In the one instance where a (staff development) teacher dropped the state units entirely, substituting a curriculum devised from general math, career math, and pre-algebra textbooks, he chose this route

> because these kids, they need the basic foundations. These kids do not have the basics, and the state assumes a kid has an eighth-grade background in math when he comes into high school. Well, [you] don't want to assume anything because these kids do not have it.

As his comment indicates, this teacher viewed Math A basically as a mismatch between a product and its market. His primary concern was that no course options remained for juniors and seniors who had not succeeded in algebra or geometry. The value of Math A, in his terms, was the freedom it offered from district guidelines regarding the content and pacing of curriculum. He used this freedom to interact more with students and to focus the course on basic skills and concepts that he believed his students never learned.

In short, six teachers across these cases (three network, one staff development, and two support group) described positive and enthusiastic assessments of Math A. Five additional teachers across the cases (one network and two each in the staff development and support-group cases) articulated concerns about the quality and use of Math A, but they also assessed the course's potential positively and related stories of its efficacy with students. One staff development teacher, in contrast, viewed Math A as a mismatch between a product and its market and abandoned the state units in favor of a basic skills curriculum.

Bases of Teachers' Evaluations of Math A

Teachers' evaluations of Math A indicated that the course, at some level, "worked." As a support-group teacher explained, "Most of the teachers in this district would probably say that I'm sold on this thing and, therefore, that's why I'm optimistic [about Math A's potential]. But I wasn't sold per se. I'm sold because I see it work every day pretty well." Reflecting on the broader effort demanded of Math A students in writing, explaining, thinking, and understanding, a network teacher concluded that Math A is "a lot more important course." For this teacher, not only was Math A "a better way to teach" but he also felt that he was a much better teacher as a result.

Beyond general impressions, a majority of teachers across the cases cited three reasons for their positive assessments of Math A. The course in practice appeared to be a better match for students than traditional mathematics courses. All four network teachers, two staff development teachers, and one support-group teacher cited this reason in their evaluations of Math A. The fit occurred on different dimensions. Math A matched students' abilities and maturity levels.[2] That is, it facilitated students' academic accomplishments and, more than conventional math courses, it also helped to develop students' social and interpersonal skills. This occurred because the manipulatives and group work forced students to cooperate in order to succeed.

The manipulatives also provided an alternative way for students who had trouble grasping abstract concepts to approach mathematics. A support-group teacher described such an instance, saying:

> I had a girl that—I asked her what she was doing, why she wasn't in algebra. She said because she failed it twice. And she goes, "I'm a visualize person. . . . I have to learn by doing." And this girl is

[now] solving two-step equations. She had, like, 108 out of 108 points on the test. And she just said, "All of a sudden I could see what was going on, and then I understood it."

The teacher continued:

> She couldn't deal with it just on the board, the equations. But as soon as she had the algebra tiles in front of her and she could start moving things around, then she said, "Now I understand what we were doing before." And for a lot of the kids it's just—they look at you writing all this algebra on the board and first of all, they tune you out, and at least with the hands-on material, they're doing things with you.

Teachers also viewed Math A positively because they concluded that Math A provided a better approach to teaching mathematics. Two network and staff development teachers, respectively, and three support-group teachers noted this difference in their course evaluations. They argued that traditional mathematics at this applied level had failed to facilitate teachers' goals (that students succeed) or policy goals (that students go on to algebra). A network teacher characterized the difference, reporting:

> I've been teaching for 20 years now, and I started out in the traditional mode. And it wasn't working for me as a teacher; I wasn't enjoying it as much. And it wasn't working for the kids. And the kids, instead of getting turned on to mathematics, were getting turned off, because what was happening in high school, they were repeating a lot of stuff that for one reason or another they didn't do well in middle school. So just repeating something you don't do well in doesn't necessarily mean you're going to get it better the third, fourth, fifth time. You have to be taught it with a different approach, and I think that's what we're doing in Math A.

Other teachers shared the perception that the traditional approach to mathematics education at this level had failed. As a department chair explained, "We had fundamental math classes; we had general math. But those are basically skills [courses], developing those skills that the youngsters have not acquired along the way before they got here. Some of us found that wasn't doing it for them."

Another network teacher described the traditional approach similarly, saying, "I don't think it was as good for the students." As these comments suggest, the repetitiveness of fundamental or general math "turned students off" to mathematics. A staff development teacher, for example, observed that Math A students "like not having the drill and practice and the tedium of doing 37 problems over that they've done for the last 8 years and still don't get. It's just different." A support-group teacher described Math A's improvement over traditional mathematics on this dimension, noting:

> I get comments back from the kids that this is real fun, but when are we going to do any math? . . . It's because it is not the traditional math, and that's what they're used to. So I think it gives them some other perspectives on what math can be besides the stuff that every kid learns to hate.

In contrast, the network district's early attempts to implement a course called Math A using a best-available textbook promised little in terms of different student outcomes. As one teacher remarked, "it is just written in a different book in a little different way, and I think you just teach it conventionally." Like its predecessors, this ersatz Math A was not stimulating for students.

If fundamental and general math were boring, they also failed, according to one network teacher, to help students grasp mathematical concepts, like "a comfortableness with variable, which we've always thought was real poorly developed in traditional textbooks. Kids can memorize what a letter is, but they have no idea what it signifies." Shortcomings such as this directly led at least one network teacher to be open to the possibility of change. Another network teacher said of Math A, "I think it's much better than it was in the past when we were using a textbook because the students are more involved with it and the teachers are involved."

A majority of teachers across the cases also noted a third reason for their positive assessments of Math A, namely, that the course was more successful at engaging students in mathematics. All four network teachers plus one staff development teacher and two support-group teachers cited this characteristic as important to their course evaluations. Part of this assessment, discussed earlier in the chapter, involved Math A's ability to motivate students. A network department chair, himself a Math A teacher, explained:

> I think Math A really has helped them want to come to class, want to be there, because you make it fun for them. And I tell them, if it's not fun, I don't want to do it. If they can't come in here and talk and interact and verbalize mathematics, then they can't be my

student. They enjoy doing that type of thing. But these are the same kids that will cut other classes.

In this regard, Math A held students' interest; it was more stimulating.
Math A, for example, provided opportunities for students to encounter math through games. On this point, one network teacher mused:

> I think [students] see a game with dice or a game with cards, and they are interested in it. The question is, is it a fair game? They are a little more interested in figuring out if it's a fair game than figuring out how to multiply fractions together, but they're going to have to multiply fractions together in figuring out if it's a fair game. So I really think it takes their minds off of a lot of the tedious work and focuses them on something that's more interesting.

Students, thus, enjoyed the manipulatives and hands-on approach. One teacher commented that "there is no sense of boredom." Students were "involved" with the math. A staff development teacher noted that "the concrete, hands-on approach does get kids into thinking about math in ways that more abstract calculations wouldn't do. They like that." A network department chair argued that there is something about Math A that holds students in class, that

> makes them want to come in. It is activity-based. The fact that they can come in, they can write, talk, they can do tessellations, they can create their own graphs, sometimes create problems that they have seen in the community. But they have not recognized that it is mathematics. It's something that they can learn math from, those kinds of experiences.

He implied too that Math A was able to capture some students who otherwise would not be interested in continuing math because "they see the richness that's involved in some of the activities that they're involved in and some of the things that they can come up with and make."
Moreover, when students' motivation increased, their attitude toward mathematics became more positive. As one network teacher remarked, "I have seen a tremendous change in attitude. . . . I see no tension. I see no anxiety toward mathematics like I have seen. . . . They seem to enjoy the class, and enjoy their friends, and enjoy me in this process." Teachers portrayed this kind of change in part as a function of the curriculum's novelty and its different organization of instruction. In the words

of one network teacher, cooperative learning "helps the social atmosphere of the class, and kids feel good in the class. And then the new curriculum helps present some material they may have seen in elementary and middle school, but in a different atmosphere."

A network teacher also linked higher student engagement to greater student effort. He described the magnitude and consequences of this big change in his classroom, explaining:

> Much more, much more effort. I get more homework. I get more attempt. If I give them a problem, they try to do it. No one says, "I can't do this," or "Do this for me," or "How do I do this?" They'll make an attempt. They might not be successful in doing it—they are still very weak [in] skills. But that's a dramatic change. Previously, many people—the student—would sit there and do nothing. If they got to something and were given a problem [that] they felt they couldn't do, many students would just do nothing. Now I see that attempt. They'll try. They may still have a lot of difficulty, but at least they'll try.

His departmental peer attributed a similar change in his students to the different organization of his classroom. "When I look at the [Math A] students," he said, "compared to when I had students in rows, they are much more alive. They're more talkative, they're more interested, they seem to have more energy in the class. So I would use those as indicators that it is working."

A third network teacher suggested that Math A student groups caused some students to pursue math questions with peers where they might give up the pursuit when dealing strictly with a teacher. As he noted:

> Sometimes they have questions because they may think, "Well, if I ask the question, then the rest of the group will think I'm dumb," or "I'm not asking this question because I'm stupid." But if [they] have somebody, another friend, another peer, I see that they are more willing to ask. And if they don't understand, they ask again until they get it.

Also:

> I find that they understand better, quicker, if a friend or peer explains it to them than when I explain it. I guess I try to do it more in a mathematical way because that's the way I'm thinking about

it, and the kid will use a different language. That makes it easy to understand.

This teacher also believed that students working in groups encouraged recalcitrant peers to "get involved."

Notice how these changes in students also altered working conditions in classrooms. More student engagement, effort, and activity translated into a more responsive teaching environment. More responsiveness from students, in turn, enhanced teachers' motivation to pursue Math A implementation.

Evolution of Student Engagement. Student engagement did not flourish immediately, however. Students resisted participation in Math A activities, in part, because the demands it made on them, the tasks it required them to undertake, were so unusual compared with assignments in other math courses. "They are sort of unprepared for the fact that they have to write their answers," explained one network teacher. "They have to verbalize their answers. They have to get up in front and give group reports. It's not something they would expect." Another teacher noted that "a lot of students have a hard time adjusting at first; it's new, this approach. . . . A lot of them want to have those [eighth-grade] worksheets back."

Students, like teachers, had to relearn what to expect and how to behave in the classroom, participating in groups and using manipulatives, for example.

Students also had to learn to operate in the new teacher-as-facilitator relationship. One network teacher observed that "some [students] I've noticed, they still want the answer from the teacher." This was a big lesson to embrace. To elaborate this point, a network teacher compared his U.S. -born students with their classmates who were recent immigrants. The former group resisted Math A; the latter group was more accepting. He attributed this difference in attitude to the fact that the foreign-born students were trying to understand the norms and culture of their new school, whereas the native students were used to a teacher-tells model of instruction. These expectations created resistance.

> There is a certain . . . expectation of you as a teacher. "You are the teacher; you tell me how to do it. Give me the answer and that's all I need. Prepare me for the test; that's all." While the [immigrant] kids, they struggle because they don't know the language, they don't know the system, so they are learning all that at the same time. And so when you show them a way, any easy way, to

grab the [mathematical] theme, the concepts, they will take it. And they will try anything.

In this respect, Math A was more demanding than other math classes. Over time, however, teachers reported that students not only accepted but enthusiastically engaged Math A. A network teacher described his experience, observing, "At first some of them will say, 'I don't want to do that,' but once they get into it they enjoy it. . . . Yesterday, they were shaking these coins. I mean, it was like Las Vegas. Sometimes they get into it, and I think they enjoy it." This positive response took time to develop, however, as another teacher cautioned: "It doesn't happen in September. There's a big difference between our students in [Math A] now [April] and . . . September, in the way they are able to work together and in their motivation. And there is a big difference." Of course, Math A was not magic: "There are a few [students] that no matter what you try, they're going to fool around and play."

Math A and the Transition to Algebra. Beyond these three modal reasons for Math A teachers' positive assessments of the course across the cases, network teachers specifically also perceived the course as easing students' transitions to algebra. Math A will be evaluated by the state, in part and from a policy perspective, on the basis of whether it assists students into algebra. Some network teachers were optimistic that this was happening already. Their assessments were impressionistic, however. No data were available to indicate that Math A was moving students into algebra. Nevertheless, network teachers' comments were suggestive of the course's potential, and these impressions composed part of their evaluation of the course.

For example, a network department chair described a noticeable change in those Math A students who continued on into a pilot college-preparatory program that resembled Math A in concept and style. She said:

> We've started already to see some results. Those of us who are teaching in that pilot college-preparatory course see that those students who have been in Math A come to the first year of that pilot course ready to work in groups, ready to explain, ready to use manipulatives, ready to use calculators when needed, knowing that mathematics is not going to be a page of 30 problems that they have to work out and get them all correct. . . . Which is what they had in the eighth grade.

She also asserted that Math A was capturing some of those students who might not have gone into a college-preparatory sequence. Another mused:

> I don't know if it's because of the way I am teaching or because of the curriculum, [but] there are students who previously would never have taken an advanced course in mathematics but now are willing to make that challenge and go on to geometry, trigonometry, etc., etc.—a few. I remember classes when no one would want to. It's a long hard road.

Minor Themes. Other reasons for teachers' generally positive evaluations of Math A appeared in a smaller number of instances across these cases. For example, three teachers reported that Math A facilitated their own goals. "Definitely," as one network teacher was quick to remark. Another conveyed the same sentiment: "Very much so," and went on to report the resultant: "That's why it's so easy for me to change."

Other reasons involved Math A's ability to promote a better and more useful classroom climate (one teacher) and to provide students with needed and broader skills, particularly what teachers termed "thinking skills" (three teachers). Moreover, teachers regarded the lessons embedded in Math A's instructional strategies, particularly group work and joint explorations and projects, as relevant beyond classroom doors (three teachers). For example, "They're working, four of them together, and trying to solve whatever the problem is. And that will help them as they go on to algebra or whatever." Three teachers also described Math A as a better way to teach, and, importantly, as a way to improve students' attitudes and motivation to learn mathematics (four teachers).

Teachers' criticisms of Math A were discussed in some detail in Chapter 3 and earlier in this chapter. Most of this criticism sorted into three categories regarding the quality of the state-produced materials, the absence of sufficient work in basic skills, and the role of Math A in the high school math sequence.

Summary

Teachers' evaluations of Math A were generally positive and based on the curriculum's ability to facilitate student learning. In this regard, a majority of teachers across the cases viewed Math A as a better match for their students, a better approach to teaching, and better at engaging students in mathematical inquiry. More student engagement and activity yielded a more responsive work environment for teachers, which in turn enhanced teachers' motivation. Network teachers also believed that Math

A was assisting students into algebra, although no data were available to substantiate these impressions. Teachers' assessments of Math A also included criticisms, mostly regarding the issue of basic skills development at a level adequate to continue students' progress through the math sequence. But the basic, albeit early, message from teachers across the cases was that Math A demonstrated potential to facilitate math learning among their students.

REACTION OF PARENTS AND MATH PROFESSIONALS

Reactions of individuals outside teachers' classrooms also potentially affect teachers' motivation to implement Math A. Included among these influences are parents, other math teachers, and professional trends in mathematics education that predispose educators to (or against) particular reforms.

Absent Parents

Across these cases, parents were uniformly absent from teachers' implementation discussions and efforts. Staff development and support-group teachers, for example, reported no contact with parents. As one support-group teacher in the suburban district noted, "Many of the seniors are on their own, fending for themselves. They don't even have parents." Moreover, he said, "I've got kids in some of my classes who have kids— they already have kids—and they're not even married."

The contact reported by network teachers included only complaints. "The only feedback I got," said one network teacher, "was from [the parents of] a few students who had poor grades." Parents also complained that Math A students did not have a textbook and that students lacked regular days and amounts of homework, issues teachers raised independent of parental comment.

As others noted, parent contact was unexpected. "Math A student parents don't usually come to open house," explained one network teacher. "There's very little contact with the school at all. I don't think they're that interested." Another network teacher expressed her belief that there was little reinforcement of mathematics education in the homes of Math A students. Moreover, even if parents wanted to help, one network teacher doubted their ability to do so. Math A was unfamiliar to parents. In his words:

> These [Math A] things are so untraditional that parents who have been taught traditionally say, "I don't understand this." And then

if the kid is having trouble, he or she can't say to the parent, "Well, this is what the teacher said, and I just don't quite get it." The parent doesn't understand what the student is doing.

Overall, parents did not figure prominently in the motivation or implementation activity of teachers in this study.

Resistant Teachers

Eight of the 12 teachers in this study reported reactions of their non-Math A departmental peers to this unusual course. In only one instance, in the staff development district, did a Math A teacher indicate that his peers viewed Math A positively, and this opinion was tentative: "I think they will all say okay."

In every other instance, Math A teachers characterized the reaction of their peers in terms of fear and resistance. Their opposition was based on perceptions that Math A overlooked basic skills and focused instead on "highfalutin ideas" about applications of mathematics. They resisted Math A because it lacked a textbook and regular homework assignments—the canon of mathematics instruction—and because it utilized manipulatives. One teacher reported that his non-Math A peers feared the noise and movement associated with cooperative learning, and all the low-level students. Another teacher explained that his peers resisted the teaching methodology and all the "oddball" preparations. Finally, one support-group teacher noted that teachers simply feared change and, as a result, concluded that "we will still have a large faction of resistance."

An Affirming Profession

In contrast to the resistance of their school or district peers, when these Math A teachers placed Math A in the context of professional trends in mathematics, they viewed themselves in the vanguard of sweeping professional changes. A support-group teacher captured this trend and his non-Math A peers' reactions, saying:

People know it's lurking there. It's waiting around the corner for them like a New York mugger. Because it doesn't matter whether it's Math A or algebra or calculus, the whole scope and sequence of the framework says that we're going to go—or attempt to go—to more of an explorations-based, project-based sort of system for teaching math. And it may not be more effective, but it will certainly be different.

His characterization of teachers' response to the then-proposed new framework was underwhelming: "I think this framework that [the state] put out, everybody got to buzzing about it. And they said, 'Well, we'll begin to implement it by the year 2000.' Well, plenty of people said, 'I'll be retired by then. No problem.'" This automatic resistance contrasts with the assessments of Math A teachers in this study who worked through the novelty of the program in their classrooms and reported, among other things, that Math A facilitated their personal goals and represented a better way to teach.

Most of the comments regarding Math A's place in professional trends came from network department chairs. One chair described the National Council of Teachers of Mathematics standards and goals, the state mathematics framework, and Math A as reinforcing similar themes. She said:

> It pushes us in one direction. The standards are really asking students to become, as they describe it, students who are powerful in mathematics. And they're asking for students who can think, who can conjecture, who can justify, who can solve problems. And that's what Math A is after, too.

A network teacher reinforced this sense of alignment, suggesting, in regard to Math A, "I think that's the way we're going." This trend surfaced closer to home, also, through the work of the California Mathematics Project and other professional organizations. As the department chair above also noted, "We are all trying to move in the same direction."

In fact, another network department chair viewed his work with Math A as an operational extension of these national trends. He explained how

> we look at the standards and look at the framework and look at the habits of mind, and look at the kinds of things that [the framework has] done, that it's advocating—the connections, the communication, the writing, teaching for understanding; you know, those kinds of things. It is those things that we look at and what we are seeing on a national level that we are saying, yes, we can try.

Also close to home in the network district, a few nonnetwork schools "jumped on the bandwagon and [were] changing their curriculum. . . . They have taken . . . a step and are actually implementing [Math A]." Thus, professional activities within and without the network district, particularly, reinforced teachers' efforts to implement Math A.

LOCAL POLICY SYSTEM SUPPORTS

Thus far, the motivational foundation of Math A teachers' implementation behavior has consisted of their own assessments of Math A in practice, including responses and characteristics of their students, and the reactions of parents, other teachers, and professional trends. Also important to teachers' implementation motivation were material supports available to them at work, particularly those found at district, school, and department levels.

District-Level Implementation Support

Math A teachers in this study faced different configurations of district, school, and department implementation support. In Chapter 2 I discussed some of the differences among the levels and types of support proffered by these network, staff development, and support-group districts. With the addition of classroom teachers' comments here, a fuller picture of district-level implementation supports emerges.

The network district, for example, offered symbolic policy-level support but provided substantial material resources at the level of the district math coordinator. As one network teacher remarked, "They [meaning the district] are tremendously supportive of Math A."

Beyond pronouncements of support, material advantages also were evident. For example, the network pilot itself was launched under the auspices of the district. The district, that is, was a partner in developing the network proposal, an important symbolic step that also structured the district's material involvement. Furthermore, the district designated federal Chapter 1 funds to support Math A staff development activities. The district, too, found other ways to organize and support relevant staff development activities. As one network teacher remarked of this willingness to bring teachers together, and to find and fund the substitute teachers that made these sessions possible, "If you have the support from the principal and from the main [district] office, it makes [implementation] a lot easier." The district also reproduced Math A materials for classroom use, in itself a prodigious undertaking due to the loose-leaf nature of the curriculum. The schools did not themselves have the resources to handle the photocopying required by Math A.

Still, the specific parts played by the district were not always clear to teachers. As a network teacher commented, "I don't know exactly what they're funding, but they are funding a portion of the Math A. They play a big role." Another network teacher offered a contrasting view. To him, district support was unclear and problematic: "I don't hear anything from the district. Money probably didn't come from the district; it probably came from the state. I don't know what the district's outlook is on [Math A]."

Three additional points are relevant to support in the network district. First, the network district, as a matter of philosophy, delegated significant implementation responsibility to teachers, for example, in designing staff development activities. In this sense, the district per se was supporting but not leading Math A implementation. Second, the district's embrace of Math A was motivated by the high number of failures in algebra classes, again coinciding with teachers' goals and the state's purpose for Math A. Third, to teachers "the district" largely meant district-level math subject coordinators rather than the superintendent or school board.

The staff development district operated under a strong yet incremental district model of Math A implementation but with few material resources forthcoming during the implementation pilot. One staff development teacher, for example, reported that material supports were promised but never delivered. Two of his staff development peers confirmed that district supports were not forthcoming. He also indicated that he was free to do what he wanted with the Math A curriculum. In his view, "Nobody cares [what I do] as long as I have the classes, create no waves, and I don't flunk every one of my kids. . . . You create no waves, everybody is happy." In this case, the district planned Math A implementation and established the pilot and the pacing of subsequent implementation efforts, but the district's support during the pilot did not extend beyond this level.

In contrast, the support-group district exhibited a strong presence down to the classroom level, even though district decision making was rife with political bargaining and the role of Math A was contested. "I don't know of anybody who's given more effort to [Math A implementation] than our district has," said one teacher. At the same time, his peer across town noted how Math A had become "a political hardball that's been thrown all over the place." Yet the district provided substantial monetary resources to teachers and offered continuing symbolic support for implementation. From one support-group teacher's vantage, the district was "very positive on the program. They like what they see, and they want to see more of it."

Ironically, this heavy district involvement created problems that constrained teachers' motivation. In effect, the district wanted to align Math A with the state framework, meaning that Math A would serve ninth graders primarily; the math council (composed of all math department chairs) preferred to reserve Math A for juniors and seniors who had failed algebra. The effect of this district-level, decision-making process was to confuse teachers about the appropriate role of Math A in the high school curriculum. Thus, instead of ascribing the state-intended mission to Math A of bridging a gap between eighth-grade arithmetic and college-preparatory algebra, a value the network teachers clearly possessed, support-group teachers were uncertain about their own effort or investment in Math A. One result was the "dumping ground" characterization of the program described earlier in this chapter. In this case, the local policy-level conflicts impeded progress toward state implementation goals.

School-Level Implementation Support

Teachers across these cases uniformly reported little or no site-level activity regarding Math A implementation. In one staff development instance, a teacher indicated that his principal "thinks it's fantastic" regarding his work with Math A. Another staff development and a support-group teacher also noted that they received some financial backing, either to purchase manipulatives, to meet with other Math A teachers, or to work on curriculum revisions. Otherwise, principals across the cases did not figure into teachers' classroom implementation efforts. In other words, behind classroom doors, principals were not visibly important to teachers.

The network, however, demanded substantial logistical support from site administrators. Principals' important and necessary contribution to the network implementation of Math A involved rearranging school master schedules so that network teachers could meet in a common preparation period. In this way, principal support enabled the network to operate. Also, Math A students in the network district needed to stay with their Math A teachers over an entire academic year, rather than one semester, which also placed demands on the master schedule.

In one network school, garnering this logistical support required a concerted effort on the part of the department chair and network coordinator (herself a chair at another school) to change the administration's unwillingness to adapt the schedule, and the accommodation was not reached until the end of the first year of network operations. As the department chair at this school characterized the process, "We really had to fight." Moreover, one of the Math A teachers in this school described the effect of this struggle in his class and the change that occurred subsequently, saying:

> There was resistance from the principal because they couldn't get the master schedule to work. So I was ending up with people who weren't supposed to be in the program at all. . . . There was no support there. This [second] year is different. [The schedule accommodated common preparation periods and continuous enrollments.]

It works better because the kids get to know you and you get to know the students better.[3]

In addition, principals had to hire teachers to pick up the demand created by network teachers meeting in a common preparation period instead of teaching additional sections. One network department chair, thus, offered a different perspective regarding support from her principal: "Our administrative staff here at [the high school] has been extremely supportive and very positive." The chair explained why she believed her principal was so supportive of Math A and the network, noting how

> they [that is, principals] can keep teachers. Each year the district keeps losing teachers, and we keep having to consolidate. And by having these extra periods, our principal, in fact, has one extra position, which means that she has something that she would not have otherwise. So that is positive. There are monies [from Math A] that come into the school for materials and supplies; that's positive. I think our principal—she is an ex-math teacher, so she has a tender spot for math—and she is the first one to admit that she taught it the old-fashioned way and she would have to go back to the classroom to learn. But I think she is impressed with what she sees because she can recognize the different dynamics in the classrooms that she visits nowadays. So she's happy about that. I think it makes her very supportive.

Also, while teachers identified no direct implementation role for principals beyond arranging the master schedule, neither did teachers necessarily desire their principals to be directly involved. One network teacher said of his principal, for example, that "she is very supportive of the math department, but on a concrete daily level—I know she is real pleased with what we are doing—they trust us that we'll be able to manage it ourselves."

This classroom control may explain, in part, why teachers seemed not to mind the absence of greater school-level implementation supports. The presence or absence of support from some quarter clearly was important. And when support was not forthcoming, teachers voiced frustration. However, the added flexibility teachers experienced within the implementation pilots, regarding the amount of material they covered and its pacing, and the deeper engagement in instruction that resulted, offset potential frustrations regarding a lack of specific school-level supports. Also important, more substantive and symbolic support for Math A implementation came from district staff and from within teachers' academic departments, and teachers' expectations of support were oriented more in these directions.

Department-Level Implementation Support

Teachers across these cases experienced widely differing levels of support within their academic departments. In the network case, teachers' departments were uniformly viewed as strong and facilitating Math A implementation. In fact, the network emerged from collaboration among department chairs. And as one chair recognized, "There is more of a department–district connection."

Next, support from department chairs fueled network and Math A activity. "The key person in the school," according to a network teacher, "is the head of the math department. I would say [that] without her there would be no [Math A]." The same sentiment was expressed by a teacher at the second network school regarding her chair: "Probably without him a lot of this collaboration wouldn't go on."

Finally, because of the district–department connection, and because the district decentralized staff development activities to departments, and particularly with the network operating at the department level, departments formed a locus of professional activity for teachers. These opportunities and responsibilities helped to structure teachers' professional interactions and they provided substantial up-close support for Math A implementation.

In contrast, teachers in the staff development and support-group cases lacked this up-close, departmental support. There were two exceptions, even if they were primarily symbolic. One staff development teacher reported that his department chair, a 35-year veteran teacher, was planning to take the Math A staff development training when it was next offered in the summer. Also, a support-group teacher remarked that his department chair was "pretty in tune with the state framework and kind of understands where Math A is headed, and has been supportive in that respect." Otherwise, teachers in these nonnetwork cases described no specific department-level implementation support.

Network Advantage: Organizing Implementation Support

Two other conditions distinguished network teachers' implementation contexts from those in the staff development and support-group cases. On one hand, the network organized and made available to its teachers implementation resources found beyond school district boundaries. In this regard, a collection of external financial and professional resources became available to network teachers. Network teachers at one high school, for example, arranged network support from a local education foundation. Network teachers also had opportunities to draw on professional resources beyond their schools. Local universities provided access to multiple resources and expertise. An Urban Math Collaborative operated nearby. The Collaborative offered workshops and provided a networking role that facilitated and broadened teacher interactions and, through its various contacts, led to grants and other fiscal resources. Similarly concerned with professional development, and operating nearby, was the California Mathematics Project. Important, too, network teachers had a sense from these professional contacts that math professionals elsewhere were moving in the same direction as Math A.

Other professional connections existed. District staff, for example, were involved with the state in developing portfolio assessments, an emerging policy issue at the time. One network department chair served on the state writing committee that produced one of the Math A units. Network teachers themselves played growing roles in their professional associations. As one network department chair argued:

> We had more sessions, more people willing to do workshops, to do presentations. I mean, it's an indicator that we are conscious of what's going on in the mathematics [community]. And [we are] providing stipends for people to attend [the] NCTM [National Council of Teachers of Mathematics] conference [and] the math collaborative, [and we are] encouraging other teachers—mentor teachers—to do demonstrations for their colleagues.

In short, network teachers, who had a relatively rich environment at their disposal, were organized to draw on outside expertise and experience.

Furthermore, network schools participated in activities that reinforced Math A's philosophy and pedagogy. Recall how Math A required substantial change on the part of its teachers. But the demands of this policy on practice were not unique at one network high school. The school was engaged in another pilot curriculum, sponsored by a university-based science institute, that placed similar pedagogical demands on teachers; it had the same feeling as Math A, according to one teacher. This pilot curriculum combined algebra, geometry, and trigonometry in nonsequential order, mixing their ideas and important themes in a 3-year program.

One Math A network teacher also participated in a pilot project for a college-preparatory curriculum. (This pilot operated in only three high schools in the state.) Because these pilot classes, like Math A, stressed group organization and cooperative learning, they provided another resource to Math A teachers. For example, a different Math A teacher at this school observed the college-preparatory pilot classes, rather than Math A classes, to gain a sense of how he could manage student groups in his own classroom. Although the Math A implementation network was a unique enterprise, it drew support from other reform activities in the same school.

Three factors seem important in this high school's simultaneous implementation of two unusual mathematics curricula. First, most (if not all) math teachers in this high school were involved in the implementation of new and quite different curricula. As one network teacher noted, "At this school, it's hard to find a math teacher who isn't either involved in Math A or the other program. . . . And anybody who's involved in those programs more or less believes in what we're doing." To an extent, therefore, all math teachers were struggling with similar changes in their practice. As such, they provided a unique resource to one another.

Second, the new curricula were reinforcing. They moved teachers in complementary directions. Their messages indicated that group instruction, a reliance on mathematical themes, integrated topics, and the like, were good for students of all ability levels. Math A and the college-preparatory pilot, thus, validated each other's changes in practice.

Third, the fact that the department undertook both curricula indicated a clear openness to change on the part of this faculty, disconcerting as change must have been at times.

In summary, network teachers had a variety of resources organized and available to them, some of which reinforced their efforts regarding Math A implementation and the changes implementation implied for classroom instruction. Staff development and support-group teachers did not share the network's organization of external resources or similar and reinforcing reform activities within their departments. On the contrary, one staff development school had been a demonstration site for a Saxon math project. Relying on repetition of discrete and incremental basic skills—an approach antithetical to the values underlying Math A—the Saxon approach to mathematics education continued to influence the Math A teacher at this site.

ADDITIONAL MOTIVATING FACTORS

Beyond teachers' goals and evaluative thoughts, these data suggested five specific factors that motivated teachers' implementation behavior. These five factors were suggested individually by different teachers; they did not appear across the cases or teachers.

First, Math A's flexibility enhanced teacher motivation. As one network teacher commented, "Math A is very, very flexible, and that's the beauty of the course." This sentiment was echoed by others. Flexibility made Math A more interesting to teachers. The teachers' interest was maintained by Math A's "different approach [that is] that you are using something that is different and that you can change it yourself, you can turn it around and play around with that."

Second, the "freshness" of Math A materials enhanced teacher motivation. A network teacher explained that Math A is

> new material for everyone in the class. [For] the top kids, it's new material. [For] the weak kids, it's new material. . . . So it's fresh. That's a success in that we're looking for curriculum that is fresh for high school kids. Even though many of these high school kids, let's say, have remedial skills, they still deserve the opportunity to get new material; they don't have to get rehashed material that they've already seen.

The freshness of the material to this teacher, too, created an advantage. As he declared, "I haven't gotten burned out or tired where I'd say, 'I've taught it enough and I'd like to teach some other class.' . . . I still enjoy it." Said another, Math A is "more fun because it's not the same routine things that you have every day."

Third, a network teacher reported that the opportunity for professional collaboration itself, via the network, motivated him to become involved in the pilot project. "I just heard about [the Math A pilot]," he explained, "and I would say the most attractive thing [was] that there was an extra prep period to meet with other teachers. And so I said, 'That was great; sign me up.'"

Fourth, all motives are not forward looking; obligation influenced teacher motivation as well. One network teacher admitted to joining the Math A project in order to repay a debt of gratitude she felt to the district for allowing her to keep her job when another teacher in her school (who was slated for a network spot) was laid off. As she described it, "I did it out of obligation in a way, because I felt guilty that I got a job back that the other teacher did not because we had cutbacks."

Fifth, financial remuneration enhanced teacher motivation. The time required by the intensive summer training sessions was offset to a degree by monetary compensation: "You're getting about $200 per day in materials and some stipend," recounted one network teacher. "So there's financial incentive to go." The flip side of this issue involved fairness. One support-group teacher explained: "I think better teaching goes on if the teachers are working together and sharing together. But the bottom line is, no, I think they really have to be compensated for that. I think that's a fair thing. . . . It's a lot of extra work."

Finally, in one instance the data indicated that belief and commitment followed practice. "At the beginning I was forced to have a Math A class, even though I didn't want it" recalled a reluctant network participant. "But now after 2 years, I'd rather have Math A classes than advanced algebra classes." As these factors enhanced teacher motivation, they also facilitated implementation.

MOTIVATION AND CURRICULUM IMPLEMENTATION

This comparison of motivational factors among network, staff development, and support-group teachers yielded three major findings. Teachers across these cases expressed personal goals and confronted implementation environments that were similar on several dimensions. Of the 12 motivational factors discussed, for example, six contributed similar influences to the direction, persistence, and vigor of teachers' implementation behavior. In this regard, teachers' goals, which animated their implementation activity, were expressed primarily in terms of fostering students' success. This success was defined variously, but the personal cast of the desired outcomes teachers described was constant across cases.

In addition, teachers across the cases confronted similar students in terms of their academic abilities but also in terms of students' positive responses to Math A strategies. Professional responses to Math A were similarly positive and supportive at a distance, in the form of professional trends and policy pronouncements from organizations like the National Council of Teachers of Mathematics and the California Mathematics Project, but up close, among one's teaching peers, were characterized by fear and resistance. Parents across the cases, however, played no role in teachers' construction of Math A practice.

Finally, school-level implementation supports across the cases were rare. In some instances, small material supports were available. The network also negotiated crucial logistical support in the form of master schedule changes, but this assistance came grudgingly and slowly. Overall, however, teachers viewed site-based material support as a minor, even absent, influence in shaping their implementation efforts and practice.

A second major finding is that teachers' assessments of Math A in practice, the most important influence on their motivation to continue the implementation pilots, were generally similar and favorable across the cases. Eleven of the 12 teachers regarded Math A positively, citing the potential and efficacy of Math A content and instructional strategies.

Six of these teachers expressed enthusiasm for Math A, based on their classroom experiences. Five others noted the course's potential, but also elaborated reservations grounded in concerns regarding the quality and use of Math A. One teacher also abandoned the state Math A units altogether in favor of a basic skills, drill-and-practice curriculum.

Moreover, the pattern of teachers' evaluations across the cases followed the pattern of implementation results described in Chapter 3. That is, the most positive assessments and the smallest variation among teachers within a case were found in the network (3 high evaluations and 1 medium). The widest variation among teachers within a case and the lowest overall assessment of Math A came in the staff development case (1 high, 2 medium, 1 low). Teachers in the support-group case fell between the others both in terms of variation and overall assessments (2 high, 2 medium). Broadly speaking, however, on this critical factor, 11 of 12 teachers regarded Math A positively based on their classroom experience.

A third finding indicated by the comparison of motivational factors is that on the five factors that differed among these cases, the network reaped advantages in each instance. In this regard, teacher, district, and state policy goals were clearly stated and aligned in the network, but not in the other cases. Also, district-level material resources were available to network teachers without confusing signals about the purpose to which they should be put. Network teachers, too, unlike their staff development and support-group counterparts, enjoyed up-close and vigorous department-level support for Math A implementation. They also benefited from the organization of resources outside the district and from activities within the district that reinforced the direction of change in their practice demanded by Math A. Each of these advantages augmented the motivational foundation of network Math A teachers and aided their classroom construction of Math A practice: Conflicts regarding purpose were minimized, resources were organized and available up close, and other department-level undertakings supported the direction of change demanded by Math A.

The advantages in motivational factors enjoyed by network teachers raise two points important to implementation efforts generally and to the assessment of implementation strategies coming up in Chapter 5. On one hand, network teachers recognized a common purpose in their use of Math A, that is, to foster greater academic success among minority students and to assist students to make a better transition to high school. This common purpose undergirded teachers' implementation efforts.

On the other hand, teachers' implementation activities were nested within reinforcing local policy system goals. In the network case, teacher, district, and state policy goals promoted similar outcomes, which reinforced the direction and vigor of teachers' implementation behavior. In contrast, in the support-group case, district support regarding Math A implementation was strong, but signals emanating from its decision-making process were mixed. Local conflict among administrators and department chairs regarding the place and use of Math A in the district left teachers confused regarding Math A's ultimate purpose. This confusion led in one instance to the "dumping ground" characterization of the course. The conflict also left teachers uncertain in terms of their own investment in Math A in terms of time, energy, and commitment.

These classroom implementation effects of policy system goal conflict or alignment—among policy makers, administrators, and teachers—illustrate the importance of viewing implementation activities in a classroom as embedded within activities at other levels of the policy system. Other analysts already have addressed this point. Purkey and Smith (1983) raised the issue of embedded contexts within a review of effective schools research. They viewed school systems as "nested layers" in which each organizational level sets the context and defines the boundaries for the layer below, although they recognized reciprocal influences among the layers. Therefore, "the quality of the process at the classroom level will be enhanced or diminished by the quality of activity at the level above it" (p. 428). Within their analysis of school reform as "steady work," Elmore and McLaughlin (1988) provided the most succinct statement of the roles and relationships played by different levels of a school system.

> Educational reform operates on three loosely connected levels: policy, administration, and practice. Each level has its own rewards and incentives, its own special set of problems, and its own view of how the educational system works. Policy can set *the conditions* for effective administration and practice, but it can't predetermine how those decisions will be made. Administrative decisions can reflect policy more or less accurately and can set the conditions for effective practice, but it can't control how teachers will act in the classroom at a given point. Practice can reflect knowledge of more effective performance, but this knowledge isn't always consistent with policy and administrative decisions.
>
> Reform can originate in any of three ways: (1) changes in professionals' view of effective practice, (2) changes in administrators' perceptions of how to manage competing demands and how to translate these demands into structure and process, and (3) changes in policy-makers' views of what citizens demand that result in authoritative decisions. There is no necessary logical order among these sources. (p. v, emphasis in original)

If there is no logical order among these sources of change, it nevertheless should be clear that the probability of change increases as conflict among the levels of policy, administration, and practice diminishes.

Furthermore, implementation tasks can be viewed as embedded within two types of contexts. On one dimension, classroom implementation is nested within departments, schools, districts, and state and national governmental entities—levels of the policy system, in other words. On another dimension, classroom implementation is embedded within other competing or complementary goals, policies, commitments, and resources that exist simultaneously in the policy system; these may be called demands within the policy system. Thus, the simple notion of embedded implementation contexts introduces substantial complexity to implementation processes.

In closing this chapter, three final observations are noteworthy. First, as the implementation results in Chapter 3 demonstrated, when Math A "worked" in classrooms, success was hard won in the sense that teachers struggled with new content, unfamiliar pedagogy, reluctant students, and uncertain outcomes. Implementation results evolved over time as practice was constructed. As one network teacher suggested, the practice of Math A depends on "how teachers implement it in the classroom." Thus, facilitating teachers' motivation—the direction, persistence, and vigor of their implementation activity—is crucial to the transformation of policy into practice and, in terms of these Math A implementation pilots, to ascertaining the classroom potential of a different and demanding approach to mathematics education.

Second, teachers' attention and activity across these cases were centered in their classrooms. This is not surprising, but it is worth mentioning because the isolation that often is its corollary constrains implementation insofar as it limits a teacher's opportunities to learn. Several teachers mentioned that they felt impeded by this isolation. One network teacher, specifically, linked isolation to frustration and lack of performance. In the next chapter, I explore the role of different implementation strategies in breaking down this isolation and the effect this had on teacher learning and implementation. The immediate point is that teachers across these cases were alike in this fundamental respect. As a staff development teacher noted, "I'm out here on my own, strictly on my own."

A third point, related to teachers' focus within their classrooms, is that teachers generally were unfamiliar with implementation activities beyond their department level. "I guess I'm not [in touch] any farther than our [network] monthly meetings," one teacher commented. This also is not surprising. I report it only to suggest, by contrast, the need for implementation strategies to be grounded in teachers' immediate contexts and daily activities.

Teachers in this study indicated that Math A at some level "worked." Why did it work? In part, its implicit theory, that is, its own assessment of causes and consequences regarding mathematics education between remedial and college-preparatory tracks, may have merit. In part, also, teachers were able over time to make sense of the demands of policy on practice and to construct Math A practice that, in their judgment, benefited students. In other words, teachers were developing a capacity to deliver Math A to students. How? Central to understanding the implementation role of a teacher professional network, one must understand how teachers across these cases evaluated different implementation strategies. Did these different strategies affect teachers' capacity to implement Math A? As teachers discuss the role of the network, staff development offerings, or support-group contacts in implementing Math A, they demonstrate how motivation and capacity are reinforcing and how teachers become learners in forging Math A practice.

CHAPTER 5

Implementation Strategies and Teachers' Capacity

> I've always said that if you want to improve education, you give teachers in their disciplines common preps and then give them a format, a form, a guided task, something that they are to do that will, in fact, create dialogue among [them and] their students. And I think it will improve education.
>
> —A network teacher

IF MOTIVATION ESTABLISHES a foundation upon which implementation builds, then capacity provides the wherewithal to erect the structure. When asked to implement Math A, teachers, of course, bring a measure of motivation and capacity with them to the task, based on their backgrounds and prior experiences. Each teacher possesses values, goals, interpretations, and emotions that fuel the direction, persistence, and vigor of his or her behavior.[1] Teachers also possess knowledge, experience, credentials, and expertise that form the basis of their capacity.

Furthermore, motivation and capacity are closely linked to an individual's environment. One's environment provides the material, information, support, and opportunities to practice that enhance motivation and develop capacity. Of course, one's environment may not provide these things, in which case individuals' capacities and, by extension, implementation are constrained rather than aided.

While teachers in this study varied somewhat in terms of education and experience (Appendix A), their work environments were comparable on several important dimensions. The fundamental organization and culture of teaching, for example, were similar across these cases. This is important because the organization and culture of teaching are such salient factors in teachers' day-to-day work experiences and because, on the whole, they constrain change (Lampert, 1988).

Other aspects of these teachers' environments also were similar. All, for example, were grappling with the same policy. In each instance, Math A meant the state-produced Math A materials, the 15 or so units that emerged from various teacher writing committees during the late 1980s. However, Math A also was taught from texts that bore little resemblance to the state-produced units. In District 1, where Math A implementation was primarily a function of a network, Math A outside the network often was defined by these textbooks.

Teachers in these cases also interacted with students of similar achievement and experience with mathematics. Students form such a large part of a teacher's world that differences in the characteristics of one's students could appreciably alter a classroom environment and, thus, strongly affect a teacher's motivation. But Math A served a niche in the high school curriculum, the effect of which was to place academically similar students in Math A classes across schools and districts.

Important to the interpretation of findings in this study, the contextual factor that differed most among these teachers was the implementation strategy that structured their experiences with Math A. Two basic strategies were represented: a network strategy and one based on staff development. A third case broached a middle ground, namely, a support-group strategy. In practice, the support group paralleled the staff development strategy but added a periodic support-group meeting for teachers. In fact, all three strategies shared a staff development component. One district then added a support group, another added a network. This chapter examines the similarities and differences among these implementation strategies and the influence they exerted on teachers' implementation capacities.

STAFF DEVELOPMENT AS STATE IMPLEMENTATION STRATEGY

To facilitate the statewide implementation of Math A, California's State Department of Education (SDE or department) initiated a broad staff development program to introduce state-produced Math A units to classroom teachers. This section of the chapter sketches the scope and organization, content, reinforcing conditions, and expected consequences for classroom teachers of the department's training.

Scope and Organization

In the summer of 1989, after the first 13 Math A units became available, SDE offered inservice workshops to Math A teachers in nine locations around California. The state model for this training included a 3-day workshop in August followed by 5 additional training days spaced throughout the academic year. State officials believed this model to be "successful." In the first year, more than 400 teachers participated on a voluntary basis.

During the second year, the locus of control for these workshops shifted from the department to 14 regional sites, usually country offices of education, although some schools also sponsored workshops. The state could no longer fund the program; regional providers assumed the responsibility on a cost-recovery basis. Department staff continued to meet with workshop hosts to plan the sessions. The state also trained workshop presenters, which it had not done the prior summer. In this second year, approximately 875 teachers participated. As one state official described the results, "That's almost 8,000 days of inservice to these teachers. Now for those teachers to keep coming . . . time after time, there must be something worthwhile going on, or otherwise they wouldn't come." Most of the teachers in year two had not participated in year one.

Federal funds in the form of Eisenhower block grants enabled the department to initiate the training and to sustain it over time. According to department staff, "If we didn't have those block monies from the federal government, we would never have been able to do it," that is, SDE never would have been able to initiate the Math A staff development effort.

A second source of funding was anticipated. Royalties from a planned Math A textbook would accrue to the state and be distributed to school districts where teachers helped to develop Math A units. These royalties were earmarked to fund local Math A staff development activities.

One result of the scope and organization of the state's Math A staff development strategy was that Math A teachers across the state had opportunities to meet and work together in ways that algebra, geometry, and other math teachers did not. "Nobody has ever set up such a big inservice program," claimed a state official. "I mean nobody has ever done it. Have we done it on a district level? Yes. Yes. [One district that is among the top ten largest in the state] used to bring the teachers in every month." This level of commitment and activity was unusual, continued that state official: "But it's a good model. It's a model of inservice training that [the state] developed to make sure that we had long-lasting effects. You just can't go in and take one shot, or you can't go in and take 1 year, because in 3 years everything is lost."

Department staff described the state's Math A staff development model as facilitating bottom-up activity with support from above. According to one official, the ongoing and reinforcing character of the strategy— that teachers are able to meet periodically throughout a school year—distinguished Math A implementation from the state's attempts to implement other curricular frameworks. How? The cost-recovery strategy maintained the training over time. As a department official remarked:

> Most of the time it's, "Put something out there, give everybody a shot of what it is, a smattering of what it is, and then let it de-

velop and get going." . . . [In the case of Math A, the implementation model is] cost effective because [of] . . . the percentage of change that has occurred . . . in regards to the amount of money the department has put in. We have never had such a cost-effective program. Never.

SDE officials portrayed this staff development strategy in positive terms. Clearly, they believed that something out of the ordinary was occurring. In part, this was attributed to the state–local partnership that formed around the provision of training. A department official described this relationship, saying:

> It's important to understand that the training was orchestrated by, produced by, the state, but the trainer body is 2 dozen California high school teachers who are also the basic developers of the course. So we managed it, we orchestrated it. . . . But this is not a state department curriculum. . . . This is a wonderful example of what can happen if you put some resources into, give support to, a system and you take advantage, in this case, of 2 dozen of the most progressive teachers, who have already understood the point, understood the vision, and who are willing, able, and ready to go for it, who have gone for it. And now we have a thousand [trained] teachers in California, over 10% of all the high school teachers, and we expect to get four or five hundred more teachers annually going through the workshops on Math A. [The state] doesn't even run the workshops anymore; they are now regionally organized. And registration, scheduling—the whole bit—is now done regionally. . . . The one thing we continue to do is set up the annual get-our-act-together [session] and prepare the workshop leaders. So we're still playing an important role in nurturing the leadership. But we don't have to manage the workshops themselves anymore. I'm very pleased with what [state department staff] have done; I'm very pleased with what county office math people have done in buying into this. It's been a winner all around.

Staff Development Content

Each workshop primarily introduced one or two Math A units. In addition, as department staff noted, "the nice thing about [the training] is that not only did we talk about the mathematics but we talked about management techniques and strategies, about asking questions, about not putting kids down." Presenters addressed questions about Math A materials, the mathematics underlying the course, Math A's purpose, its philosophy, professional and policy directions or trends, and the rationale behind the state's plans. Content included use of manipulatives, cooperative learning, calculators, and some discussion of classroom management strategies.

Moreover, teachers had an opportunity to share classroom experiences: "When you have teachers meeting eight times a year, they network. Every time they come back, they network," said a state official. "Network" in this instance meant that teachers shared experiences, talked about what worked, what didn't work, and how they changed the course. They received information, but they also shared experience.

Reinforcing Activities and Conditions

One state official suggested that this Math A staff development training was reinforced by the course's growing presence in professional conferences and other proceedings. As he explained:

> What happens is that there are so many conferences now, like the [California Mathematics Council] conferences, that on every agenda there are the Math A talks. For example, at Asilomar last year, I think we had 10 talks on Math A. And so all of those teachers would come. . . . This year we had five or six 2-hour workshops on Math A down in Riverside and Palm Springs. In November [at an upcoming statewide math conference], there will be talks on Math A and B.

Beyond the inservice experience itself, this official suggested that, in order to implement Math A, teachers "have to like kids" and have to believe that they are no longer "the god of instruction but the facilitator of learning." Administrator support also was necessary, first, to pay for the inservice and to allow teachers time to attend and, second, to foster a school culture that asserted: "Students are the most important thing."

Consequences for Teachers

SDE staff judged the consequences of this inservice strategy in three ways. First, more districts were participating and many teachers were receiving training.

> There are more districts involved. There are more teachers that have been inserviced and have been changed in their teaching. They have had quality inservice in use of manipulatives, in use of

cooperative learning, in use of calculators, in use of management strategies. They have never had that before. They may have had some in their education classes, which they didn't like. They've never had a succinct management strategies course in which they could take that thing and understand exactly what it is and be able to use it the next day.

Second, the training provided a philosophical base that supported a new concept of teachers' work. As an SDE staff member explained:

What happens is [the training] can turn teachers around for people who are very bitter or for people who are stuck in these general math classes where they don't like to be there and the kids don't like to be there. [It gets] them sort of thinking, "This is going to be fun. This is going to be enjoyable. And I'm not exhausted mentally at the end of the day for a negative reason, but I'm exhausted for a positive reason." When you're exhausted for a positive reason, then that's a good exhaustion.

In other words, when the attitudes of teachers change, their teaching styles change. Moreover, according to department staff, these changes were occurring not over the course of a year, but of 2 months, or even just a summer workshop.

Third, these inservice experiences attempted to create a new culture among teachers. Because Math A required different content, organization of instruction, pedagogy, and ways of relating to students, it also required teachers to rethink their relationships to the subject and to students and to change their style of teaching. The demands of policy on practice, recall, are substantial, significant, and material. Were these changes taking place? Department staff believed they were.

Not only is it taking place in those [Math A] classes, it's taking place in their other classes. [Teachers are] changing their questioning strategies and teaching strategies in their Algebra 2, in their geometry, in their Algebra 1. Remember I told you about the tower problem, which [involves mathematical] sequences? Teachers are now teaching it in their Algebra 2 classes, where they normally teach arithmetic sequences, by using that [Math A] model. And so, therefore, there are major changes. In fact, if there is one major change, that's it: If there is no change in content whatsoever, but if we were able to change the attitude and pedagogy of what these teachers are doing in their classrooms with regards to what they do with the kids and how they act toward the kids, we've done a major, major change in secondary mathematics.

In short, the state hoped to expand teachers' participation in Math A, to communicate the course's philosophy and technology, and to begin changing the relationships among teachers, students, and curriculum across the whole of high school mathematics.

STAFF DEVELOPMENT–BASED IMPLEMENTATION IN DISTRICTS 2 AND 3

Districts 2 and 3, a large, urban district and its smaller suburban neighbor, respectively, adopted the state's staff development strategy as their primary means of implementing Math A. Inservice offerings in these districts even were combined initially, although separated subsequently. Still, the training in each district shared essential characteristics. The greatest difference between them involved the addition in District 3 of a Math A teacher support group.

Components of the Training

The staff development implementation strategies in these districts shared two principal components: a summer workshop and follow-up training during the academic year. In District 2, this local training included a 5-day summer inservice. This summer workshop was followed by 5 additional days of release time spaced throughout the academic year.

Teachers in District 3 organized their training similarly. Few suburban teachers attended the state-organized staff development summer workshop in District 2. Three of the four suburban staff development teachers in this study, however, did attend these District 2 sessions early in the implementation process. These teachers then formed the nucleus of a staff development effort in their own district. One teacher described this process, saying:

> Myself and [two others] were the only ones in our district that really extensively went to those [sessions in the adjacent urban district]. So we sort of became the committee to oversee our implementation and our [course] development. And we felt that . . . we could train our teachers—not so much that we personally could train our teachers, but we could put together a workshop to train

our teachers. And we brought in outside people to do the actual training.

Training in District 3 involved a summer workshop for 17 teachers plus three Saturday sessions during the academic year.

Local training, too, included a combination of local and state presenters. In District 2, training was conducted primarily by a Math A classroom teacher and by the district mathematics coordinator. In District 3, training was conducted by a presenter from a regional office of the California Math Project (but not the local regional office) and by the same Math A classroom teacher from District 2 who provided training for the urban teachers.

Content of the Training

The content of these professional development activities included at least five elements. Content included an introduction to Math A materials. Introducing content clearly was the main purpose of the workshops. "What we try to do," said one support-group teacher, "is take two units in that 4-hour time, go through them with people, demonstrate things, and let people try things. And if we've taught the unit before, like I have, and there are any perils or pitfalls, you might try to point those out." This same teacher later summarized the benefits of this materials-based training to teachers.

> What you get out of [the training] is an opportunity to look at the materials in advance with other people, and to go through them with someone who's taught it, and to be alerted to some of the special features, and to have a chance to bounce ideas around with other people concerning particular portions of it. That's about what you get.

Other teachers suggested similar themes: that the focus on material exposed teachers to materials they could use in their classrooms, provided some opportunity to practice Math A exercises, and addressed changes or adaptations because "we're continually changing and updating this stuff."

Practice with the materials composed part of teachers' workshop time. For example, a staff development teacher described how workshop presenters "gave us a packet, and [tried] to get us to look through the packet, see what's there, maybe tell us do page this, that, that, and that.

So we get a little practice working on it in a group with teachers, so you can see what you are up against."

Content also included discussion of teaching strategies, focusing on classroom management issues, absenteeism, grading, and "a lot of different things that crop up—and they cropped up in the other county workshops, too. These are the concerns of all teachers." Teaching strategies included the use of manipulatives. In addition, modeling by workshop presenters composed a large part of the training experience. As one staff development teacher remarked, the training was helpful "because it has given me some techniques. [The trainer] down here—I mean, some of the techniques and some of the things that he has done have been fantastic. I was able to pick up a lot of things." Other teachers expressed similar sentiments, one saying, "Just getting ideas and seeing a guy like [the trainer], who is a master at this stuff. It helped me see what someone else was doing." Another teacher also praised the presenter: "[He] is real good at showing us all his sponge activities." She summarized the value of this component of the training by saying, "It's good to get reminded as to what the other techniques are."

A third aspect of training content included the sharing of lessons and experiences among participants. One advantage of following up a summer workshop with release days or Saturday sessions was that teachers were able to discuss Math A in the context of their classroom experiences. Reported one staff development teacher, "After your summer session, when you're coming back in after you've done it, you do a lot of networking as to what you are doing, how it is going, that type [of interaction]."

This opportunity was important particularly because Math A implementation in these staff development districts (like the network district) was still in the early, pilot stage. Implementation traversed uncharted territory; teachers' repertoire of experience was limited. A teacher reinforced the importance of these contacts, saying, "You can talk to other teachers around the district. Remember, we're all piloting this. So [we] find out what was working for them, what wasn't working for them." The novelty of the program encouraged teachers to meet. One explained that "you definitely really need that. You need to find out what works with other people, how they did it. You can find out things, you know. Somebody says, 'Okay, I tried this and it didn't work.' Or 'Oh, yeah, I tried that and I sort of modified it a little bit and we did this.'"

The coordinator of implementation efforts in District 3, himself a Math A teacher, described the advantage to teachers of meeting together in terms broader than Math A or implementation. He suggested that "more of this should happen all the way across the board. I think better teaching goes on if the teachers are working together and sharing together." Teachers reflected this sentiment in comments regarding how interaction with peers would help them draw on others' experiences, discuss student reactions, and seek guidance "to make the cooperative learning a little more effective."

On the other hand, some teachers had a more limited view of this interaction. One mentioned how other teachers could help her catch misprints in the materials. Another suggested that colleagues could "sit down with [me] to cut out squares of paper that get used; maybe steal stuff from her for dividing up groups. I know [one teacher] has a whole set of ideas for handing students things as they come in the door [that assigns them to groups]."

Training content also included encouragement for teachers to change. A staff development teacher, though, brushed off this aspect, noting, "There's a lot of pep talking going on." Another teacher, however, placed the changes in terms of the spirit of Math A. According to him, "The training just doesn't involve what's in the packets, but it involves, again, how do you catch the spirit of Math A in your teaching. So a lot of it had to do with changing the teachers' perspective as to who they were in front of the classroom."

Finally, the main advantage of Math A teachers working together throughout the year, one teacher suggested, was to reduce the isolation associated with teaching, and especially of those Math A teachers who were the only Math A instructors in their schools. The collaborative training also was designed to foster risk taking among Math A teachers. A staff development teacher reflected this notion, recalling that

> one of [the trainer's] famous sayings—and I'll say the same thing here—is you can see my face print all over the floor on things that I've flopped on. You know, bring it back, try it. So in that aspect, I think it is very, very helpful because you can pick up some new ideas.

This freedom to fail was an important norm, particularly given the demands Math A made on teachers' time, beliefs, knowledge, and practice. Initially, implementation results were sometimes devastating to teachers. One adherent recounted her early experiences, remarking, "It was real tough at the beginning of the semester, first part of the year. I would just—I hated them, they hated me. They hated the class. . . . It was brutal. It was horrible." "They," in this instance, were her students. This same teacher described the advantage of the monthly support-group meetings available to her in District 3 as "more of a self-esteem boosting, because some of us needed it at that point. So I just think getting together and hearing other teachers' horror stories—to know that you weren't the only one."

A SUPPORT-GROUP COMPONENT

District 3 added a support-group component to its implementation strategy. All 17 of the district's Math A teachers met once a month in this special format. These support-group meetings were held after school, and teachers were compensated each session for 2 hours of professional development time at a "curriculum writing fund" rate of $17 an hour. One teacher described these sessions, saying, "Initially it was a crying the blues, woe is me, or 'hey, this is really going great.' Because this is what happened: Teachers would be real up or real down." Another teacher characterized these meetings as "a support group where we just kind of came and bitched and griped and said, 'This is how things are going.'"

The support meetings sometimes focused partially on curriculum materials, but according to one participant mostly they encompassed

> just interaction—hearing. We would go around the table, and everyone would say how they're doing. And many of them were excited about an activity they had just done or how well it went. Or some were down in the mouth because their kids just didn't seem to be turned on. And many commented on how it helped them to learn what other teachers were doing and so on.

One teacher captured this dual focus on materials and support by describing these meetings as "rewrite and review, or just for unburdening."

The unburdening in these sessions provided an opportunity for teachers to hear each others' problems and to develop their understanding of Math A. One teacher recalled, "We share problems. And I would say that one of the things that we did was as we go through the units, we bring in the problems that we had. You say, 'I didn't understand this,' or 'this was worded incorrectly.'"

More important, perhaps, support encompassed teachers' emotional well-being. One of the suburban teachers described how the "hearing" that occurred in the support-group meetings provided teachers with "a little emotional lift. You are able to realize that you're not alone in terms of—if it's a negative experience—in terms of, in fact, there are others experiencing the same thing." Another teacher affirmed that "you build a little camaraderie that way."

Attendance at these support meetings, however, was problematic.

As one of the lead, or original three, teachers explained, "I only went to one. I usually had other meetings that they conflicted with." In fact, the suburban teachers decided to forgo these support meetings in order to use the hours, instead, to revise curriculum. One teacher described this shift in purpose as a move toward a "group curriculum-writing effort." So the "support-group" meetings ended in March; the staff development workshops ended in February (interviews were conducted in May).

The support-group concept was extended to the site level also. District 3 attempted "to set up a mini support group" by placing two Math A teachers in each school. "Whether they get paid or not," explained one teacher, "I know on that local site level they're still meeting because they can benefit from one another's experience in the classroom."

Interestingly, District 2 also attempted support-group meetings, on a weekly basis, after school on Fridays. But these meetings foundered before the district's implementation pilot commenced. They foundered for lack of financial support and of sustained leadership (too much depended on one person) and because of their reliance on "tired time."

District 2 staff development teachers found other channels of support. Recalling the opportunity, one teacher noted that the district "did have some support groups for people getting together, but [the other Math A teacher here in my school] and I work really well together. . . . I didn't go [to the support-group meetings]." Would support of this type be helpful? "Oh, sure. For those who want to go to it, it would be great," concluded a staff development teacher. This teacher suggested that informal contact among Math A teachers within a school would be important, in those cases where that opportunity was available. Promoting this kind of informal, school-based interaction was District 3's intent in assigning two Math A teachers to each school.

A NETWORK IMPLEMENTATION STRATEGY

In Chapter 1, I defined a (Math A) teacher professional network as the linkages and voluntary interactions among teachers, their colleagues, and professional organizations that are instrumental in shaping teachers' beliefs, values, and substantive knowledge regarding Math A. At base, such a network links teachers with professional expertise and fosters the development of a common perspective through repeated interactions.

Fundamentally, a network is a series of nodes connected by lines. These linkages and the valued commodities they convey—labor, knowledge, opinion, influence, affect, evaluation, and the like—characterize a network. In brief, five factors elaborate a network's operation: (1) access, or the way network participants are connected; (2) content, or the kind of material transmitted; (3) relationships among the participants; (4) frequency, or how often participants interact; and (5) strength, the extent to which network participants have multiple connections.

The Math A network in District 1, for example, linked teachers within schools, across schools, and to policy and professional resources beyond the school district's borders. Figure 5.1 illustrates the network's structure.

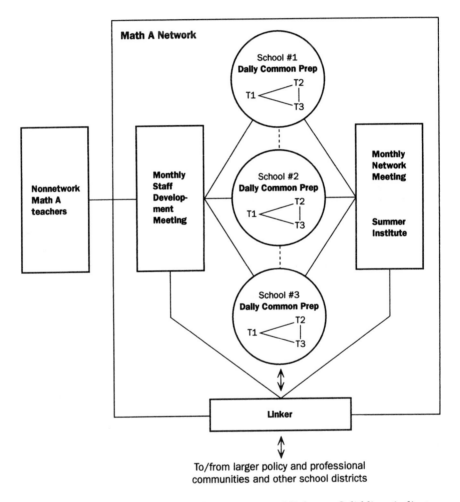

Figure 5.1. The network structure: Components and linkages. Solid lines indicate structured connections; broken lines indicate informal connections. "T" denotes "Teacher."

In short, this structure includes six components: a within-school common preparation period, cross-school monthly meetings, cross-school monthly staff development workshops that link network and nonnetwork Math A teachers, intensive summer training with students, a "linker" (that is, an individual who connects network teachers to a broader circle of professional experience and expertise), and unstructured or informal linkages among network teachers. These components represent one model of network implementation, and within this model the centerpiece of the network in District 1 was clearly the teachers' common preparation period.

Within-School Common Preparation Period

The first component of District 1's network implementation strategy involved a within-school common preparation period. Three Math A teachers in each of three high schools shared a common preparation period for the sole purpose of implementing Math A. These nine Math A teachers[2] formed the core of the Math A network. Peripheral, but important, participants included department chairs, a math resource teacher (who ran a math lab in one of the high schools), and outside experts. The network teachers' common preparation periods met daily during sixth period.

The common preparation period was scheduled in addition to the teachers' regular preparations. As a result, each teacher taught four sections of mathematics instead of five, a 20% reduction in their teaching loads. In turn, each school hired an additional teacher to cover the class sections normally taught by teachers in the network. A National Science Foundation grant and school district resources together funded the cost of the additional teacher at each high school. This financial support created the opportunity to schedule the additional, network preparation period, but money alone was insufficient to deliver the common period to network teachers.

The additional preparation period could not have materialized without key administrative support at the site level. Principals had to adjust their master schedules to accommodate the teachers' need for common meeting time during the school day. The logistics of rearranging master schedules and the willingness of the principals to undertake these changes played an important role in enabling the network. Principals, however, responded differently to this fundamental network requirement. Garnering administrative support still was an issue at the time these data were collected. Almost 2 years into a 3-year grant, one participating high school had yet to arrange its master schedule so that all three network teachers shared the common preparation period; only two of the three teachers were meeting at the time.

Network teachers gained access to the common preparation period by design; that is, their access was built into the structure of the network. However, only three teachers at each participating school shared this access. Other Math A teachers at these schools did not. Limiting access to only a portion of Math A teachers at each site was a function of limited resources. In fact, the network utilized three strategies to expand the benefits of the common preparation period to nonnetwork Math A teachers in the schools.

First, participation in the network at one high school was rotated annually among the pool of Math A teachers in the school, although not every one was rotated every year.

Second, also at this high school, nonnetwork teachers were encouraged to join their network colleagues in the common preparation period whenever time permitted. Other demands on these nonnetwork teachers, however, made this interaction problematic. As one teacher noted:

> The [nonnetwork] Math A teachers know that we [network teachers] have a sixth period meeting. . . . Other teachers come in from time to time that coincidentally may have their own prep period at that time. . . . That [picks up] two more [Math A teachers], but not all the time because it's just too much.

Too much, that is, in the sense that nonnetwork teachers must use their only preparation period for planning, grading, assembling materials, contacting parents, and myriad other activities. The combination of these demands precluded nonnetwork teachers' regular participation in the common preparation period. Noted one network teacher, in addition to the two nonnetwork teachers whose preparation periods coincided with that of the network, "there are a few others that we talk with, but not as regularly."

Third, a second high school in the network integrated a math lab into its Math A curriculum and implementation strategy. Run by a mathematics resource teacher, the math lab exposed students to activities that reinforced what they were learning in the classroom. Of the three work stations in the lab, one dealt with computers, another with "hands-on" applications of math concepts, and the third with exercises or games from the Math A curriculum. Lab activities were developed jointly between the resource and network teachers.

The math lab extended opportunities for teacher collaboration regarding Math A implementation. The department chair explained:

> The whole idea is the fact that there is collaboration that goes on before the class comes into the lab, where the resource teacher will

sit with the classroom teacher and plan, and ask, "What are you doing in your classroom? What are the units you are working on? What kinds of activities can we now put together so that these kids can come in and have some hands-on experience with the math that goes on in the classroom?"

The lab also extended network experiences to nonnetwork Math A teachers. The two groups of teachers were linked through the resource teacher, and they all sent their students to the lab. As the resource teacher recounted, "I work with [the nonnetwork teachers] after I've talked with the [network] teachers, who have met and are going through the materials and [who] tried out the materials first." According to a department chair, the benefit of this connection to nonnetwork teachers was that teachers "get exposed to some activities—cooperative group work type thing—that filters back into the classroom." Could the nonnetwork teachers pick up these techniques elsewhere? Not likely. Again, the department chair stated:

> My sense is that if you took teachers and just had a workshop once a month, or what have you, just did a workshop with them, and [they] go back into the classroom, and you don't have the op-portunity to see it happening with students, then there is some in-hibition for them to try [what they learned] in their own isolated classroom situation. Whereas if the teacher comes into the lab and the resource teacher . . . is involved in the process, then the chances are that it gets back into the classroom.

Other high schools in the district had math resource teachers, some of whom attended monthly Math A staff development workshops (described below) and, thus, conveyed lessons from the network to their respective departments.

While the resource teacher provided important linkages between network and nonnetwork teachers, her collaboration with the former was limited to once every 2 weeks, infrequent compared with the daily common preparation period.

The common preparation period enabled network teachers to collabo-rate daily regarding their Math A practice. Beyond structure, however, the content of the collaboration during this common time provided an indication of the implementation role of the network and the possible utility of the network to both policy and practice. How did teachers use the common preparation period? What did they talk about? How did they spend their time?

Teachers made several uses of their common time. Before examining each, however, it is important to view these transactions as a whole, because the broad scope of teacher exchanges within the common preparation period was, in part, what defined this network's implementation potential. A network teacher summarized the domain of this collaboration as "total management":

> You're sharing your ideas. You're collaborating. You're not just talking about the materials themselves, you're talking about how the students are adapting to them, about how students are picking up different materials, other things you can do. It's not just the curriculum itself. You're talking in general about everything that's going on: how you're structuring your class, how you're doing your groups, "This works for me; this will work better in teams than in groups," or whatever it is. It's not just curriculum. You're talking about total management. And when you're working out of a textbook [like most math teachers do] basically that may not be the case.

"Total management" encompassed at least six components. First, teachers planned what material to present in class, deciding "what unit we're going to use and how we're going to present it."

This planning had both a prospective and a retrospective character to it. Teachers compared their immediate experiences and projected these into upcoming lesson plans. A network teacher explained that

> we go through the lesson; we say: "How did it go? What happened? How did yesterday go? The day before go? Did it work well? What was wrong? What helped? And what are we going to teach tomorrow? What's the concept of the ideas? And what do we want to get across?" And we look ahead: Do we need to give a test? Do we need to make up tests? What can we use for homework? And we talk about some problems we have and how we can handle [them]. And we get our material ready.

This same type of discussion surfaced in other comments. For example, the network department chair said, "The common planning time [is used] to deal with the units, to discuss the units, to look at what's going to work, what we have tried, what has worked, what hasn't worked, how are we going to modify it, and that type of thing."

The planning was immediate—teachers "discuss the lesson that we just did that day and what we're planning to do"—and it drew on lessons over time as teachers "talk about different ideas: 'This is the way I did it last year.'"

Second, teachers solved problems associated with their practice. "We talk about some problems we have and how we can handle it," one explained. In this sense, problems were placed on the table and addressed by the group. One teacher described the process as "[we] just start comparing notes, like what we're going to do." These problems arose immediately from teachers' classroom experiences, and teachers' approach to problem solving exhibited a character similar to that of an NFL coaching staff on Monday morning: "The people who are doing the same program . . . meet and talk about what went wrong, what worked, what different approach I did that worked for me. And the teacher could come and visit my classrooms, so we could make these arrangements."

The common preparation period facilitated cross-class comparisons (which these teachers viewed as positive and helpful), broadening each teacher's understanding of what worked and what did not. "I meet with the other teachers and compare how their classes did, said one teacher. "And we always talk. We talk about how we did today, what we got accomplished."

Third, teachers adapted the state Math A curriculum for best use in their classrooms. Adaptation composed an integral part of teachers' implementation activity. As one remarked, teachers "meet together, plan the lesson, decide which activities they're going to do or not do; how they're going to do them and adapt them and change them from what's already there. And try them out."

While teachers recognized that they individually adapted material as they used it ("I'm sure each teacher does it individually"), network teachers also acknowledged that their Math A adaptations were, at base, a group effort and, thus, a collective responsibility. This group role and responsibility was implied by one network teacher as he described the adaptation process.

> We get the units in advance, and I know what my kids can do and what they cannot do. And then what we do is sit as a group and say, "I think this unit doesn't reflect the reality of the kinds of kids that we have in the class," so we don't have to do it. We have that flexibility. . . . [But] it's not that I'm going to make that decision my-self, alone. That's why we meet during the sixth period [common preparation period]. [We do it] as a group of teachers.

The decision rule regarding adaptations was: "You do what you think your kids will need." Overall, however, teachers seemed to recognize three self-imposed controls on the adaptations: (1) that changes benefit students, (2) that other teachers consent to the changes, and (3) that the changes reflect the spirit of Math A. This last criterion mitigated the "dumbing down" of the state curriculum.

Teachers shared adaptations of Math A curriculum within the network; they also negotiated them there. Such give-and-take suggests that, within the network, teacher collaboration produced a professional consensus of best practice regarding the state Math A curriculum, a sense shared among network participants. In fact, as I described in Chapter 3, implementation results looked similar across network teachers' classrooms. In District 3 also, where the support group operated, variation in Math A practice was narrow. This was not the case among staff development teachers in District 2.

In a fourth component of "total management," teachers discussed appropriate instructional strategies, including, for example, how to present material. They asked each other, "What kind of manipulatives do you use, how to present it, how to use the blackboard better, how to make it clearer." These questions seek both how to communicate better and how to use technology better.

Fifth, much of network teachers' conversations addressed their perceptions of student needs; in other words, how better to match students and material. For example, one teacher mentioned the special concern he had related to his students' language ability: "Because [of the immigrant students] we're dealing with at our school . . . the explanation is real important. . . . Because of their limited English, we may be using the wrong vocabulary word. So we [teachers] share a lot of that experience."

Sixth, teachers challenged and supported one another. A network teacher recalled these interactions, explaining:

> We have the opportunity to discuss an issue with one another, to clarify our ideas, to question our ideas, to challenge one another, to spark enthusiasm in one another, to support one another emotionally when various teachers are going through a tough time, to share the successes as well as the failures.

Another teacher phrased it similarly: "And so we do a constant sharing of ideas and seeing what works and what doesn't work and what to try out; successes in the class and share our frustrations and what doesn't work and what we have to improve next year." This function is similar to, if more intensive than, the support-group component in District 3's implementation strategy. Both the network and support group allowed teachers to move beyond the intellectual component of implementation to the visceral realities of the change process. In terms of this study's theoretical framework, emotions underlie motivation and capacity. They encourage implementers to engage or to avoid subjects, tasks, and situations.

It is also worth noting what the content of these network interactions did not encompass. Of the network teachers interviewed, none mentioned spending their common time socializing or complaining about administrators or students, or using a portion of their time for non-Math A-related purposes. If these types of activities did occur, their salience was low enough not to come to mind when asked.

Cross-School Monthly Meetings

The second component of this network implementation strategy involved a cross-school monthly meeting of network teachers. These meetings occurred after school for a couple of hours. The purpose of this meeting, in part, was to develop and reinforce a "vision" of what teachers were trying to achieve. Teachers came together and worked on curricular issues. The network coordinator described one of these meetings that had occurred just the day before.

> Yesterday we had a problem presented to the group, and we worked on it and discussed what students would be getting out of this problem that was different. So we showed the teachers the problem written in the "old way" and the problem written in the "new way" and asked them what was the difference and what would the students get out of the new way. And [the teachers] could see that the problem was more open-ended, that students were not being led to an answer. [Students] were given the situation, and they had to come up with their own solution; that there could be many different approaches to the solving of that one problem, and it wasn't defined for them. So students were allowed to think more creatively, and the teachers could see this. So that type of thing, actually getting teachers into how students learn and how we can create this environment. We constantly revisit the issue of cooperative groups because teachers have varying degrees of success with that. Now that's kind of typical.

From this one example, readers can discern at least four characteristics of these monthly network meetings: (1) the content was driven by the network coordinator's perception of topics that needed to be covered, (2) one purpose was to learn how mathematics education was conceived within Math A, (3) the group experimented with specific problems that would be posed to students, and (4) an objective was to build teacher capacity regarding the underlying demands Math A made on practice—in this example, learning how to handle cooperative groups.

The main differences between the common preparation period and the monthly meeting related to their content (or orientation) and leadership. According to a network teacher, the monthly meetings were

> much more structured by [the network coordinator], and it's where she has some overall goal that she needs all of the teachers to participate in. It could be emphasizing writing by the students and how we are going to assess that. In the meeting last night we talked about implementing the sequencing unit and using tiles to do that and also some other assessment problems that they have rewritten that she wanted us to look over and see how we might solve those problems ourselves and what we'd expect from the students. So generally there isn't discussion really about how the program is going in individual classes during those [monthly] meetings.

The monthly meetings, thus, were more conceptual than practical, in the sense that they focused on issues like alternative assessments or the introduction of manipulatives rather than specific classroom situations.

One teacher explained that the monthly meetings helped to link teachers with Math A resources and experiences beyond their school district. This external resource was often university staff.

> And there are people from [the local university who] . . . bring ideas to us at that meeting. And they bring the new units and problems that we could use for homework; so problems that we could use in the classroom, or exercises that have been used in [another county] where the program started initially, and something they have done that they've had some success [with] that we could apply here. So it's a meeting where we disseminate what's going on and we ask questions and all of that.

Still, network teachers introduced their own experiences in these sessions as a contrast. As one described the process, "We bring with us material that we have used that has worked with us, and then [we] have a chance to exchange ideas and talk about what is going on."

Cross-School Monthly Staff Development Workshops

A third component of the network strategy enabled some network teachers and all other teachers who were interested in teaching Math A to meet once a month in a workshop format. These workshops were handled more like traditional staff development offerings and included teachers from nonnetwork high schools who wanted to introduce Math A in their classrooms. Presenters included the network coordinator plus staff from a regional office of the California Mathematics Project.

The monthly workshops served two purposes. The workshops introduced Math A materials to interested teachers, and they disseminated experiences of the network to nonnetwork Math A teachers. As a department chair described it, "We are inviting other schools who are not among the original three [network schools] to look at what we are doing and sharing." In effect, the strategy was to create a secondary network of Math A teachers, where the district and department chairs both attempted to share Math A materials and lessons learned in the network with nonnetwork sites and individuals. How extensive was participation by network teachers in this meeting? According to the department chair:

> Actually there are only three [network teachers] who attend those meetings. They are there as leaven. They are my shills in the crowd. But the others are just teachers from other schools in the district who expressed interest, and some have joined a little later because they heard about it later, . . . but it's a very representative group of the district. Almost every major high school has someone there.

Intensive Summer Training with Students

In a fourth component of the strategy, network teachers met and worked together for 4½ weeks in the summer. During this session, teachers taught in teams in the mornings and devoted afternoons to evaluating and shaping their curriculum. The purpose of the summer session was threefold: (1) to serve as a transition for students moving from eighth grade to high school, allowing students to work with teachers who would become their high school mathematics instructors; (2) to allow teachers to practice the content and pedagogy of Math A, both by instructing students themselves and by observing other teachers (through team teaching); and (3) to provide common time for teachers to critique Math A materials, to alter or otherwise hone the materials for use in the upcoming academic year. In a word, to "see whether it is going to work."

Typically, students and teacher teams worked together in the mornings. In the afternoons, sans students, teachers "discussed what went right, what went wrong, what were the things [they needed] to change." As one teacher concluded, the large number of teachers working on the curriculum simultaneously was helpful.

> It's not like I was team teaching with somebody else and we were the only people teaching the same unit. There were like two more couples doing the same thing at the same time. So we would get together in the afternoon, not just two teachers, but now six or ten, and talk about the units.

The strategy involved focused interaction. The previous summer, for example, the network sponsored an inservice workshop on Math A for approximately 20 district teachers. As the network coordinator described it, "We zeroed in on one unit and we conducted inservice on small groups." Similar sessions were planned for subsequent summers.

A "Linker"

A fifth component in District 1's network implementation strategy involved a network coordinator who served as a link among all network teachers and schools and, importantly, who connected network teachers to a larger world of professional experience and expertise. She described her own role, saying:

> I am the link, and I am going to start playing a stronger role next year [in the third year of the network's operation] by visiting [all] the schools. And, in fact, during the month of May I'm going to try and set up my going to three or four schools and modeling lessons with their classes so that they can get a feeling of what [Math A] is; to see this lesson in their own particular Math A class.

Specifically, she was describing how she planned to spread the lessons learned by network Math A teachers to other Math A teachers around the district. There were at this time three other high schools where one or two teachers were attempting to implement Math A in a manner consistent with state policy but outside the district's Math A network. These experiments resulted from the staff development opportunities. The network coordinator planned to facilitate implementation of Math A in these and other places in the district where interest in Math A was developing.

The importance of the linker was acknowledged by network teachers.

Then we have [the coordinator], who is the department head and one of the major forces in the Math A curriculum and is also very active at the [state] level. So we are very fortunate to have her input and her contact with the [state] and many other districts. So she is abreast of all this information.

As I discuss shortly, the coordinator's contacts with local university staff helped garner resources and facilitated the network's creation. These and other university and professional resources enhanced the network's implementation effort.

Informal Collaboration

This network provided several opportunities for teachers to meet, plan, evaluate, adapt, and otherwise address the classroom implementation of Math A. However, their connections extended beyond these structured opportunities. In fact, they were phoning each other. Referring to these casual calls, one teacher said:

I have done that a lot. Because I know that I have to teach some part of the unit [and] I don't have the foggiest idea what it's about, and so I may call one or two other people, and they give me ideas and sometimes they are quite ahead of me and they say, "Well, we did this; try that."

More often than not, these calls were placed to teachers at other schools, as one teacher explained, because

I know that I have met with [the network teachers in my school] and we couldn't reach any agreement, or we couldn't understand. And then I call somebody from [another high school]. . . . And then that person will help. And they are always there. I guess that's a key point there, the networking.

Evolution of the Network

How did this network come to be? It developed from a set of complementary desires, resources, and opportunities that converged during the 1988–89 school year. Teachers at one high school shared two concerns. They felt that something needed to be done at the high school level that would help students bridge the gap between the demands of middle or junior high school and the requirements of high school.[3] Moreover, teachers at this high school were sensitive to the fact that a number of African-American and Latino students were not succeeding in college-preparatory math classes, and somehow teachers needed to address this. A teacher recalled, "That's a real concern. There's an inequity in the way we are teaching them."

Subsequently, the mathematics department chair from this high school received a sabbatical, which located her for a time in a professional development program at a nearby university. Once she was there and working with the program's staff, "it just dove-tailed." The university became interested in doing a project with the high schools. By cooperating with the schools, the university increased implementation resources available to the teachers, schools, and district. After visiting a number of candidate high schools in the district, three surfaced as being potential successes.

At this point the mathematics department chairs from the three network high schools met a number of times with university staff and with the district mathematics coordinator, thus including district resources in the effort. A proposal to the National Science Foundation resulted from these meetings, which, when funded, launched the Math A implementation network.

Some Math A information was available to teachers in one high school prior to their undertaking formal implementation of Math A. This early, unorganized trickling in of information may have helped to lay the ground work for Math A implementation.[4] Teachers at this high school engaged the Math A materials more quickly than their counterparts in other network high schools. According to the network coordinator, "Here at [this high school]—because we had those 2 years of introduction, because of the stuff that I was bringing them—our teachers were like one step ahead of the other teachers, at least half a step." Teachers at other network high schools acknowledged the head start enjoyed by their colleagues at the first high school. One teacher at the second school, for example, commented that "most of the time they [at the first high school] are quite ahead of us."

Once established, the network still required time to become established. The department chair described the first year of operations as chaotic.

> We were just implementing it. Different schools were at different places. Some schools never really implemented it until the last 3 weeks of school or some such thing like that—even of the three

core schools I'm talking about. This [the second year of the network operation] was the first year there has been a greater concentrated effort to implement it at these three schools.

Although network operations were smoother subsequently, some problems remained, like arranging the master schedule at the third school.

Evaluating Components of the Network Strategy

It is worth noting how teachers viewed two components of the network strategy: the common preparation period and the relationships teachers developed within it.

Common Time. The network coordinator clearly felt that common time was the critical component of the entire network strategy. She described the common preparation period as

> an essential ingredient to [the network] without which I would not be its project coordinator. I made that very clear. Without which whatever success we have, we would not have. Our success may be limited, but it's only because the teachers have been given time. It's an overwhelming job, I think, to implement new curricula and new teaching strategies and new ways of assessing without being given support, and by that I mean . . . common time. Because I also think that teachers, like students, learn better when they work together in groups.

Teachers in the network shared her assessment. One asserted that he and his colleagues would not meet if not for the common preparation period. As he explained:

> If we didn't have the extra prep period, I don't think we would meet together. The only way that would happen is let's say that somebody who is the head of the department . . . said, "Okay, I think it would be a great idea if the [Math A] teachers met once a month or once every other week, and let's do it at lunch time." So if . . . some strong force or personality in the department took the initiative and said, "Let's do it," and organized and got everybody motivated to meet, we might give up some time to do it. But if we didn't have the extra prep period that means we have another class and with that class is an extra prep and extra grading. So not

only do you have less time, you have more work. So I don't think
we would do it.

The centrality of common time to teachers' sense of success was
evident throughout the network. For example: "Time is of the essence."
And: "You have to have that teacher collaboration time or I don't think
it would work." One teacher summed up their efforts, saying, "I guess
what we are trying to create is a network in the district. . . . We have to
meet and exchange ideas and bring materials that work, that if we want
to use it, you use it, and if you don't want to, just don't use it."

Another teacher pointed out that other endeavors had come and gone
in the district with little sustained effect. In part, she mused, this was
because the demands on teachers' time precluded sustained attention to
an innovation. Outside support was required. In its absence, only a few
teachers continued with a change.

> It seems to always happen with anything that we get into. There
> will be a teacher who will continue it no matter what, but the ma-
> jority of teachers will not continue it unless you have some kind of
> support there. They won't continue it in the same capacity. And so
> I think you really need that outside support; it's not just in terms
> of having good curriculum. You need to have that outside sup-
> port, whether it be workshops or collaborative time. I think the col-
> laborative time with teachers is essential.

Thus, she suggested, good curriculum alone cannot sustain efforts at
change. And although exceptional teachers always will be able to carry
on, "that's not the case for most of the teachers. They need to have that
support."

Relationships Among Network Members. Networks are built upon informal
exchanges and reciprocal relationships. In theory, the information shared
among a network's constituents may lead to common understandings,
common purpose, even collective action (Rogers & Kincaid, 1981). In such
a situation, network members act as reference points for one another's
decisions. The informality and reciprocity within a group fosters trust,
which fuels interaction. Did the Math A network in District 1 approximate
these conditions?

According to one teacher, network relationships were characterized
by "a spirit of rapport, so if we need help we ask each other." This
same teacher also described network relationships as "very good, very

harmonious, supportive, friendly. There has been no friction at all. We meet as peers. There's no idea that someone knows more than another person. Very open. It's good."

As it happens, this teacher "goes to some extra meetings outside of school [on behalf of the network] and gets more information on how to implement some of the lessons." He then conveyed the information to his peers during their common time. Nevertheless, as another teacher remarked, "I feel like we're clearly peers. There is someone who goes to these other meetings and brings information to us and has more experience with the program, but we really act just like peers. Nobody is telling somebody else what to do. It's all shared."

Similarly, a spirit of mutual support was expressed by several teachers. For example: "So if I have something that I have translated, I take and give it to somebody else that has Spanish-speaking students. And sometimes [in return] I get translations in Chinese." Another teacher described similar interactions, saying, "'Gee, I don't have a balance, I can't weigh these things.' 'Well, I can get it for you [responds another].'" Or, one teacher writes and another types. These are small things, but they facilitated teachers' interactions and interdependencies.

Beyond this characterization of support, these data revealed little regarding the strength of relationships among network teachers, that is, the multiple types of relations they maintained. One relevant point on this dimension, however, was that the social and professional aspects of teachers' relationships were viewed as reinforcing. As one network teacher described his experience in the summer workshop, "There are probably about 12 of us all together, and we're doing this [training] all day long and talking about it and getting ideas from each other and [saying], 'This works, this doesn't work; here, would you like some of my soda pop?' and that kind of thing." By this he implied that the rapport among network teachers became a resource in their learning.

DISCUSSION

The foregoing descriptions of staff development, support-group, and network implementation strategies accomplished three things. They introduced a model of network implementation, contributing detail and context that grounded this study in practice. This information then highlighted similarities and differences regarding the structure and content of the various strategies. Finally, the data suggested problems and lessons that begin to elaborate a network's implementation potential.

The Network's Operation

Description of the implementation network in District 1 addressed the central question regarding how a teacher professional network operates. In this case, the network included six components: a daily, extra, common preparation period for Math A teachers within network schools; cross-school monthly network meetings that promoted teachers' professional development and their connections across schools; monthly staff development workshops for some network teachers and any interested nonnetwork Math A teachers; intensive summer training that spanned a month and involved students, team teaching, peer observation, and post hoc group assessments of teachers' classroom experiences with Math A; a "linker" who connected the network with a larger world of professional expertise and experience; and informal, unstructured contacts among network teachers. These components constitute one model of a teacher professional network.[5] The model links classroom teachers within schools, across schools, and to professional expertise and practice beyond the school district's borders.

Comparing Implementation Strategies

These data also demonstrated similarities and differences in the structure and content of these implementation strategies. For example, the network provided teachers with more opportunities, and with more intensive formats, to collaborate on Math A (Table 5.1). The frequency of teacher contact thus was greater in the network. Network teachers also shared more common, and more immediate, experiences than did their counterparts in the staff development and support-group districts. All three districts, for example, required summer training. In District 1, training involved a 5-day workshop; in District 2, 5 half-day workshops. In the network district, summer training involved teachers in classroom instruction for 4 weeks, teaching together and observing one another in the mornings, and collaboratively evaluating Math A materials and classroom experiences in the afternoons.

Similarly, follow-up training in District 2 included 5 release days spaced across the academic year; in District 3, it entailed 3 half-day sessions on Saturdays. District 3 also initiated a Math A teachers' support group, which met monthly after school for 2 hours. In the network district, follow-up included monthly 2-hour meetings after school, plus a daily common preparation period devoted to Math A. Support was embedded within the network's common preparation periods.

The significance of the network's more frequent and intensive teacher

Table 5.1. Structure of Implementation Strategies Compared

Structure	Staff Development	Support Group	Network
Summer training	Workshop: 5 days	Workshop: 3 half days	Class format: 4 weeks with team teaching, peer observation, group evaluation
Follow-up workshops throughout the school year	5 days release time	3 half-day Saturdays	Monthly 2 hours after school; monthly release day (some network teachers only)
Support group	No	Yes, monthly 2 hours after school	Embedded in common prep
Common prep period	No	No	Daily, in addition to regular prep
Linker	No[a]	No[a]	Yes
Informal connections among Math A teachers	Department-based when available	Department-based when available	Department-based, all schools and across schools
Common experience	Indirect, periodic sharing	Indirect, monthly sharing	Direct through summer teaching, daily sharing

[a]In this case, the linking function was performed by a district math resource teacher. In contrast, the network included a coordinator who performed specific linking duties beyond those undertaken by the district's math resource teacher.

interactions is evident in several ways. Frequent interactions expanded the time teachers could attend to implementation demands. In terms of the study's theoretical framework, implementation capacity is enhanced through individuals' greater attention to implementation tasks. On this dimension, the dailiness of the network enabled teachers to address implementation tasks more frequently than did other strategies.[6]

The network structure also provided network teachers with immediate and common experiences. Again, the summer training is illustrative. Network teachers instructed students, taught in teams—and so observed their teammates—and together evaluated course materials and class sessions. Teachers' implementation of Math A, thus, began with a shared and commonly defined classroom experience. Math A practice and teachers' collaboration regarding this practice also developed simultaneously, which may establish expectations of collaboration and foster teachers' joint work over time.

In the same manner, the daily common preparation period allowed immediate evaluation, planning, and support. Teachers conferred when questions, problems, frustrations, or successes arose, not days or weeks later when a meeting was scheduled and when the press of intervening classroom events had focused their concerns elsewhere.

Frequent collaboration in the network also allowed teachers to move beyond introductory matters, like discovering the content of the next Math A unit, to issues more closely associated with the curriculum's use in practice. I base this observation on the language teachers used to describe the content of their interactions, and this varied among staff development, support-group, and network teachers (Table 5.2). Content in staff development and support-group districts focused primarily on introducing new Math A materials, but teachers there also practiced, discussed teaching strategies, shared classroom experiences, explained adaptations they found useful, and encouraged other teachers to change.

Table 5.2. Content and Relationships of Teachers' Interactions Compared

Factor	Staff Development	Support Group	Network
Content	Introduce materials (main purpose) and allow some practice, discuss teaching strategies, share classroom experiences, discuss curriculum adaptations, encourage teachers to change, reduce isolation		Plan what materials to present in class, solve problems, adapt units, discuss instructional strategies and student needs, challenge and support
Expertise	Primarily presenters, with peers sharing experiences during workshops	Mixed: presenters in workshops, peers in support group	Primarily peers, with presenters in monthly network meetings
Control of agenda	State/local providers	Mixed	Classroom teachers
Format/ relationships	Formal, workshop, experts, others	Mixed	Some formal, more often informal, round table, colleagues

In Districts 2 and 3, implementation efforts also were designed to reduce teachers' isolation.

The language that network teachers used to describe their interactions reflected purposes similar to those cited by staff development and support-group teachers, but implied a deeper level of engagement. For instance, network teachers planned what materials to use in class, based on recent experience and expectations gleaned from the state units. They solved problems by comparing the day's classroom experiences, and together they negotiated adaptations of the Math A materials. In the process, like their staff development and support-group counterparts, network teachers discussed instructional practices, talked about students' needs, and challenged and supported one another. The difference on this dimension between network teachers and those in Districts 2 and 3 was one more of degree than of intent.

The network structure also established the context of expertise and control over teachers' professional development agenda (Table 5.2). Expertise in the staff development setting resided primarily with workshop presenters who offered prepared information and addressed teachers' questions. These presenters also controlled workshop agendas. As a result, the staff development setting cast its participants as "experts" and "learners." Logically, a workshop format, limited time, and voluminous material are conducive to expert–learner interactions. This arrangement also is familiar, employed routinely in high school classrooms, but exactly the opposite of how Math A sought to restructure teacher–student relations.

The expert–learner orientation of staff development structured teachers' professional development experience in terms of "training" rather than construction of practice. This was clear in teachers' comments. As a support-group teacher put it, "All of our teachers were trained in the packets or the material of the state." A staff development teacher, reflecting on her inservice experience, said, "I've done that, yeah. I hope that they'll have at least one workshop a year for those previously trained to just get refreshed on it. That would be great." Still another said, "I want to go back again and see what else they have." These comments reflect teachers' reliance on outside experts.

Components of the network strategy also involved these expert–learner relations, principally in the monthly after-school meetings and staff development workshops. But the primary network interactions—primary because of their frequency and embeddedness in teachers' daily routines—those in the common preparation periods, reflected a different relationship, a peer-explorer model, one based on reciprocal interaction, an informal setting, and unfamiliar material. Network teachers sat around tables in their math department offices every day and discussed Math A issues of immediate importance to them. As one network teacher remarked, "Nobody is telling somebody else what to do. It's all shared."

The support-group strategy hewed a middle course, utilizing the expertise of external presenters in workshops and classroom teachers in the support group. The difference between this mixed approach and the network, again, seems to be a matter of degree, with the network utilizing its frequent interactions and embedded setting to foster group work and exploration of math concepts among math teachers. Because group work and mathematical explorations are central themes of Math A itself, professional development in the network setting more closely resembled the philosophy and strategy of the course these teachers were developing.

Potential and Uncertainty

Beyond observations regarding the structure of staff development, support-group, and network implementation strategies, five points illustrate the potential and uncertainty of teacher professional networks.

First, staff development, support-group, and network teachers alike judged their respective implementation strategies positively. In assessing these strategies, the question for all groups was: compared with what? Was Math A inservice helpful? As one staff development teacher suggested, "Rather than just say, 'Here it is'? . . . Oh, definitely." In fact, Math A staff development offerings brokered several advantages. They connected teachers with instructional assignments, convened teachers who shared similar assignments, focused on content and pedagogy, and extended over the course of an academic year. These desirable attributes often are missing from typical inservice activities. On the other hand, Math A inservices still were distanced from teachers' daily work, structured, intermittent, and brief. In addition, they failed to reflect the assumptions of the material they introduced regarding how persons learn.

The main difference between the cases on this dimension was that staff development and support-group teachers characterized inservice opportunities as helpful, while network teachers portrayed their interactions as integral to their practice. This distinction was evident earlier in the chapter in network teachers' comments about the focus of their interaction—planning, problem solving, and the like. Other evidence included network teachers' comments regarding their increased sense of efficacy, for example, "Professionally I feel like I'm a much better teacher." This sentiment was absent from staff development and support-group data. Still, all three strategies compared favorably with teachers' usual professional development experiences. Compared with each other, differences related to the level of integration between implementation strategy and daily practice.

Second, the salience of these implementation strategies was higher among network teachers than their staff development and support-group counterparts. Network teachers said a lot about their network, and the network composed an important part of teachers' implementation experiences, permitting daily interaction across a great range of topics.

Conversely, staff development and support-group teachers said comparatively little about their training. These teachers' inservice experiences occurred less frequently, covered many topics quickly, lacked a daily connection to teachers' classroom experiences, and provided little reinforcement for lessons learned. Lacking reinforcement, lessons were more likely to languish than to be incorporated into instruction. According to one staff development teacher, "Each week we brought in our ideas on probability, our ideas on algebra, and then we duplicated them off. And everybody got them, and we took them home. And they're sitting in that closet right there. And then the next year I didn't go [to Math A workshops], but they did some more Math A stuff. And I'm not sure what they did then." Her last statement implied how a lack of reinforcement also may affect dissemination.

Third, in terms of implementing and sustaining curricular innovations, isolation courts failure: "You need to have that outside support," concluded a network teacher. "I think the collaborative time with teachers is essential." Most teachers, she asserted, did not possess the capacity to carry on alone, and good curriculum alone cannot sustain change. Uniformly, network teachers credited their progress to the common preparation period.

In this regard, teachers' collaboration was fostered to a greater extent through network than through staff development or support-group experiences. All four of the network teachers said that they directed questions and problems to the network. None of the staff development or support-group teachers made similar claims regarding their structured support. Meeting infrequently was helpful but did not substantially change the isolation that characterized their teaching. Recall the staff development teacher's lament, "I'm out here on my own, strictly on my own."

Fourth, the link between isolation and implementation failure raises a question about the kinds of interaction that can diminish teachers' insularity. The data across these cases indicate that isolation may be reduced and implementation facilitated by centering teachers' interactions within their academic departments. Network teachers did seek and find assistance in their common preparation period, while staff development and support-group teachers lacked such structured assistance. However, when the question focuses not on the strategy of assistance but its locus, the result changes. Teachers across the cases who had other Math A teachers in their departments relied on these departmental peers for assistance and support. One of three staff development teachers and three of four support-group teachers took advantage of such opportunities. Recognizing the value of these "mini support groups," District 3 attempted to place two Math A teachers at each school.

The importance of departmental collaboration indicates two things regarding a network's implementation potential: that proximity and immediacy count; and because proximity and immediacy occur naturally in academic departments, grounding strategies of teacher support in their departments may enhance the efficacy of implementation efforts overall. Lieberman and McLaughlin (1992), for example, described how the Los Angeles Urban Math Collaborative required whole departments to participate in a network in order to ensure that teachers would have a moderately receptive environment in which to try out new ideas. The cases here indicate the utility of at least teaming teachers within departments for the purpose of mutual support.

The value of immediate and department-based teacher contacts illuminates a fifth point. These cases demonstrate that networks are problematic. Some form of network was attempted in all three cases but sustained in only one. In District 1, the network flourished and teachers integrated the network with practice. District 2 launched a Math A support group, but it faltered. District 3 incorporated a support group into the district's implementation plan. It operated for half a year before teachers abandoned it, preferring instead to focus on curriculum revisions.

Why was structured collaboration sustained in one district and not the others? Support groups in Districts 2 and 3 relied on "tired time," and other meetings and obligations precluded teachers from attending regularly even if they wanted to. Financial compensation also failed to encourage participation over time. Moreover, as the earlier comment of a support-group teacher indicates, "support" in this format assured teachers that they weren't the only ones having problems; the "hearing" and camaraderie lifted one's spirits. But this type of support didn't connect directly with practice. In contrast, the network structure enabled teachers to challenge and support one another in the context of daily practice. Structuring collaboration within the daily schedule provided regular opportunities for interaction; it also may have signaled the importance of interaction.

SUMMARY

These descriptions of staff development, support-group, and network implementation strategies introduced a model of a teacher professional network and highlighted similarities and differences among three implementation strategies. The network's particular structure and frequent interactions expanded teachers' time to attend to implementation tasks, provided more immediate and common experiences, allowed teachers to move beyond introductory issues to ones closely associated with the use of Math A in practice, and established a context for expertise and control over teachers' professional development agendas. Still, differences between the strategies appeared to be ones of degree rather than of intent.

These comparisons also indicated that all teachers viewed their particular professional development opportunities favorably, but that the salience of the network strategy, and thus its importance to practice, was higher than the others. The network, too, fostered greater collaboration and sustained it over time.

If these observations indicate a network's potential, two issues arose that elaborate its uncertainty. While network teachers raised questions and problems within their network common preparation periods, all teachers across the cases who had the opportunity directed similar concerns to teachers in their own departments who also taught Math A. The efficacy of this network model may derive from its design, namely, grounding network interactions in academic departments, rather than from an ability of networks qua networks to sustain teachers' connections.

Similarly, networks themselves are problematic. In two of the three cases, networks failed to sustain teachers' participation over time, even though the demands and challenges of implementation remained high. District 1's success may have depended fundamentally on the frequency, proximity, and immediacy of teachers' connections and interactions. Like the network teacher suggested, common time among teachers that is focused on their practice builds professional capacity to change education.

CHAPTER 6

The Contribution of Teacher Networks: Linking Policy, Practice, and Professional Development

> I think better teaching goes on if the teachers are working together and sharing together.
>
> —A support-group teacher

WHEN PRESENTED WITH THE hypothetical task of implementing Math A across his district, one network teacher responded immediately, saying, "Phew, I've got a headache." In that the demands of Math A policy on practice are substantial (involving broad changes), significant (focusing on curriculum and instruction), and material (allocating teacher and student resources differently), his headache is understandable. In this study, too, the headache was greater for some teachers than for others. Within these network, staff development, and support-group strategies, school districts and teachers approached implementation in different ways. Comparing teachers' early implementation experiences across the cases reveals the implementation potential of teacher networks. Of note first, in this regard, is the need to view networks and implementation in the context of teachers' learning.

LEARNING AND MATH A IMPLEMENTATION

All implementation involves learning on the part of the individuals who are responsible for the change that implementation implies. Even relatively straightforward, programmed implementation tasks, like obeying a new speed limit, require adaptations in thinking and behavior. Is the higher speed equally safe in ideal and inclement weather? Is increased speed worth a trade-off in decreased gasoline efficiency? Can I handle my auto as competently at the faster pace? Still, such straightforward changes are relatively easy for individuals to command.

Learning associated with the implementation of Math A is more problematic. The uncertainty of learning with Math A lies in its demands on teachers' practice. For example, Math A was organized around large math themes, exploration and application of mathematical concepts, and cooperative learning. It utilized concrete models and hands-on manipulatives. It asked students to be active learners, and it required teachers to facilitate students' learning rather than simply to transmit a body of knowledge. These changes affected teachers' conceptions of mathematics, the content and instructional materials that shaped their courses, and the ways teachers and students interacted.

Math A fundamentally asked teachers to rethink the whole of their teaching practice. Teachers confronted new and uncertain instructional technology, novel and vague goals, slim institutional supports, and few—if any—models of successful practice. In these circumstances, teachers must discern the demands of policy as well as appropriate responses in practice. One network teacher directly conveyed this need when she observed that students and teachers both were "learning and developing through this [implementation] process." Her departmental peer likewise noted that "teachers have to learn. . . . [Implementing Math A is] like an experimental process for us." In the context of this study, teachers' classroom-level perspectives on implementation revealed six characteristics of the learning demands associated with the complicated curriculum changes Math A represented.

Novel Demands

One characteristic of the learning associated with Math A entailed both the novelty of the curriculum and the uncertainty associated with it. The content of Math A challenged teachers because it presented mathematics differently and because it expected teachers and students to act differently in relation to it. "It's a completely different way to teach, and for the kids, it's a different way to learn," asserted a support-group teacher. Similarly, a network teacher explained that "a lot of it is new for us. You know, how do we do this? And what's it going to be like in the classroom?" His counterpart across town described how "Math A is new and different and harder, harder in that the teachers have never had it before." In this same manner, a 15-year veteran math teacher noted that Math A "is a brand-new experience for me because I never taught this kind of material." Thus, the novelty of the curriculum itself demanded learning.

Novelty also created uncertainty. At the outset of implementation, teachers' expectations were unclear. In this regard, a network teacher described how "when you just start maybe you don't know what to expect from the [student] groups. You don't have it in your head exactly what it's going to look like, and how they're going to work, and when they're going to be quiet, and when they're not."

This uncertainty turned up in teachers' instruction. He continued:

> So if you're unsure about it, then you're not sure where to draw the line. At least that's what happens with me. But as I get more experience with it, or I see it with other teachers and I work with them, I know where to draw the line, and then the students know where it is.

Teachers were unsure, that is, exactly where implementation would lead. For instance, a network teacher noted, "When you are implementing a program that is so new, there are things that will not work." And because "things" do not always work, implementation involved risk. "You have to take a risk," explained a support-group teacher. "You might fail. You might get all this stuff out and start going somewhere and say, 'Where is this leading?' And I think there is a risk of failure there, too. You have to be willing to admit that you don't know all the answers." With Math A, teachers and students both, in a real sense, were "trying it out."

Broad Scope of Change

Another characteristic of learning in the Math A context involved the broad scope of change associated with Math A practice. Policy required learning on multiple dimensions. For example, course concepts were different. One teacher admitted, "I don't know quite what the concepts [are that] they want out of it." Materials also were unusual and untested. "When the new curriculum was developed," recalled a network teacher, "I needed conversation and support with fellow teachers to understand the material." Moreover, the technology of change was unfamiliar. Pondering this difficulty, a network teacher remarked, "Like if we're going to use tiles to teach sequences, how do we do that?" In this regard, also, cooperative learning presented challenges and sent one teacher on a search for staff development options that helped him to reorganize his classroom around student groups and to utilize and manage cooperative structures. In short, learning and implementation—improving teachers' understanding and facility with the curriculum—involved conceptual and operational challenges.

The number of changes demanded simultaneously by Math A implementation deepened teachers' implementation challenge. A network department chair recounted the problem, explaining:

> I had one of the teachers say to me just recently that "you are really asking a lot of us. You are not only asking us to use new curriculum, you are not only asking us to expect students to produce a different kind of mathematics, you're asking us to look at math differently and teach it differently." And that's what it really boils down to. For some teachers, it's a very easy change. For others, especially if you've been in this business at least 20 years, and many of them have, it's very hard to change old habits.

Teachers confronted new content, novel instructional techniques, unfamiliar technology, a different organization of instruction, new roles for themselves and their students, unfinished materials, even a reconstituted vision of mathematics education. All these changes immersed teachers in a variety of conceptual and operational issues related to practice and required that teachers manage and make sense of the aggregate demands of change.

Ongoing Process

Math A implementation also evidenced an evolutionary character. Learning and implementation are, as a network teacher suggested, "a constant growing process." His departmental colleague similarly explained that implementation "doesn't happen all at once." Students and teachers were learning and developing as they defined Math A in practice, and learning occurred gradually. Math A students, for example, worked ideally by design in groups of four. But, as a network teacher lamented, "I haven't worked to that point. I've only worked up to two or three. I have to build that up. Myself, you see, I'm not used to [groups] either."

At first in this implementation process, teachers' learning curves were steep. A network teacher remarked how "in the first year of [Math A] there are so many things that I learned about how to run my classroom that, of course, I'm anxious to do them over again next year." Similarly, another teacher described how his own learning and instruction were connected, saying:

> I've been teaching Math A for 3½ years,[1] and each year I'm improving. I'm not doing the same thing every year. I may be using the same curriculum, but I'm presenting it maybe in a slightly different manner from just what I've learned or shared with other

folks and how they're presenting it and what kind of manipulatives are used.

Simple trial and error sometimes underlay this learning process. Referring to his experimentation with student groups, a network teacher recalled how he required students to reconfigure their rows of desks into small clusters every time they started a group activity. Eventually, he concluded that "as we gradually worked more and more in groups, it [got] to be more of a hassle to keep turning the desks back and forth. So the second semester I just put them in groups and left it that way." This was a simple enough lesson, but one that developed only with experience. Moreover, once students configured themselves routinely in small groups, other opportunities and benefits emerged, particularly regarding students' mutual assistance. The key point, for both teachers and students, was that implementation and learning unfolded over time. As the network teacher quoted earlier asserted, "It doesn't happen in September."

Constructed Knowledge

Closely related to the nature of implementation as an ongoing process, teachers, like students, constructed their knowledge from multiple exchanges with individuals, materials, or events in their classrooms and professional contexts. The network linker outlined this learning process, explaining:

> It's very hard. As you look at the teachers, you will find them at different places. It's a continuum. And just as the students need time to develop their learning and understanding of math, teachers need time to develop their learning and understanding of how students learn. And studies are indicating that students in fact do construct their knowledge and we do not hand it to them in a parcel and that many experiences, many exchanges, many articulations, that's how knowledge takes place. But the teacher, too, has to have those experiences, those opportunities, that developmental process so that his and her understanding of what it is to be a mathematics educator will take form.

A similar notion emerged from the analysis in Chapter 3 where teachers' adaptations of Math A materials evolved from knowledge they gained through classroom experience.

Motivation

In the case of Math A, learning also fostered teacher motivation. This cuts both ways, of course. Familiarity could breed disinterest, even contempt. In this study, however, some teachers suggested that learning expanded their willingness to pursue implementation. For example, during the first organizational meetings regarding Math A implementation in the network district, teachers participated voluntarily but reluctantly. As the network coordinator remembered:

> They weren't exactly thrilled with some of the ideas we were espousing. . . . If you had been there the very first time we met together in August or September, there would have been strong negative reactions to every single thing we would have done. It was extremely tiring, it was very negative kind of vibrations. They would say things like, "Oh yes, this will work, but never with my kids." Or "you must have different kids." Slowly, more teachers are buying into it. Now not everybody, but the atmosphere is different. . . . Some have bought the whole thing, and they're doing it, the whole package; others are just taking parts of lessons and trying them out.

Other teachers shared this impression. A resource teacher in the network district described teachers' changing attitudes, saying, "The very first meeting I went to this year, I thought, 'Oh, my gosh!' These teachers were totally complaining the whole time. And now there's a different attitude among those teachers; I can tell." Similarly, her departmental peer recalled how "at the beginning of the year in September or October, the resistance [of teachers to Math A] was very much higher than [it is] now [in April]." This network teacher, himself, had been resistant to Math A in the beginning, asserting, "That won't work for me, no way." After almost 2 years of experience with Math A in his classroom, however, he preferred his Math A classes to his advanced algebra assignment because, he said, it was more fun and because it engaged students more readily in mathematics.

Smallest Unit

Finally, the underlying importance of learning to Math A implementation arises from the preeminence of the "street-level bureaucrat"—teachers, in this study—in shaping implementation outputs, namely, the curriculum that is presented to students. As one teacher noted, the gulf between curriculum and its effect on students is spanned only by a teacher. He explained that Math A "curriculum is good at one level, but it depends on the teacher, how [he's] going to implement the curriculum. And every teacher has [his] unique style and unique way of implementing it." Another network teacher expressed this sentiment succinctly: "It's a matter of how we implement it, you know." In terms of the analytic framework of this study, implementation is a function of the motivation and capacity of individual implementers, the smallest units (McLaughlin, 1990a) in the implementation process.

These learning demands associated with Math A implementation cast networks in terms of teachers' professional development. As Lieberman and McLaughlin (1992) concluded, "In this period of intensive school reform, when traditional in-service training and staff development have been shown to be inadequate, networks can provide fresh ways of thinking about teacher learning" (p. 677). The linkage between networks as implementation agents and as professional development mechanisms was particularly close in the case of Math A because the implementation task was grounded in the content and instruction of California's mathematics framework, a key component in the state's instructional guidance system (cf. Smith & O'Day, 1991) and the central features of learning. Moreover, given the character and demands of learning associated with Math A implementation, the introduction of teacher networks raises a question about even what constitutes the smallest implementation unit or most important locus of professional development. Networks become particularly important when change is fundamental, uncertain, evolutionary, and dependent on the interaction of multiple actors, as with Math A. In circumstances such as these, the professional understanding, agreement, and action needed to define policy in practice emerge from ongoing contacts among classroom teachers (and related others). As one network teacher concluded, "You have to have that teacher collaboration time, or I don't think [Math A] would work." Thus, the smallest unit that matters in a case like Math A may be the network or community of practice to which teachers belong.[2] Professional discourse that develops within such a setting merges the demands of policy and practice in an operational definition of instruction.

IMPLEMENTATION AND MATH A PRACTICE

Of note, also, in terms of elaborating a network's implementation potential are findings in this study that distinguished components of network, staff development, and support-group implementation strategies and that revealed differences across the cases in terms of classroom practice.

In terms of the implementation strategies themselves, teachers received increasing amounts and types of implementation support, in turn, from the staff development, support-group, and network strategies. Key differences between the network and other implementation strategies involved the network's provisions for team teaching, peer observation, and collaborative evaluation of Math A materials and instruction (through the summer institute); emotional and professional support embedded in a common preparation period and teachers' daily experiences; and more frequent collaboration and attention to implementation tasks. Other differences relate to ongoing connections among classroom teachers; a deeper exploration of Math A materials and problems of practice; better organization of implementation resources within the district and with expertise and experience beyond the district's borders; and greater teacher control over implementation resources and professional development activities.

In terms of Math A practice, teachers' experiences across the network and nonnetwork cases were similar on several dimensions. They all were involved in limited district pilots of Math A, and thus their experience with the curriculum was similar. Also, teachers displayed a general knowledge of Math A concepts and teaching strategies. In this respect, teachers knew what Math A demanded of them. Moreover, teachers used the state-produced Math A units as their basic instructional material. With one exception—in the staff development case—teachers adapted the state materials, and their adaptations were similar: filling gaps in existing material, including basic skills materials; expanding coverage of existing topics; fine-tuning the state-produced material; and, in the network case, addressing departmental goals. Adaptations across the cases also were undertaken based on teachers' assessments of students' needs. Furthermore, teachers across the cases taught students who were low-achieving and of low socioeconomic status, and teachers expressed personal goals regarding their students in terms of fostering students' success, which often meant simply persisting in school, working with others, and solving problems. In short, the cases were similar in terms of the structural components of implementation, teachers' knowledge of policy goals and expectations, and teachers' desired outcomes for students.

On the other hand, differences among the cases emerged regarding teachers' practice of Math A, collectively and individually; their evaluations of the course based on early implementation experiences; and teachers' facility with Math A instruction.

Collectively, that is, the strategies through which teachers engaged and adapted Math A materials differed across the cases, and the different implementation strategies affected practice differently. Network teachers negotiated adaptations—the town hall model. Practice was similar across their classrooms, and it reflected the state framework. Staff development teachers, in contrast, adapted the material (or did not) separately—the solo performer model—and practice varied widely, from pushing the boundaries of the course within the spirit of Math A to abandoning the state units altogether. In yet another manner, support-group teachers adapted Math A materials individually but subsequently cycled their changes through a curriculum revision committee. This committee in turn disseminated the collective revisions to all teachers—the clearinghouse model. In this case, adaptations were mainly consistent with state policy, although more varied than in the network. Also, variations in practice were assumed to narrow over time as teachers indirectly shared revisions and as instructional materials became more similar.

Network teachers generally demonstrated greater facility with the organization of instruction and new instructional role asked by Math A, and they expressed a higher commitment to Math A than their counterparts in other cases. For example, network teachers integrated cooperative learning into their instruction more frequently and appeared to be more confident in their use of student groups (three of four instances versus one of four instances in both the staff development and support-group cases). Network teachers also articulated more clearly and worked to implement their intended instructional role as a "facilitator of learning" (three of four instances versus two of four instances in both the staff development and support-group cases).

In short, implementation patterns and teachers' capacities differed across the cases, with more positive implementation outputs found in the network case, more problematic outputs in the staff development case, and support-group outputs falling in between. Teachers' evaluations of Math A followed this same pattern and illustrated it simply: In the network case, the course rated three high marks and one medium one; in the support-group case, two high and two medium; and in the staff development case, one high, two medium, and one low; that is, network most positive, staff development least positive, support group in between. The question of importance involves ways in which the network itself contributed to the differences in Math A practice that one sees across these cases.

THE NETWORK'S CONTRIBUTION TO IMPLEMENTATION

What did the network contribute to Math A implementation that fostered the differences in practice among network, staff development, and support-group classrooms? Lessons from this comparison of implementation strategies are usefully summarized as a series of propositions that indicate the contribution and implementation potential of teacher professional networks. These lessons involve the implementation role of networks, their critical components, and needed supports.

Proposition 1

Networks facilitate implementation to the extent that they provide classroom teachers with common time to attend to implementation tasks.

The importance of this conclusion stands out in two ways. First, common time enabled teachers to focus their attention on the tasks of implementation. A staff development teacher, for example, related the importance of time to the scope of demands Math A placed on him, saying:

> If I had 4 years of experience teaching Math A, it would probably be okay. But I'm trying to develop materials and integrate manipulatives into curriculum and explore some areas that I've never explored before in terms of how to teach using manipulatives. And that takes time, it takes a lot of time.

In the network case, common time in the form of a common preparation period devoted to Math A allowed teachers to pursue Math A implementation free from the constraints of other preparations, grading papers, contacting parents, attending meetings, securing supplies, Xeroxing tests, or other tasks that teachers juggle in the course of a work day. The common preparation period devoted 50 minutes a day to joint planning, learning, and assessment. In fact, network teachers argued for the importance of the common preparation period per se, but other network models (Giganti, 1991; Lieberman & McLaughlin, 1992; Wisconsin Center for Education Research, 1992, for example) indicate that common time is the central issue, not the location of it, although time outside of the school day raises logistical and other difficulties.

Common time enabled collaboration among teachers regarding Math A practice, and this collaboration enhanced implementation in several ways. For example, collaboration reduced teachers' isolation. As one network teacher suggested, he and his colleagues began to develop friendships *and* ideas, which had never happened before. He explained why this was unusual: "I have a tendency to become insular," he said, "What is it? This is my island, this is my room. And the only people that ever come to my island are the students. And I never get a chance to talk to the other teachers. . . . I never see many people."

A network department chair reinforced this perspective, explaining that isolation is built into the organization of teaching.

> If [teachers] are not meeting together they tend to go back to their classrooms. And part of that is because of the way our preparation periods are scattered. There is no reason not to be in their classroom. There is no one else out there to talk to or share ideas. That's why the common prep is so important.

In the absence of collaboration, teachers acknowledged frustration. One teacher compared the opportunities teachers experienced inside the network and out, noting directly that

> one of the problems is frustration. Some [teachers] are alone. There is just one person teaching the Math A class, so there is no way for that person to go immediately there at the school site and find the help of a person. [In contrast,] I guess what we are trying to create is a network in the district, [where] we have to meet and exchange ideas and bring materials that work.

The network served as the vehicle for collaboration.

Collaboration also placed teachers' work in a larger professional context, enabling them to learn from each other and to track their progress individually in regard to the experience of their peers. For instance, a network teacher remarked that

> I like and I need the communication with other teachers to see how it's going in their classes so that I can understand better if what I'm doing is on the right track. And the sharing is real important.

Similarly, another network teacher explained:

> This prep period, I think, has been one of the positives—one of the pluses—of the program because it has given me a chance to learn from the other two teachers. . . . They use a different style that I would never have thought about [attempting], a different way, and so we share ideas.

Sharing helped change teachers' ideas and attitudes "because you start to see, too, it's not just your classroom. And you're getting ideas from somebody else, and you feel that you're not alone in this, too." A department chair noted that the result of this collaboration filtered back into the classroom and encouraged teachers to experiment with new techniques. He concluded, therefore, that "you need the [common] time . . . to develop, to try things out."

Collaboration also engendered network teachers' concern for students. The network department chair explained:

> To be honest, really, I think [teachers'] attitudes have changed now. It's a caring that you show for the students, the concern if they are not learning: "What else [do] we need to do? Let's put on the brakes and rethink this through to see what else we can do." That type of collaboration will continue.

Moreover, collaboration promoted teachers' sense of efficacy: "Professionally, I feel like I'm a much better teacher." Another network teacher elaborated this judgment, explaining:

> I've gained the strength, the ability, the confidence of teaching Math A and knowing that the way I am teaching it is the way we have decided that we want it to be taught. . . . I understand the curriculum. I've learned how to implement it. I have an understanding of which teachers have expertise in certain areas: Some teachers are better in manipulatives; some teachers are better in making problems; some teachers are better in classroom management. So I know who to seek out if I need some help. . . . All of these little details that we sometimes take for granted in the management of a class because it's so much and it's real hard for one person to do it all himself. So I know that we can share material. That's real helpful. So in the future I hope that we continue getting this [common preparation] period. But should it be cut back, because there is so much cutbacks right now, it's helped me personally a lot.

Collaboration also facilitated teachers' common success. According to a network teacher:

> We help each other be more successful so we feel better about [Math A] and are more sold on the idea. We find that it works. A teacher who doesn't have the [common] prep period and is out on their own implementing a program that's all these handouts and there's no book, may not be able to make it work and [consequently may] feel like this whole idea is a failure.

Thus, in the end, some network teachers attributed a higher level of implementation performance to their collaboration. From her vantage working with network and nonnetwork teachers in one school, a resource teacher observed that "other teachers are doing [Math A] that don't have the [common preparation] period, but they're not doing it at the same level." These comments indicate the potential of collaboration to reduce teachers' isolation, enable cooperative learning, expand teachers' professional context, enhance concern for students, promote a sense of efficacy, and facilitate common success. Common time opened opportunities for teachers to attend to implementation tasks, collaborate, learn, and construct practice.

Proposition 2

Networks facilitate implementation to the extent that they organize resources in support of teachers' implementation efforts.

The importance of this conclusion was evident in the different organization of learning resources across these cases. The network, for instance, organized resources within the school district; linked network teachers to experience and expertise in other districts, networks, universities, and professional organizations; pooled the expertise of classroom teachers within the network; and provided these resources to teachers on a continuing basis. Information included daily discussions of practice with Math A teachers within schools through the common preparation period; periodic discussions of practice with teachers from other schools through monthly network meetings; the introduction of new Math A materials, ideas, and strategies through monthly workshops; sustained periods of practice and evaluation with students and colleagues through summer institutes; and tips and techniques through informal, unstructured communications among network participants. Professional development opportunities, thus, were embedded in teachers' daily work.

In contrast, the pattern of assistance in the staff development and support-group cases was intermittent, professional development opportunities arose outside teachers' daily routines, expertise was isolated in the sense that there were few connections among classroom teachers, and access to external resources was haphazard. Although these attributes characterize staff development offerings generally (Corcoran, 1990; Little, 1990a; McLaughlin, 1991; Smith & O'Day, 1991) and in California (California Commission on the Teaching Profession, 1985; Koppich, Gerritz, & Guthrie, 1986; Little et al., 1987), the state cautioned against this more traditional approach to professional development regarding implementation of the state mathematics framework.

Teachers need the same opportunities to develop their understanding and their ability to apply their knowledge to new situations as students do, and such development does not occur in a one-time, 2-hour workshop on a single topic. Rather, well-planned, extended programs are needed in which teachers have the opportunity to see new techniques demonstrated in classrooms, try out new methods with their own students, and reflect on change in the curriculum. Further, teachers must receive coaching and support over a period of time to build their confidence and to see for themselves how content and methodology are related in their teaching. Most in-service programs will have to be substantially overhauled for these criteria to be met. (California State Department of Education, 1985, p. 5)

With broad changes demanded of teachers, and learning closely linked to implementation success, implementation resources and supports that are organized and immediately available to teachers are likely to facilitate implementation capacity to an extent that more traditional staff development supports, or even intermittent support-group sessions, will not. In short, the network's organization of implementation resources was more commensurate with the demands of Math A on teachers' practice than were the approaches involved in the staff development and support-group implementation strategies examined here.

Proposition 3

Networks facilitate implementation to the extent that they foster professional discourse, which leads to a common definition of practice.

Network teachers in this study used their common forum to negotiate a common definition of Math A practice. Math A was similar across network classrooms, just as it closely reflected (and elaborated) the state's vision of Math A. Network teachers' capacity and commitment to Math A also were somewhat higher than among their nonnetwork counterparts. Variations on these dimensions were wider in the other cases. This may not be an unusual finding in cases regarding textbook-driven, programmed curricula—algebra, for example. However, given the formative nature of Math A; the substantial, significant, and material demands of Math A policy on practice; the uncertainty of its technology; the novelty of its theory; and the broad scope of its curricular adaptations, consistent practice across classrooms and schools is an interesting finding in itself.

Why did practice appear to be similar across network classrooms? In general, it seems, because network teachers learned together, and these lessons shaped their practice. They shared expertise, and this expertise influenced their practice. Within network teachers' ongoing, structured, collaborative attention to Math A implementation, questions were raised, problems solved, frustrations voiced; experience was shared, policy tested, and practice defined. In this context, teachers could explore the meanings of policy in practice. In contrast, if faced with a curriculum that failed to address student needs, teachers presumably may use a network to circumvent policy prescriptions. In other words, bad policy well implemented is still bad policy, and a network could make short work of it.

Seven points appeared to be important in this respect. First, the discourse associated with the network's common time was focused by teachers' instructional tasks, namely, presenting Math A to students in a meaningful and efficacious manner. This distinguished the character of the network as a "professional" undertaking.

Second, the domain of teachers' dialogue within the network encompassed what one network participant termed the "total management" of change. In this context, teachers planned what materials to use in class, solved problems associated with practice, adapted Math A materials, discussed and refined instructional strategies, evaluated students' needs, and challenged and supported one another professionally and emotionally. This depth of activity extended beyond activities undertaken within the staff development and support-group formats.

Third, the immediacy of teachers' discourse contributed importantly to facilitating Math A implementation. Teachers grappled with issues and problems as they arose, rather than days or weeks later in a scheduled support-group or staff development setting. A corollary to this immediacy involved teachers' heightened control over the resources of implementation, in terms of their own time and attention and in terms of the topics and pacing of these activities.

Fourth, professional dialogue created a mutual dependence and openness among network participants. One network teacher characterized this change, saying of network teachers, "You're really dependent on each other. In this particular [instance, that is, Math A], you're dependent on each other." The network coordinator expanded this notion, linked it to teacher learning, and suggested that the emerging level of teacher interdependence was an exciting development in itself. When teachers work together, she remarked,

> you create, number one, a very supportive network among those teachers. And, two, you create in teachers—because of the network you give them the right and the privilege to take a risk and sometimes fail. You're not out there all by yourself. . . . You can come back [from the classroom] to your peers and say, "I tried this, and it fell flat." Ten years ago, teachers would never confess failures to one another. They were very protective of their domain.

And now they exchange their failures and successes. To me it's one of the most exciting elements of the project.

Network teachers, the coordinator asserted, maintained a cohesive group identity. This contrasts sharply with the norm of privacy that exists among teaching staffs (Little, 1990b).

Fifth, the involving character of teachers' professional discourse had a leveling and reassuring effect on network participants. One relieved network teacher explained this influence. "You know something," he said,

> before these [network] meetings, I thought I was the only one in the district who was having some difficulties on how to reach students. "It may be just me," I would say. But when you go to these [network] meetings, you find that everybody else has the same problems, too. And what we do then is that we try to—where's there's a common problem here—let's try to reach an agreement and find a solution. So it is not just you trying to find a solution. And I feel, myself, as though I'm not alone, just left alone in my classroom, no. . . . What I'm finding out is that now I'm not afraid to seek help. Because before if I didn't know what was going on or what to do, I wouldn't say anything. I would keep it to myself. I guess I had the [concern that] if I go and ask, they would say, "How are *you* teaching? How good a teacher are *you*?" And that's not the reality. Everybody else has the same problems. So now I'm not afraid to cry for help, I guess. And that makes me feel a lot better. I'm more comfortable.

Importantly, when he cried for help, it was available: "All the time," he said. The other teachers "are always there. I guess that's a key point, the networking."

Sixth, support generated within teachers' collaboration played a key role in developing implementation capacity. Every network teacher mentioned its importance. Why? Because support was enabling. In most comments, teachers linked support with motivation. One teacher, for example, linked the support he found in the common preparation period to his persistence and success in Math A. According to him, teachers' ongoing collaboration made a "big difference":

> You have that time where even if you don't discuss a specific lesson, you at least are with the other teachers getting support. You know that they're [teaching] in groups. It's like a student in a classroom. If everybody is in a group and working, then they're more

motivated to work in their group with the other students in the group because they see everyone else doing it. So when I go to a meeting and the other teachers have their students in groups and they have their expectations and they're going through the lessons, then I know I can do it and I have to do it. So their success builds up my success.

In this instance, support, motivation, and capacity resulted from the daily collaboration he experienced in the network.

His case is interesting because he had started teaching, then abandoned, Math A the year before, and he attributed his dropping out to a lack of support. As he explained:

Last year I tried to do a little bit of [Math A] at the beginning of the year, and I wasn't part of the [network] group where I had the extra prep period. I had one Math A class. I decided not to continue after a couple of weeks, or a few weeks. By not being in that group and not having the extra prep period, I didn't have the support for trying to implement a new curriculum and trying to do something new, having students in groups, and trying to figure out how this stuff worked without a book.

This teacher was not the only one to give up amidst the uncertainty of implementing a new and unusual course. As another recalled, "If you are all by yourself, like I was last year, I give up. It was frustrating because there was nobody around to [answer] questions." The support he found in the network helped to maintain his interest in Math A. "The other thing is the networking, the support," he said. "There is a lot of support out there for me from other teachers. And without it, I wouldn't be in the Math A classes."

Finally, professional discourse contributed to the legitimization of changes wrought by implementation. The fact that teachers themselves were piloting and adapting the Math A curriculum and sharing their experiences provided a level of authenticity and legitimacy that would have been unavailable if the curriculum had been delivered to teachers as a finished product. As a network teacher explained, "I think it will be easier to sell everybody on the concept of Math A if [teachers have] had a chance to look at it and to participate in the evolution of the program." Among network teachers, that participation led to a sense of ownership of the curriculum they presented in class. "I learned a long time ago," cautioned one teacher, "not to try to get teachers to do things just by telling them they have to do it. Make it so that there's a group of experienced teachers who can carry the ball and say, 'Hey, this works,' and hopefully through a peer type of thing, get the Math A to work."

Conversely, a teacher predicted resentment for cases where decision makers failed to consult teachers.

> If somebody up in the board of ed[ucation] decides that this is the textbook that we're going to use, then a lot of us [teachers] have resentment. But if we've been using it and testing it for years, letting things work, and then we say, "This works" and "This doesn't," ... there's some sense of ownership.

In short, teachers' comments indicate how professional discourse focused by instruction, extending over a range of implementation issues, and connected immediately to teachers' practice can shape a common definition of practice, create a sense of community and mutual endeavor, communicate enabling supports, and legitimate changes demanded by policy but tempered by practice.

Proposition 4

Networks facilitate implementation to the extent that they are structured by (a) a common purpose, (b) frequent interaction, (c) immediate and common experiences, and (d) a linker to bridge the gap between network and other resources.

If, as this study indicates, the contribution of networks to implementation involves common time to attend to implementation tasks, the organization of implementation resources, and professional discourse regarding practice, then the study also indicates that these contributions are neither automatic nor self-activating. Here as elsewhere (Lieberman & McLaughlin, 1992), networks appear to be problematic. All three districts attempted a network in one form or another. One succeeded. Why did the network succeed in District 1 but not in the others? What factors enabled the network, which then facilitated teachers' implementation efforts?

The cases in this study revealed important structural factors that fostered teachers' collaborative work. For example, the network benefited from a common purpose. Network teachers viewed their work in terms of promoting important shared goals, in this case assisting at-risk students through their transition to high school and improving minority students' success in college-preparatory mathematics. Teachers used Math A to facilitate both goals, specifically, to move students into algebra. These common goals imbued the network with a mission larger than implementation per se and animated teachers' implementation efforts.

The network also benefited from frequent interactions among its participants. Frequent interactions expanded the time implementers had to attend to implementation tasks. Frequent interactions also provided immediate opportunities for planning, evaluation, and support that grounded the network in teachers' daily routines and practice. Frequent interactions, moreover, moved network participants beyond introductory issues—what's next?—to issues more closely associated with implementation—in the case of Math A, planning material, solving problems, and refining instructional strategies based on practice, challenge, and support. This factor most distinguished the network and support-group strategies. Finally, frequent interactions provided the multiple, ongoing exchanges among network participants that fostered mutual understanding and the construction of meaning.

The network benefited as well from immediate and common experiences among its members. The intensive summer training that involved network teachers in instruction, peer observation, and collaborative evaluations of materials, instructional strategies, and personal capacities defined implementation at the outset in terms of a shared and commonly defined classroom experience. Teachers discussed these experiences in terms of developing the collaboration and trust that supported and expanded network interactions. In this sense, the network benefited from the reinforcing nature of teachers' social and professional relationships. As one teacher suggested, "On a social level as teachers, we've gotten to know each other better, but on a work level, we've gotten so many ideas from each other."

Finally, the network benefited from a linker, someone who connected the network to implementation resources beyond its boundaries, to a larger world of professional knowledge, expertise, and experience. This linker infused the network with new material, ideas, and alternatives. In this important sense, the linker expanded the network's resources. Without such a function, the network would be only as good as its constituents at any moment, their possibilities for professional growth limited by their immediate abilities.

Proposition 5

Networks facilitate implementation to the extent that they (a) are supported by materials that demand attention, engage teachers in instruction, and foster a sense of experimentation, and (b) are embedded in a reinforcing local policy context.

One can conclude from this examination of curriculum implementation that instructional materials affect teachers' interactions. Textbook-driven courses—the "page-a-day-and-no-time-to-play" curricula—provide few incentives for teachers to interact. On the contrary, programmed curricula reinforce teachers' isolation.

In the case of Math A, teachers' implementation task was more difficult because of the in-progress status of the state-produced Math A materials. Teachers asked, "How do we implement this?" but also, "What do we implement?" "What meaning should this have?" "What else should we be doing?" The unfinished character of these instructional materials fostered a sense of experimentation and collaboration. This experimentation formed a context essential to defining the practical effect of Math A, insofar as it enabled teachers to test, revise, and improve the draft materials. These works in progress created frustrations but also opportunities for teachers to exercise leadership and expertise and to control and influence practice. For example, network teachers uniformly were leery of a future Math A textbook. As one teacher noted, "If you're working out of a text, you're basically working in isolation, and this way [in the network] you're not. You're sharing your ideas. You're collaborating." The strong sense among network teachers was that policy evolved as curriculum was tested in classrooms and evaluated among themselves. To them, the joint work enhanced the legitimacy of the changes demanded by Math A.

This Math A network also benefited from a coherent policy context in which signals and actions within the area of mathematics education were reinforcing rather than conflicting. This second essential support served strategic and operational purposes. In strategic terms, policy coherence focused and imputed meaning to network teachers' actions. The alignment of the network with state and local policy goals—moving students into algebra—reinforced the mission of the network and clarified the place and importance of Math A in the curriculum. In the same way, the complementary nature of Math A and the integrated mathematics pilot curriculum that also was being implemented at one network high school implied that the direction of change demanded by Math A had broad applications, was beneficial for all students, and was embedded in wider professional trends. The coherent state and local context, thus, conveyed a foundational level of support for network teachers. In contrast, the contested purpose of Math A in the support-group district provided teachers with mixed signals about the place and importance of Math A in the constellation of course offerings available in their district and opened Math A to the moniker, "dumping ground."

In operational terms, administrators remained important players to the extent that they created conditions within which the network operated, even if school and district administrators played little direct role in shaping network interactions. In this study, if master schedules were not rearranged, then common preparation periods were not available and students could not remain with their teachers over both semesters of an academic year. Thus, administrative support was enabling. Not all networks, of course, involve common preparation periods within a school work day, but other operational needs may arise, such as materials, substitutes, conferences, travel, and the like. With regard to the development of Math A, a state official reflected:

> It's bubbled up from the bottom, but it's had to be fostered from the top. You have to have support and you have to have some direction and you have to give the grass roots their support. You can have a lot of grass-roots movement, but if they don't get anything to support them, it's not going to work.

LINKAGES AND FUTURE QUESTIONS

This analysis fits into a stream of past and future inquiries about school change, policy implementation, and professional development. In indicating how teacher networks can positively affect teachers' motivation, capacity, and practice, for instance, this study of networks and curriculum implementation complements and expands a growing body of knowledge regarding teachers' professionalization and improvements in teachers' professional development (Crandall, Bauchner, Loucks, & Schmidt, 1982; Giganti, 1991; Johnson, 1990; Lieberman, 1995; Lieberman & Grolnick, 1996; Lieberman & McLaughlin, 1992; Little, 1990b; National Commission on Teaching and America's Future, 1996; Rosenholtz, 1989; Rosenholtz & Kyle, 1984; Secada & Adajian, 1997; Stocks & Schofield, 1997; Wisconsin Center for Education Research, 1992, for example).

Casting implementation in terms of teachers' motivation and capacity also follows a path traveled by others. Hawley (1978), for example, argued that "the crucial determinant of any given innovation's success is the *willingness* of teachers to employ it and do so creatively and selectively in the context of the needs and abilities of their students" (p. 229, emphasis added). Notice also Hawley's reliance on the classroom context. The RAND Change Agent study similarly concluded that "project success is unlikely unless teachers want to work hard to make it happen" (McLaughlin & Marsh, 1978, p. 72). In other words, innovation develops through goals that motivate individuals, groups, and organizations alike to act purposefully.

Other analyses, too, have cited the importance of viewing change in the context of learning. Lieberman and Miller (1991) described the need for continuous growth and development of teachers as "one of the most vexing problems of educational change" (p. vii). Earlier, McLaughlin and Marsh (1978) suggested that "even the 'best' educational practice is unlikely to fulfill its promise in the hands of inadequately trained or unmotivated teachers" (p. 69). The literature on school change also focuses on the importance of learning and views change as proceeding over time, requiring constant problem solving, ongoing attention, and collaboration (Fullan & Miles, 1992). The lesson here is that implementation and practice evolve from learning over time.

Conclusions that define networks' implementation role in terms of task orientation, collaboration, and professional discourse complement similar lessons that prescribe the importance, for example, of ongoing contact among teachers, concrete training with follow-through, nurturing structures of communication, and a central role for teachers (McLaughlin, 1991). Other lessons from research involve a focus on curriculum and instruction, time sufficient to ensure gains in knowledge and skills, and collegial norms (Little, 1984). Important, also, in the change process are opportunities for teachers to observe one another and to discuss new techniques with peers (Lampert, 1988), like those opportunities presented by the intensive summer network training in this study. McLaughlin (1990b) identified teachers' professional community, problem-solving structures, and teacher control over practice as workplace factors that support teachers' goals for students. Smith and O'Day (1991) and Little (1990a) highlighted the importance of linking professional development with teaching assignments. As teachers in this study indicated, teachers work better when they work together and when their collaboration is grounded in practice. This notion was echoed by teachers across California (Koppich, Gerritz, & Guthrie, 1986).

A fundamental issue here regards support for learning, implementation, and change. As Huberman and Miles (1984) concluded, "Innovations 'lived and died' by the amount and quality of assistance that their users received once the change process was underway" (p. 273). Cuban (1993) concluded simply that classroom innovations fail, in part, because teachers lack help to put complex ideas into practice, and Odden (1991) deemed ongoing support to be the sine qua non of classroom change. His assertion highlights the important role networks can play in expanding and organizing implementation supports within districts, across districts and other entities, and among classroom teachers.

Future investigations of networks should further explore and test the propositions developed in this study. They also might focus productively on questions such as the following:

- What different types of teacher networks exist and with what prevalence? What relative advantages or disadvantages do these models exhibit in promoting teachers' professional development and implementation behavior?
- What factors are related to teachers' interactions within networks? For example, whom do teachers rely on and why? What characteristics or circumstances within networks facilitate or constrain the trust and reciprocity among participants that fuel network interactions?
- What factors relate to networks persisting over time?
- How does the introduction or operation of teacher professional networks redistribute control locally over curriculum and implementation resources? What impact does this have on programs and professional relations?
- Can teacher professional networks foster closer state–local linkages? What impact do these linkages have on policy and practice? How, in other words, do networks affect the composition of policy or the response of practice?

These and related questions would develop researchers' and practitioners' understandings of the role, operations, and utility of teacher professional networks in terms of fostering learning, implementing policy, and shaping practice.

POLICY IMPLICATIONS AND CONCLUSIONS

Did the Math A teacher professional network affect the implementation of this novel curriculum? Findings here indicate a positive contribution of networks to classroom-level policy implementation. The network facilitated implementation by providing common time for teachers to attend to implementation tasks; organizing professional, policy, and expert resources in support of teachers' implementation efforts; and fostering a professional discourse that led to a common definition of practice. These contributions arose from a common purpose among network participants, frequent interactions focused on practice, immediate and common experiences, and a "linker" who connected the network to a larger world of professional experience and expertise. These contributions, in turn, found support in curricular materials that demanded teachers' attention, engaged teachers in instruction, and fostered a sense of experimentation that expanded practice, and in a coherent policy context that clarified the importance and position of Math A in teachers' work.

These findings suggest several implications for policy. For instance, networks may provide a way of approaching teachers' professional development and implementation of policy that addresses shortcomings of traditional inservice strategies. The staff development offerings organized by the California Department of Education to promote Math A began the process of improving teachers' professional development opportunities. Teachers across the cases, all of whom participated in staff development activities targeted at Math A, indicated that the state-organized training was helpful. But the state's strategy was restricted to delivering traditional supports in a better way. In contrast, the network fundamentally changed the nature of professional development activities from a training model to one commensurate with teachers' construction of practice. This transforming function indicates the utility of pursuing networks as a tool in policy implementation and of exploring ways to integrate networks into the constellation of professional development activities available to classroom teachers.

Yet we know that networks are both powerful and problematic (Lieberman & McLaughlin, 1992). If they are powerful, policy makers may rush to mandate them or to craft incentives that initiate them. If networks are problematic, then mandates by themselves will fail and incentives will be misplaced. By illuminating attributes of a network's success—in this case, a common purpose, frequent interactions (to move beyond introductory matters), immediate and common experiences (to stimulate collaboration and build trust), and a linker (to broaden a network's reach and expertise)—this study began to explore the source of networks' power and inherent difficulties. Such knowledge will assist policy makers to craft more efficacious incentives and structures.

A second policy implication revolves around teachers' affirmation of Math A and similarly styled curricula. Because the material was "fresh" and because it presented mathematics to students in a novel way that peaked their curiosity and held their attention, some teachers here asserted that Math A "worked."[3] Teachers in this study shared this assessment to varying degrees, and several expressed reservations. But only 1 of the 12 teachers in these cases abandoned the materials during the pilots as a poor match between a product and its intended market. This implies the efficacy of the theory and operational components of such state mathematics policy.

The sum total of teachers' voices from this study suggests a third, simple and powerful, policy implication. That is, the meaning and effects of curriculum policy depend on practice. Teachers in this study viewed Math A as a "work in progress." The material was far from polished and far from complete. Transforming policy into practice required substantial local adaptation. The Math A that "worked" was a product of teachers' elaboration of Math A's meaning in the context of high school classrooms. The idea that Math A would improve as it evolved is consistent with early state expectations regarding both curriculum content and its effect on teacher professional development. Alternatively, if offered initially as a finished product, the state-produced Math A material clearly would not have worked. Success in these circumstances reinforces the definition, invoked earlier, of implementation as a stage of policy making rather than simply the application in classrooms of materials developed elsewhere. In the case of Math A, policy depended on practice.

This dependency of policy on practice was evident in the degree to which local adaptations of state Math A materials formed a routine part of teachers' classroom implementation. Given the discussion in the previous paragraph, this dependency comes as no surprise. Its importance, though, lies in its implications for the relationship between state policy and local practice. If local adaptations occur routinely, how can the state ensure implementation consistent with state goals? Similarly, how can teachers develop a professional, rather than idiosyncratic, conception of practice that addresses their students' needs?

The adaptations in these classrooms were not exotic. They filled gaps in existing material, expanded topics covered in insufficient depth, fine-tuned existing material, and addressed specific departmental goals. As a whole, these changes were designed to address student needs. In part, changes also addressed subtle conflicts among policy goals, for example, that Math A students subsequently move into algebra but that conventional, pre-algebra–type material not appear in Math A course content. When policy conflicts occur, the street-level accommodations teachers undertake (potentially) ensure that the aggregate effects of multiple policies on students make sense.

To the extent that one understands policy and practice as related undertakings, at least in the context of implementation, the more likely opportunities will arise to bridge the gap between the two domains. Rather than speaking of "policy" and "practice" as independent realms, education systems would benefit by recognizing linkages between macro- and micro-level policy domains. In this sense, macro policy establishes goals and pushes practice in directions commensurate with those goals; micro policy then gives voice and practical effect to legitimate goals.

Ideally, practice informs policy, which, in turn, establishes working conditions that motivate and sustain student *and* teacher learning. This function implies the advantages of relating policy more closely to practice and of seeking an appropriate balance between the goals and operational components of policy. Classroom teachers should be viewed as critical players in coordinating components of a state's instructional guidance system, including state goals and frameworks, school curriculum, professional development, and assessment mechanisms.

Finally, like other policies, Math A was not self-executing. It required learning and a context that fostered implementers' motivation and capacity. On both dimensions, this study indicated the power of action emanating from a professional community nested within a coherent policy context.

As education changes, policy will attempt to accommodate and shape this change. In the case of curricular innovations, policy gains voice and practical effect only as it is translated into practice. Since this translation requires motivated and capable teachers, implementation strategies must strive to foster these attributes. Teacher professional networks may serve this role. Therefore, future investigations of networks can productively expand understanding of professional learning, implementation, and the construction of practice. The potential of networks is that they expand policy implementation from a series of discrete and idiosyncratic classroom-level actions into a collective venture among teachers and state officials as they address the meaning and management of educational change.

APPENDIX A

Study Methods

THE METHODOLOGY SUPPORTING this study arose from the confluence of six factors: an exploratory research question, implementation focus, adaptive policy, particular theoretical assumptions regarding individual-level implementation behavior, availability of a critical case, and California's reliance on staff development as an implementation strategy.

AN EXPLORATORY RESEARCH QUESTION

The research question asks about two relatively unknown phenomena: teacher networks and Math A. Researchers had concluded that networks could be "powerful and problematic" factors in teachers' professional development and school change (Lieberman & McLaughlin, 1992). Still, networks are relatively unexamined, and a specific focus on their role in curriculum implementation is new.[1] Similarly, notwithstanding a 1985 California math framework adoption, Math A implementation in 1991 was newly underway. The state-produced instructional materials that catalyzed implementation efforts in the districts I studied were not available until 1988–89. In 1990–91, when data were collected, these districts were engaged in limited implementation pilots. Little state or local information was available about the progress of implementation in classrooms. With little knowledge at the time about networks or Math A, I opted for an exploratory study. Following George's (1979) conception of such studies as opportunities to learn more about the complexity of a problem or to develop an explanatory framework, I aimed to generate propositions useful to subsequent research (Lijphart, 1971).

IMPLEMENTATION FOCUS

Because the study focuses on implementation, process questions play a central role (Patton, 1990): What did teachers do? How did they do it? What motivated them? How did they feel about the policy and its practice? How did they interpret policy and implementation events? The resultant analysis would need to address teachers' perceptions as well as activities.

179

Implementation and process considerations led to qualitative methods, in order to produce detailed descriptions of implementers' contexts, actions, and responses. Such data better capture how Math A developed and what personal or contextual factors most affected teachers' practice.

Also, implementation research predominantly has involved case studies (Palumbo & Calista, 1990), which have been employed to investigate curriculum implementation (Fullan & Pomfret, 1977). A case study design, too, has the attribute of easily accommodating the complexity of implementation, lack of researcher control over implementation events, and multiple sources of data (Yin, 1989).

LEVELS OF ANALYSIS

The adaptive nature (Berman, 1980) of Math A policy—vague goals, broad changes, uncertain technology, and little management control—suggested that variations in practice likely would occur. Accordingly, the study would need to explore implementation beneath the level of the network, in Math A classrooms. Classrooms are where implementation outputs occur, where students engage a curriculum.

Assumptions in the theoretical framework regarding individual-level implementation behavior reinforced this need to study implementation at the level of classrooms. A constructivist perspective on implementation, for example, requires research attention to the perspectives of the teachers who define Math A in practice. If practice is idiosyncratic (Cohen & Peterson, 1990), then curriculum implementation must be, too. The analytic framework describes implementation in terms of teachers' goals and evaluations of themselves and their work contexts, and in terms of their capacities to do the job. Variations in motivations and capacities that lead to different practices would be clearest at the level of classrooms.

Theory and policy, therefore, demanded two levels of analysis. First, the network. After all, I intended to explore a network's role in curriculum implementation. Second, individual Math A teachers, the street-level bureaucrats embedded within the network who shaped policy outputs as they constructed practice. Implementation cases, then, would involve subunits of analysis.[2]

A CRITICAL CASE

An exploratory, qualitative case study design seemed most appropriate, on the grounds that such a strategy would best describe classroom-level implementation processes and variations in practice. But what case, or cases? Even within the definition of a teacher professional network, wide structural or functional variations could occur. Could I define a "typical" network?

Here, as in other aspects of life, timing was everything. At the time I conceived the study, a California school district had launched a unique, 3-year experiment in Math A implementation through a teacher network. I "discovered" this network during exploratory interviews with state and regional math educators regarding site selection. The network's applicability defined my case selection strategy: This network presented a critical case (General Accounting Office, 1987; Patton, 1990) that promised particularly rich information about a teacher network's implementation role and potential. Not only did participants recognize the network and their participation in it (not always the case with networks), but this network was attempting to implement Math A in a manner consistent with state policy, which allowed me to address a state-level implementation concern regarding how to facilitate policy outputs that reflect state curriculum goals.

CALIFORNIA'S RELIANCE ON STAFF
DEVELOPMENT-DRIVEN IMPLEMENTATION

Implementing policy through a teacher network is an unusual, which is to say, nonroutine, strategy for putting policy into practice. Policy makers usually rely on traditional staff development supports. One analyst commented that "staff development has moved from a position of disregard in policy circles to become a taken-for-granted component of almost all education reform initiatives"; describing staff development's transformation from "policy afterthought" to "policy requirement" (McLaughlin, 1991, p. 61).

In fact, California crafted an entire implementation strategy for Math A around professional development. In its first 2 years, this strategy provided approximately 8,000 days of inservice training to 1,200 Math A teachers statewide. Training was offered through 14 regional centers that used a cadre of state-trained classroom teachers as presenters. A state official characterized the magnitude of this effort, saying, "Nobody has ever set up such a big inservice program." Another state official described the program as "a winner all around."

Why rely on professional development? If students learn more and perform better when their teachers are highly motivated and increasingly capable, then policy makers' concern will be to facilitate teachers' motivation and capacity. The policy question becomes: What strategy best facilitates these outcomes? (Alternatively, what levels of motivation and capacity can be expected with different types or amounts of investment?) As this study casts implementation in terms of teachers' motivation, capacity, and context, and determines that teacher learning is a key lever on motivation and capacity, implementation strategies must be judged, in part, by their ability to enhance teacher learning. In terms of the "winner all around" characterization, students win as teachers learn; and because learning undergirds professional development, teachers win, too.

The state's wide use of staff development to implement Math A encouraged a research comparison between network and staff development strategies and outputs. In this context, implementation outputs refer to the curriculum teachers present to students. And because curriculum is presented by teachers, teachers' adaptations of policy govern the nature of policy outputs. A comparison between network and staff development strategies raises three questions. First, how are network and staff development strategies similar or different? Second, is Math A practice in network and staff development classrooms similar or different? Third, beyond implementation strategies, are the contextual opportunities or constraints of network and staff development teachers similar or different?

The utility of this comparison is framed by the research question: Do teachers' professional networks affect the implementation of Math A? In policy terms, do teacher professional networks build capacity to implement Math A? The juxtaposition of network and staff development implementation strategies, therefore, is presented in a manner intended to elaborate a network's implementation role: How do the strategies compare? What are their respective consequences for teachers' learning, motivation, and capacity? A comparison case was necessary, one in which implementation was supported by staff development. Ideally this case would be comparable (Goggin, 1986) to the network case in all aspects except its implementation strategy.[3]

CASE SELECTION

I selected cases using two steps. First, I contacted State Department of Education, California Mathematics Project, and California Mathematics Council staff and asked them to suggest comparable districts that were using network and staff development implementation strategies. These conversations yielded a short list of district names. Second, to confirm these assessments of district activity and to gain access to the districts, I contacted school district officials (associate superintendents and/or math subject-area coordinators) in the nominated districts.

From this process, I selected three districts. District 1 included the network. District 2 relied on a staff development implementation strategy, providing the study with its requisite comparison district. At this point, I also included a third district. I did this initially because Districts 1 and 2 appeared to be broadly comparable except with respect to their overall commitment to implement Math A. District 1's commitment was relatively low (not striving for district-wide implementation of the state framework but supportive of teachers' activities); District 2's commitment was high (moving toward district-wide implementation of the framework). In terms of the study's theoretical framework, this difference might be important if it affected teachers' motivations and capacities variously. Since this could not be predicted at the outset, I included a third district, one with a high commitment to implement Math A and a network to facilitate implementation.

As it happened, the "network" in District 3 introduced to the study a network structure that was more likely to occur elsewhere, namely, a periodic, after-school support group. However, Math A teachers in this district did not see their support group as constituting a network per se. District 3's implementation strategy, in essence, steered a middle course between a clear, intensive network, as in District 1, and sole reliance on staff development support, as in District 2. I dubbed this middle ground a "support-group" strategy and kept it because of the variation it added to the study's cases.

Table A.1 contrasts the cases. I refer to them throughout the study as instances of network (District 1), staff development (District 2), and support-group (District 3) implementation. All three cases are similar in terms of their prescribed curriculum, stage of implementation, and availability of staff development support. All three are different in terms of their Math A implementation strategies.

On other dimensions, two districts are large and urban; one is medium-sized and suburban. Two exhibited high commitment to implement Math A; one did not. Finally, the cases differed in their use of Math A. In District 1, Math A served as a transition course between eighth-grade arithmetic and algebra. In District 2, the district intended Math A to be a transitional course, but in two instances the course served mostly juniors who had failed algebra. Similarly, in District 3, administrators defined Math A as a transitional course, but this use was contested by department chairs. During the fieldwork, Math A in District 3 served mostly tenth and eleventh graders, some of whom were moving from lower-level math toward algebra, while others had failed algebra.

Table A.1. District Case Selections Compared

Factor	District 1	District 2	District 3
Size	Large	Large	Medium
Type	Urban	Urban	Suburban
Prescribed curriculum	Framework, state units	Framework, state units	Framework, state units
Implementation strategy	Network	Staff development	Support group
Stage of implementation	Pilot	Pilot	Pilot
Staff development training available	Yes	Yes	Yes
Local university support available	Yes	Yes	Yes
District commitment to Math A implementation	Low[a]	High	High
Use of Math A	Transition to algebra	Mixed: District intent was transition to algebra; in practice some transition and some post-algebra failure	Contested: District wanted transition; pilot year serving mostly jrs./srs. after algebra failure

[a]But supportive of teachers' efforts to implement.

TEACHER SELECTION

Within each case, I asked district or school officials to nominate teachers to participate in the study. The selection criterion was an individual's potential to serve as a key informant, that is, a teacher who could speak knowledgeably about his or her experiences with Math A. In District 1, these suggestions came from the network coordinator, who was a department chair; in District 2, a math resource teacher at the central office; in District 3, a Math A teacher who served as the district's resource

teacher for Math A. I contacted nominated teachers through their department chairs (to gain permission to proceed) and asked them to participate.[4]

Four teachers composed the subunits in each case. With two exceptions, all had volunteered to participate in their districts' Math A pilots.
These two were network teachers whose department chairs had committed their departments to participate and needed to fill positions. Across
the cases, teachers' years of experience ranged from 2 to 26, but all were
new to Math A, teaching for only a year or two. Two of the teachers were
math majors, five, math minors; two entered teaching by passing the math
component of the National Teachers Exam, and one held a graduate
degree in nuclear engineering (teaching was a second career) (see Table
A.2).

Table A.3 indicates that students across the cases were similar, too.
In Districts 1 and 2, students were predominantly minority; in District 3,
the suburban district, they were predominantly White. In all districts,
however, Math A students exhibited poor math skills and were described
as at-risk for educational failure. Most students were poor economically,
and many were recent immigrants.

DATA COLLECTION

Data collection involved four directives: (1) compare Math A policy (the
state framework) with the curriculum presented to students, (2) seek
teachers' perspectives regarding their construction of Math A practice,
(3) verify teachers' perspectives through multiple sources, and (4) organize
the process loosely enough to discover unanticipated influences on teachers' practice. Data came through interviews, observations, and document
reviews.

Interviews

The study's primary data included interviews with Math A teachers. The
purposes of these interviews were (1) to describe Math A implementation
on five dimensions of practice: materials, organization of the classroom,
teaching role, knowledge of Math A, and teacher commitment; (2) to
explore teachers' motivation, capacity, and context; and (3) to describe
teachers' backgrounds.

I conducted interviews late in the school year (April and May), at
the end of a full year's classroom experience. I used a semistructured
interview protocol (Appendix B) organized around factors in the theoretical framework: teachers' goals and evaluations of self and context, with

Table A.2. Characteristics of Math A Teachers Compared

	Placement	Education	Yrs. Exp. Math	Yrs. Exp. Math A	Other Experience
District 1					
Teacher 1	Volunteer	Math minor	20	2	Algebra, geo., mostly remedial math, Spanish, social studies
Teacher 2	Volunteer	English major, NTE math	6	1	Computers
Teacher 3	Assigned, felt obligated	Math major	15	1	Geometry, middle school teacher for 11 years
Teacher 4	Persuaded (reluctant volunteer)	Industrial arts major, math minor	15	2	Advanced algebra
District 2					
Teacher 1	Volunteer	Industrial arts major, math minor	21	1	Lower math, algebra, wood shop
Teacher 2	Volunteer	—	—	1	—
Teacher 3	Volunteer	Nuclear engineering grad. degree	2	1	Calculus (former submarine commander)
Teacher 4	Volunteer	Science major, NTE math	2	1	Algebra, eighth-grade math, technical math
District 3					
Teacher 1	Volunteer (asked to take lead by district)	Math minor	26	2	District math resource teacher for Math A
Teacher 2	Volunteer	Music major	15	2	Former high school band director/10 yrs.
Teacher 3	Volunteer	Math major	9	2	Algebra, Math 2 (= seventh/eighth-grade math)
Teacher 4	Volunteer	Health/PE major, bio and math minors	17	2	—

Table A.3. Characteristics of Math A Students Compared

	Grade	Level	SES	Ethnicity
District 1				
Teacher 1	9	Weak skills	Low: recent immigrants, broken homes, work nights, LEP	Minority (Latino)
Teacher 2	9	Not ready for algebra, don't know fractions	Low	Minority (Latino/African-American)
Teacher 3	9	Immature, low skills	Low	Minority (Latino)
Teacher 4	9	Could not survive algebra	Low: most from Central America, LEP	Minority (Latino)
District 2				
Teacher 1	11/12	Missing basic skills, can't add/subtract fractions	Low: Chapter 1, most falling through cracks, bilingual	76% minority (Latino)
Teacher 2	Mostly 11/12	Some from math 8, some failed algebra	Low: Chapter 1	40% minority (Latino/Asian)
Teacher 3	9/10	Few skills, concrete thinkers, "really the pits"	Low: Chapter 1	95% minority (Latino/African-American, Asian)
Teacher 4	9	Poor skills	Low: poor, racial tension, immigrants	Minority (African-American, Latino)
District 3				
Teacher 1	11	Low	Low/middle	72% White
Teacher 2	10/11	Weak, aren't strivers, low motivation, prior failures	Low/middle	100% White
Teacher 3	10/11	Low, weak math skills	Low/middle	100% White
Teacher 4	10/11	Low	Low/middle	93% White

Note: "LEP" is limited English proficiency. "Chapter 1," now Title I, Part A, is education for disadvantaged students.

context encompassing policy prescriptions, student reactions, local implementation environment, and implementation strategies. This approach standardized basic questions across interviews, ensuring consistent coverage of important concepts. This process also left room to follow leads, ideas, or issues that emerged during the conversations as important to teachers' implementation experiences and practice.

I conducted interviews at teachers' convenience, usually during preparation periods or before and after school. Interviews were audio recorded and transcriptions prepared to preserve an accurate record and to allow subsequent coding and analysis.

I interviewed state and district officials as well. These conversations explored Math A policy goals and implementation resources and strategies. They expanded the study's information regarding implementation contexts beyond classroom doors. At the state level, interviews included State Department of Education officials, California Mathematics Project staff, and authors of the 1985 state mathematics framework. At the district level, interviews captured math subject-area coordinators, who were chiefly responsible for the course's implementation. I also interviewed others whom teachers identified as important to their implementation efforts. This step brought department chairs and resource teachers into the data base.

Observations

I observed two settings: Math A classrooms and network meetings. Observations constituted a smaller component of the study. Their purpose was twofold. In the classroom, observations provided another source of information regarding a teacher's role and organization of instruction, and student reactions. In network meetings, observations provided information about who participated and about the content and tone of discussions. In addition to observation chronicles, I followed up observations by asking teachers or network coordinators whether the session was typical, and, if not, how. Like the interviews, observations were audio taped to allow subsequent review.

Document Review

Interviewees identified and contributed relevant documents. These documents elaborated policy content, curriculum frameworks, instructional materials, background papers, and examples of students' work. Documents were reviewed, labeled (by level and subject), numbered, and filed.

The case record involved some 600 pages of interview transcripts, 160 pages of field notes, and 53 documents ranging from 1 to 500 pages.

DATA ANALYSIS

The study set out to explore the implementation potential of a teacher professional network. It assumed a constructivist perspective on implementation, adopted a comparative case strategy, and employed a constant comparative method. The analytic process involved five steps: organizing the data, categorizing its content, searching within and across cases and subunits of analysis for patterns of experience and interpretation, displaying findings in a cross-case narrative, and interpreting these findings in the form of propositions or lessons that addressed basic research questions.

Organization

The organizational component of this process readied the data for analysis. This meant two things: first, to order the mound of transcripts, notes, and documents and to facilitate recalling and citing these data. This required nothing more complicated than a series of folders and files on a personal computer, cross-referenced by alias files. Second, I checked interview transcripts for completeness and accuracy by reviewing, and thus experiencing again, all of the interview sessions.[5]

Content Analysis

Once satisfied that the primary data were complete and accurate, I coded and categorized the interviews. I started by reading through the transcripts, jotting questions and ideas in the margins. My initial coding scheme came from the theoretical framework and interview guide. At the same time, I gleaned other categories and codes inductively from the data. This resulted in nine categories and 73 separate codes (Appendix C), a number surprisingly easy to work with. Next, I clipped and sorted the coded data into a series of stacks. These nested stacks corresponded to the study's central concerns and their constituent parts, for example, (1) teacher motivation, then (1a) teachers' evaluations of context, then (1aI) evaluations of other math teachers' reactions, and so forth.

Cross-Case Analysis

The categorized data facilitated a search across cases and teachers for patterns of practice, experience, and interpretation. This immediate cross-unit examination organized the analysis around the study's central questions. The process was governed by four directives: illustrate findings with direct quotes or vignettes, use multiple sources or types of data when available to support findings, indicate the prevalence of a finding across teachers, and watch for negative cases.

Narrative Presentation

The resultant analysis then was crafted into a narrative presentation with summary data displays. As a concluding exercise in this process, I again read through the interview transcripts and field notes to construct, inductively or logically, alternative explanations for the findings. These ruminations were incorporated into the narrative.

Interpretation

As a final step, I revisited the narrative and interview data in an attempt to capture implementation experiences in the form of interpretive typologies and propositions. The resulting metaphors and propositions harness the complexity of implementation processes and organize its important attributes for further study.

APPENDIX B

Semistructured Teacher Interview Guide

I WANT TO TALK with you a bit about Math A, about how you're teaching it, about how it's being implemented, and about the kinds of support you have or need for putting this relatively new course into practice.

QUESTIONS REGARDING MATH A INSTRUCTION

1. First of all, what is Math A?
2. How is Math A different from other math courses you've taught? [Different content? Different teaching strategies?]
3. What content or materials do you use?
4. Do you use the [state] materials directly or do you change them? [If change:] What goes into your calculation about how to adapt the materials?
5. Is your classroom organized or laid out in any special way for Math A? [Group work?]
6. Is your role as a teacher different in a Math A class than it would be in other math classes, or about the same?

QUESTIONS REGARDING STUDENT REACTIONS

7. How have your students reacted to Math A?
8. Have you changed what, or how, you teach Math A in order to gain students' cooperation?
9. Is Math A a good match for the students? That is, is it a good approach to teaching mathematics to these kids?
10. Where are the students supposed to go after Math A?
11. Will Math A help them get there?

QUESTIONS REGARDING THE IMPLEMENTATION OF MATH A

12. What are your own goals for Math A? In other words, what do you hope to accomplish with your students in your classroom?

13. Do you think the district considers Math A to be an important part of the curriculum?
14. Does the central office support Math A? How?
15. Does your principal support Math A? How?
16. Does your department chair support Math A? How?
17. Do other teachers in your department support Math A? How?

QUESTIONS REGARDING TEACHER SKILLS

18. What do you need in order to do a good job teaching Math A, or even learning to teach Math A?
19. Have you had any training or inservice regarding Math A? Please describe. [Probe for access, frequency, content, relationships, additional linkages.]
20. Do you have an opportunity to work regularly with other teachers on Math A? If so, please describe.

If Networks Absent:

21. When you have a question about what to do, how to proceed, what meaning to give something, how to structure something, whom do you go to?
22. Is there some kind of support you would really benefit from as you work to implement Math A that you don't have now?
23. Would you gain something personally or professionally from working closely with other teachers on Math A?

If Networks Present:

24. How did you start attending these meetings? Who else attends?
25. How often do you meet with other Math A teachers?
26. What do you talk about when you meet with other Math A teachers?
27. How would you characterize the relationships among teachers in the network?
28. Do you see these other teachers only in the Math A meetings, or are you connected in other ways as well?
29. What keeps the network operating? [Outside person? District person? Group commitment? Money? Common prep? Etc.?]
30. When you have a question about what to do, how to proceed,

what meaning to give something, how to structure something, whom do you go to?

31. What do you gain personally or professionally from participating in the network?

QUESTIONS REGARDING TEACHERS' EVALUATION OF MATH A

32. How would you assess Math A now, given your experience with it in the classroom and your goals for teaching math to students?
33. How would you characterize your motivation to continue teaching Math A? Why?
34. If you were in charge of the district's implementation of Math A, what would be the one or two most important things you would do to ensure that the curriculum was implemented well?

QUESTIONS REGARDING TEACHER CHARACTERISTICS

35. Did you volunteer to teach Math A, or were you assigned?
36. How long have you been teaching? Teaching mathematics? Teaching Math A?
37. What is your math background?
38. What other math courses have you taught?

APPENDIX C

Coding Schedule

Italic typeface indicates main category. Asterisk indicates code suggested by data rather than theoretical framework.

CATEGORY / SUBCATEGORY		CODE	NO.
Implementation Strategy Identified		*IS*	*1.0*
IS:	Network	IS-NET	1.1
IS:	Staff Development	IS-STA	1.2
IS:	Support Group	IS-SUP	1.3
Implementation Strategy Described		*IS*	*2.0*
IS:	Access	IS-ACC	2.1
IS:	Content	IS-CON	2.2
IS:	Relationships	IS-REL	2.3
IS:	Frequency	IS-REL	2.4
IS:	Strength	IS-STR	2.5
IS:	Underlying resources*	IS-RES	2.6
IS:	Evolution of*	IS-EVO	2.7
Implementation Results Described		*IR*	*3.0*
IR:	Content of presented curriculum (including adaptations, reasons for adaptations, and assessments)	IR-CON	3.1
IR:	Organization of classroom	IR-ORG	3.2
IR:	Role of Math A teacher	IR-ROL	3.3
IR:	Teacher's knowledge of Math A	IR-KNO	3.4
IR:	Teacher's commitment to Math A	IR-COM	3.5

IR:	Experience with Math A/stage of implementation* (including response to Math A)	IR-EXP	3.6
IR:	Utilization of Math A*	IR-UTI	3.7
Teacher Motivation		*TM*	*4.0*
	GOALS		
TM:	Personal goals	TM-GOL	4.1
	EVALUATIONS		
TM:	Values, attitudes	TM-ATT	4.2
TM:	Commitment to underlying ideas, concepts, or methods of Math A	TM-COM	4.3
TM:	Evaluation of Math A/other math	TM-MAT	4.4
TM:	Evaluation of implementation strategy	TM-STR	4.5
TM:	Reaction of other math teachers*	TM-TEA	4.6
TM:	Perception of professional goal or trends*	TM-PRO	4.7
TM:	Capability/efficacy (personal agency beliefs)	TM-PAB	4.8
TM:	Perception of district goals	TM-DIS	4.9
TM:	Perception of policy decision making	TM-DEC	4.10
TM:	Validation*	TM-VAL	4.11
TM:	Evaluation of environmental resources*	TM-ENV	4.12
	OTHER MOTIVATING FACTORS		
TM:	Flexibility of course*	TM-FLX	4.13
TM:	Freshness of course material*	TM-FRE	4.14
TM:	Professional collaboration*	TM-COL	4.15
TM:	Job security*	TM-JOB	4.16
TM:	Financial remuneration*	TM-FIN	4.17
TM:	Challenge*	TM-CHA	4.18
	ENERGIZING FUNCTIONS		
TM:	Emotions	TM-EMO	4.19
TM:	Attention	TM-ATN	4.20

Teacher Capacity		TC	5.0
	CHARACTERISTICS		
TC:	Experience/years and courses	TC-EXP	5.1
TC:	Education	TC-EDU	5.2
TC:	Credentials	TC-CRE	5.3
TC:	Assigned/volunteered	TC-ASN	5.4
TC:	Effort*	TC-EFF	5.5
TC:	Personal characteristics* (e.g., I am a concrete, sequential person)	TC-CHA	5.6
	LEARNING NEEDS		
TC:	Learning needs/available skills*	TC-LEA	5.7
TC:	Role of teacher in implementation*	TC-ROL	5.8

Student Characteristics		SC	6.0
SC:	Achievement/exposure to math	SC-ACH	6.1
SC:	Maturity	SC-MAT	6.2
SC:	SES	SC-SES	6.3

Student Reactions		SR	7.0
SR:	Change/learning	SR-CHA	7.1
SR:	Attitude	SR-ATT	7.2
SR:	Attention/cooperation/effort	SR-EFF	7.3

*Parent Reactions**		PR	8.0
PR:	Attitude*	PR-ATT	8.1
PR:	Communication with*	PR-COM	8.2

Implementation Environment		IE	9.0
IE:	Central office support/decisions	IE-CEN	9.1
IE:	Principal involvement/support	IE-PRI	9.2
IE:	Departmental support*	IE-DEP	9.3
IE:	Key person*	IE-KEY	9.4
IE:	External resources	IE-EXT	9.5
IE:	Implementation strategy	IE-IMP	9.6
IE:	Professional relationships*	IE-PRO	9.7
IE:	Organization of teaching	IE-ORG	9.8

IE:	Culture of teaching*	IE-CUL	9.9
IE:	Reinforcing activities*	IE-REI	9.10
IE:	Teacher responsibilities beyond the classroom	IE-RES	9.11

Notes

CHAPTER 2

1. For example, Boyer, 1983; Carnegie Forum on Education and the Economy, 1986; Education Commission of the States, 1983; Powell, Farrar, and Cohen, 1985; Sizer, 1984; Twentieth Century Fund, 1983.

2. As a result of Senate Bill 813 (1983) California's graduation requirements included 3 years each of English and social science; 2 years each of mathematics, science, and physical education; and 1 year of fine arts or foreign language. One semester of economics was added subsequently. Implementation of California's new requirements was swift (Grossman, Kirst, Negash, & Schmidt-Posner, 1985; Odden & Marsh, 1987).

3. The Hughes-Hart Educational Reform Act of 1983, Chapter 498, Statutes of California.

4. In contrast, see *Professional Standards for Teaching Mathematics* (National Council of Teachers of Mathematics, 1991), which accompanies the organization's *Curriculum and Evaluation Standards* (National Council of Teachers of Mathematics, 1989).

5. In contrast, a fidelity perspective asserts that the goal of implementation is faithful replication of a policy maker's intentions. The emphasis is on conformity with a policy template developed at a level removed from program operations. Granted, all implementation research implies a measure of concern with fidelity. But some policies—prepackaged, relatively explicit innovations, like the 55 mph speed limit—suggest the application of this perspective more than do others.

6. In the early 1990s, the state signed a contract with a publisher to compose a Math A textbook. The publisher produced several iterations, which were reviewed by California district staff and teachers. A district official in District 2 conveyed her satisfaction that the later drafts did indeed reflect the spirit of Math A and did improve the state-produced Math A units that teachers had been using for 3 years. Her district expected the textbook to be available in classrooms in fall 1992.

7. In contrast, highly specified, "programmed" implementation fits better with incremental change, certain technology, low conflict, and tightly coupled implementation systems (Berman, 1980).

8. Teaching for understanding emphasizes understanding as opposed to

recall, and a few generalizations rather than many rules. Other contrasts include conceptual schemes versus specific processes, global relationships versus sequential steps, broad application versus limited uses, takes longer to learn but is retained longer versus learned more quickly but is quickly forgotten, difficult versus easy to teach, and difficult versus easy to test (California State Department of Education, 1985, p. 13). See also, Cohen, McLaughlin, and Talbert (1993).

9. He continued: "Now we've got a completely different story when we start taking on Algebra 1, which is a terrible course. . . . [Algebra 1] is *the* filtering course; it is *the* gateway, or barrier, course for getting into college. So that's why it has so much support, not because of what it is, but because of the role it plays."

10. Adopted in 1991.

11. Beyond the core, students may take calculus or a recommended advanced course in probability and statistics.

CHAPTER 4

1. The number of teachers indicated in this list equals more than 12 because teachers expressed multiple goals.

2. Students significantly influence the terms of their work (Walker, 1990). A support-group teacher in this study described an instance of how these terms are negotiated in class: "It was real tough at the beginning of the semester, first part of the year. . . . [Math A is] a completely different way to teach and for the kids it's a completely different way to learn. And all they wanted to do was play, and I think we needed to reach a compromise. I couldn't be as strict as I am in my normal classes, and they had to come back from that this wasn't an hour of play time. [And was this compromise negotiated between you and the students?] Not verbally, but we worked it out. Just give-and-take here and there, and it worked out. Now we live through the day, and we have fun."

To the extent that teachers in this study interacted with students of widely differing levels of ability or cooperation, teachers' motivation to implement Math A would be expected to vary. However, network, staff development, and support-group teachers instructed students who were similar on characteristics such as achievement level, attitude, and socioeconomic status (see Appendix A). In part, this is a function of design. Math A was intended to serve a particular niche in the high school mathematics sequence, that is, post-eighth-grade arithmetic. And across the cases in this study, whether Math A served as a bridge into algebra or provided an alternative for students who had attempted algebra unsuccessfully, students possessed poor math skills and were described as at-risk in terms of educational failure—"really the pits," as one staff development teacher lamented. Most students were economically poor, and many were recent immigrants. Since teachers across these cases instructed students of similar characteristics, teachers' motivation would not be expected to vary widely based on this dimension alone.

3. Scheduling problems at a third network school, one not part of this study,

actually prevented all the network teachers from sharing the common preparation period, a central component of the network's implementation strategy.

CHAPTER 5

1. Ford and Ford (1987) defined motivation as the "selective direction, vigor, and persistence of behavior" (p. 27).

2. Nine teachers were funded, but one had a stroke and dropped out. A replacement teacher was selected but, at the time I conducted interviews, was meeting with the others only intermittently because of scheduling problems.

3. One teacher's strategy for addressing this problem involved manipulating the one part of the system over which she exerted some control. As she explained, "I've always wanted to start some kind of course, and I've tried many and I've failed many different times. I'll be the first to admit that. So it is very frustrating." Her sense of frustration was mitigated, however, by the knowledge that she was not alone: "I think if I was the only one who was feeling this way, then you just suffer alone. But it was very obvious that there was a number of us here in this school who felt exactly that way."

4. Such early information was available to teachers in Districts 2 and 3 also. A math resource teacher in District 2 attributed teachers' early interest in Math A, and their willingness to experiment with it in their classrooms, to this early availability of information and draft materials.

5. Other models are possible, even more likely, because this network drew critical financial support from a national foundation. Similar support would not be available widely nor would it be long-lived.

6. The disparity can be approximated by adding the number of structured hours demanded by each implementation strategy and dividing by eight to arrive at a days-per-year estimate of structured attention. This rough calculation reveals that staff development teachers interacted around Math A the equivalent of 10 days; support-group teachers, 6.25 days; and network teachers, 41 days. In other words, staff development and support-group strategies structured the attention of their teachers about 24% and 15%, respectively, of the time structured by the network. Thus, the opportunities for structured interaction among teachers varied widely between network and nonnetwork teachers in these cases.

CHAPTER 6

1. Two years in the district's pilot and 1½ years of informal experimentation before the pilot commenced.

2. Thanks to Milbrey McLaughlin for this insight.

3. This assessment of Math A stops short of describing outcomes for student learning. It merely reflects teachers' judgments that Math A seemed to be a good

match for their students' abilities and appeared to engage students in mathematical problem solving and reasoning in ways that other curricula failed to do.

APPENDIX A

1. Network analysis is not new to implementation studies, however (see Sabatier, 1986). My study of Math A implementation constitutes an analysis of a network's implementation, not a "network analysis" in the technical sense of mapping and analyzing teachers' interactions (cf. Freeman, 1989; Knoke & Kuklinski, 1982).

2. Teachers, of course, are embedded within departments, schools, districts, the state, and a profession. Their contexts are multiple and meaningful (McLaughlin & Talbert, 1990). Purkey and Smith (1983) argued that each organizational level in a school system establishes the context and defines the boundaries for the layer below. These embedded levels appear in this study as attributes of teachers' contexts. Teachers comment on these influences in terms of their impact on motivation, capacity, and practice.

3. An obvious potential comparison involved network and nonnetwork staff development teachers in District 1. After all, Math A was taught across the district, while only three schools participated in the network pilot. However, nonnetwork Math A teachers taught an essentially different Math A course, one based on an ersatz Math A text. As this different course never attempted to implement the state framework, comparability across network and nonnetwork classrooms was insufficient to justify a comparison of implementation experiences.

4. In District 1 I interviewed six of seven network teachers and observed four. In District 2 I interviewed and observed five of 10 Math A teachers. I dropped a sixth teacher from the study due to scheduling conflicts, and the fifth teacher, too, because he was so unlike his district peers: heavily involved in the state development of Math A, a staff development provider himself, and the "epitome" of a Math A teacher. In District 3, I interviewed five of 17 Math A teachers. Three of these had one more year of experience with Math A than other teachers in the district. The other two were teamed with one of the experienced teachers at their respective schools.

5. Interviews were transcribed by a professional typist and delivered to me on floppy disk. I corrected the transcripts by listening again to the interviews while I read along in the transcript and made appropriate corrections. This step also allowed me to revisit not only the words and thoughts but the emotions of the teachers and others involved. I printed corrected transcripts with each line of text numbered. Documents also were numbered and catalogued.

References

Adams, J. E., Jr. (1997). School finance policy and students' opportunities to learn: Kentucky's experience. *The Future of Children, 7*(3), 79–95.

Baier, V. E., March, J. G., & Sætren. (1988). Implementation and ambiguity. In J. G. March, *Decisions and organizations* (pp. 150–164). Oxford: Basil Blackwell.

Beck, L. G., & Murphy, J. (1996). *The four imperatives of a successful school.* Thousands Oaks, CA: Corwin Press.

Berman, P. (1980). Thinking about programmed and adaptive implementation: Matching strategies to situations. In H. Ingram & D. E. Mann (Eds.), *Why policies succeed or fail* (pp. 205–227). Beverly Hills, CA: Sage.

Berman, P., & McLaughlin, M. W. (1978). *Federal programs supporting educational change: Vol. VIII. Implementing and sustaining innovations* (R-1589/8-HEW). Santa Monica, CA: RAND Corporation.

Bird, T., & Little, J. W. (1986). How schools organize the teaching occupation. *Elementary School Journal, 86,* 493–510.

Bourque, M. L., & Garrison, H. H. (1991, September 30). *The levels of mathematics achievement: Initial performance standards for the 1990 NAEP mathematics assessment: Vol. 1. National and state summaries.* Washington, DC: National Assessment Governing Board.

Boyer, E. L. (1983). *High school: A report on secondary education in America.* New York: Harper Colophon.

Brooks, J. G., & Brooks, M. G. (1993). *In search of understanding: The case for constructivist classrooms.* Alexandria, VA: Association for Supervision and Curriculum Development.

Brophy, J. E., & Evertson, C. M. (1981). *Student characteristics and teaching.* New York: Longman.

Burt, R. S. (1982). *Toward a structural theory of action.* New York: Academic Press.

California Commission on the Teaching Profession. (1985). *Who will teach our children?* Sacramento: Author.

California State Department of Education. (n.d.). *Math A: A brief description.* Sacramento: Author.

California State Department of Education. (1985). *Mathematics framework for California public schools: Kindergarten through grade twelve.* Sacramento: Author.

California State Department of Education. (1991, January 29). *Math A materials for teachers.* Sacramento: Author.

Carnegie Forum on Education and the Economy. (1986). *A nation prepared: Teachers for the 21st century.* New York: Carnegie Corporation.

Carpenter, T. P., Lindquist, M. M., Brown, C. A., Kouba, V. L., Silver, E. A., & Swafford, J. O. (1988). Results of the fourth NAEP assessment of mathematics: Trends and conclusions. *Arithmetic Teacher, 36*(4), 38–41.

Cohen, D. K., McLaughlin, M. W., & Talbert, J. E. (Eds.). (1993). *Teaching for understanding: Challenges for policy and practice.* San Francisco: Jossey-Bass.

Cohen, D. K., & Peterson, P. L. (1990, June 18). *Effects of state-level reform of elementary school mathematics curriculum on classroom practice: Final report* (Grant No. R117 P8004). Washington, DC: U.S. Department of Education, Office of Educational Research and Improvement.

Cohen, S. G. (1993). New approaches to teams and teamwork. In J. R. Galbraith, E. E. Lawler, III, & Associates (Eds.), *Organizing for the future: The new logic of managing complex organizations* (pp. 194–226). San Francisco: Jossey-Bass.

Cooper, M. (1988). Whose culture is it, anyway? In A. Lieberman (Ed.), *Building a professional culture in schools* (pp. 45–54). New York: Teachers College Press.

Corcoran, T. B. (1990). Schoolwork: Perspectives on workplace reform in public schools. In M. W. McLaughlin, J. E. Talbert, & N. Bascia (Eds.), *The contexts of teaching in secondary schools: Teachers' realities* (pp. 142–166). New York: Teachers College Press.

Crandall, D. P., Bauchner, J. E., Loucks, S. F., & Schmidt, W. H. (1982). *Models of the school improvement process: Factors contributing to success: A study of dissemination efforts supporting school improvement.* Andover, MA: The Network.

Cuban, L. (1993). *How teachers taught: Constancy and change in American classrooms 1880–1990* (2nd ed.). New York: Teachers College Press.

Curriculum Development and Supplemental Materials Commission. (1990, December). *Draft mathematics framework for California public schools: Kindergarten through grade twelve.* Sacramento: California State Department of Education.

Darling-Hammond, L. (1985). Valuing teachers: The making of a profession. *Teachers College Record, 87,* 205–218.

David, J. L. (1993). *Redesigning an education system: Early observations from Kentucky.* Washington, DC: National Governors' Association.

David, J. L., & Goren, P. D. (1993). *Transforming education: Overcoming barriers.* Washington, DC: National Governors' Association.

Education Commission of the States. (1983). *Action for excellence.* Denver: Author.

Elmore, R. F. (1978). Organizational models of social program implementation. *Public Policy, 26,* 185–228.

Elmore, R. F., & McLaughlin, M. W. (1988). *Steady work: Policy, practice, and the reform of American education* (R-3574-NIE/RC). Santa Monica, CA: RAND Corporation.

Eulau, H., & Siegel, J. W. (1981). Social network analysis and political behavior: A feasibility study. *Western Political Quarterly, 34,* 499–509.

Feiman-Nemser, S., & Floden, R. E. (1985). The cultures of teaching. In M. C. Wittrock (Ed.), *Handbook of research on teaching* (3rd ed.; pp. 505–526). New York: Macmillan.

Fennema, E., & Nelson, B. S. (Eds.). (1997). *Mathematics teachers in transition.* Mahwah, NJ: Erlbaum.

Firestone, W. A., & Corbett, H. D. (1988). Planned organizational change. In N. J. Boyan (Ed.), *Handbook of research on educational administration* (pp. 321–340). New York: Longman.

Ford, M. E. (1992). *Motivating humans: Goals, emotions, and personal agency beliefs.* Newbury Park, CA: Sage.

Ford, M. E., & Ford, D. H. (1987). Humans as self-constructing living systems. In M. E. Ford & D. H. Ford (Eds.), *Humans as self-constructing living systems: Putting the framework to work* (pp. 1–46). Hillsdale, NJ: Erlbaum.

Fosnot, C. T. (Ed.). (1996). *Constructivism: Theory, perspectives, and practice.* New York: Teachers College Press.

Freeman, L. C. (1989). Social networks and the structure experiment. In L. C. Freeman, D. R. White, & A. K. Romney (Eds.), *Research methods in social network analysis* (pp. 11–40). Fairfax, VA: George Mason University Press.

Fuhrman, S., Clune, W. H., & Elmore, R. F. (1988). Research on education reform: Lessons on the implementation of policy. *Teachers College Record, 90,* 237–257.

Fullan, M. G. (with Stiegelbauer, S.). (1991). *The new meaning of educational change* (2nd ed.). New York: Teachers College Press.

Fullan, M. G. (1992). *Successful school improvement: The implementation perspective and beyond.* Toronto: Ontario Institute for Studies in Education.

Fullan, M. G., & Miles, M. B. (1992). Getting reform right: What works and what doesn't. *Phi Delta Kappan, 73,* 745–752.

Fullan, M., & Pomfret, A. (1977). Research on curriculum implementation. *Review of Educational Research, 47,* 335–397.

General Accounting Office. (1987). *Case study evaluations* (Methodology Transfer Paper 9). Washington, DC: Program Evaluation and Methodology Division.

George, A. L. (1979). Case studies and theory development: The method of structured, focused comparison. In P. G. Lauren (Ed.), *Diplomacy: New approaches in history, theory, and policy* (pp. 43–68). New York: Free Press.

George, C. (1987). *A study of the implementation of the model curriculum standards in California high schools.* Sacramento: California State Department of Education.

Giganti, P. (1991). A community of learners. *Educator, 5*(2), 5–8.

Goggin, M. L. (1986). The "too few cases/too many variables" problem in implementation research. *Western Political Quarterly, 39,* 328–347.

Goggin, M. L., Bowman, A. O., Lester, J. P., & O'Toole, L. J., Jr. (1990). *Implementation theory and practice: Toward a third generation.* Glenview, IL: Scott, Foresman/Little Brown Higher Education.

Goodson, I. F. (1990). Studying curriculum: Towards a social constructivist perspective. *Journal of Curriculum Studies, 22,* 299–312.

Grossman, P., Kirst, M. W., Negash, W., & Schmidt-Posner, J. (1985). *Curricular change in California comprehensive high schools: 1982–83 to 1984–85* (Policy Paper No. PP85-7-4). Berkeley: University of California, Policy Analysis for California Education (PACE).

Hall, G. E., & Hord, S. M. (1987). *Change in schools: Facilitating the process.* Albany: State University of New York Press.

Hall, G. E., & Loucks, S. F. (1978). Teacher concerns as a basis for facilitating and personalizing staff development. *Teachers College Record, 80,* 36ff.

Hanushek, E. A. (1994). *Making schools work.* Washington, DC: Brookings Institution.

Hawley, W. D. (1978). Horses before carts: Developing adaptive schools and the limits of innovation. In D. Mann (Ed.), *Making change happen* (pp. 224–253). New York: Teachers College Press.

Hering, W. M. (1983, April). *An analysis of the extent, method, and content of interactions among participants in an informal, interactive education network.* Paper presented at the annual meeting of the American Educational Research Association, Montreal. (ERIC Document Reproduction Service No. ED 228 187)

Honig, B. (1985). The educational excellence movement: Now comes the hard part. *Phi Delta Kappan, 66,* 675–681.

Honig, B. (1988). The key to reform: Sustaining and expanding upon initial success. *Educational Administration Quarterly, 24,* 257–271.

Huberman, M. (1982). Making changes from exchanges: Some frameworks for studying the teachers' centers exchange. In K. Devaney, *Networking on purpose* (pp. 87–114). San Francisco: Far West Laboratory for Educational Research and Development.

Huberman, M., & Miles, M. (1984). *Innovation up close: How school improvement works.* New York: Plenum.

Ingram, H. (1977). Policy implementation through bargaining: The case of federal grants-in-aid. *Public Policy, 25,* 499–526.

Ingram, H. M., & Mann, D. E. (1980). Policy failure: An issue deserving analysis. In H. M. Ingram & D. E. Mann (Eds.), *Why policies succeed or fail* (pp. 11–32). Beverly Hills, CA: Sage.

Johnson, S. M. (1990). *Teachers at work: Achieving success in our schools.* New York: Basic Books.

Jones, D. (1997). A conceptual framework for studying the relevance of context to mathematics teachers' change. In E. Fennema & B. S. Nelson (Eds.), *Mathematics teachers in transition* (pp. 131–154). Mahwah, NJ: Erlbaum.

Kirst, M. W. (1988). Recent state education reform in the United States: Looking backward and forward. *Educational Administration Quarterly, 24,* 319–328.

Kirst, M. W., & Jung, R. (1980). The utility of a longitudinal approach in assessing implementation. *Educational Evaluation and Policy Analysis, 2,* 17–34.

Kirst, M. W., & Walker, D. F. (1971). An analysis of curriculum policy-making. *Review of Educational Research, 41,* 479–509.

Knoke, D., & Kuklinski, J. H. (1982). *Network analysis.* Beverly Hills, CA: Sage.

Koppich, J., Gerritz, W., & Guthrie, J. W. (1986). *A view from the classroom: California teachers' opinions on working conditions and school reform proposals.* Berkeley: University of California, Policy Analysis for California Education (PACE).

Lampert, M. (1988). What can research on teacher education tell us about improving quality in mathematics education? *Teaching and Teacher Education, 4,* 157–170.

Lave, C. A., & March, J. G. (1975). *An introduction to models in the social sciences.* New York: Harper & Row.

Lieberman, A. (1995). Practices that support teacher development. *Phi Delta Kappan, 76,* 591–596.

Lieberman, A., & Grolnick, M. (1996). *Networks and reform in American education.* Paper prepared for the National Center for Restructuring Education, Schools, and Teaching (NCREST), Teachers College, Columbia University.

Lieberman, A., & Grolnick, M. (1998). Educational reform networks: Changes in the forms of reform. In A. Hargreaves, A. Lieberman, M. Fullan, & D. Hopkins (Eds.), *International handbook of educational change* (pp. 710–729). Boston: Kluwer Academic.

Lieberman, A., & McLaughlin, M. W. (1992). Networks for educational change: Powerful and problematic. *Phi Delta Kappan, 73,* 673–677.

Lieberman, A., & Miller, L. (Eds.). (1991). *Staff development for education in the '90s: New demands, new realities, new perspectives* (2nd ed.). New York: Teacher College Press.

Lijphart, A. (1971). Comparative politics and the comparative method. *American Political Science Review, 65,* 682–693.

Lipsky, M. (1980). *Street-level bureaucracy.* New York: Russell Sage Foundation.

Little, J. W. (1984). Seductive images and organizational realities in professional development. *Teachers College Record, 86,* 84–102.

Little, J. W. (1990a). Conditions of professional development in secondary schools. In M. W. McLaughlin, J. E. Talbert, & N. Bascia (Eds.), *The contexts of teaching in secondary schools: Teachers' realities* (pp. 187–223). New York: Teachers College Press.

Little, J. W. (1990b). The persistence of privacy: Autonomy and initiative in teachers' professional relations. *Teachers College Record, 91,* 509–536.

Little, J. W., Gerritz, W. H., Stern, D. S., Guthrie, J. W., Kirst, M. W., & Marsh, D. S. (1987). *Staff development in California: Public and personal investments, program patterns, and policy choices.* San Francisco and Berkeley: Far West Laboratory for Educational Research and Development, and University of California, Berkeley, Policy Analysis for California Education (PACE).

Lortie, D. C. (1975). *Schoolteacher.* Chicago: University of Chicago Press.

Louis, K. S., Marks, H. M., & Kruse, S. (1996). Teachers' professional community in restructuring schools. *American Educational Research Journal, 33,* 757–798.

McDonnell, L. M., & Elmore, R. F. (1987). Getting the job done: Alternative policy instruments. *Educational Evaluation and Policy Analysis, 9,* 133–152.

McLaughlin, M. W. (1987). Learning from experience: Lessons from policy implementation. *Educational Evaluation and Policy Analysis, 9,* 171–178.

McLaughlin, M. W. (1990a). The RAND change agent study revisited: Macro perspectives and micro realities. *Educational Researcher, 19*(9), 11–16.

McLaughlin, M. W. (1990b). *Strategic dimensions of teachers' workplace context* (Report No. P90-119). Stanford: Stanford University, Center for Research on the Context of Secondary Teaching.

McLaughlin, M. W. (1991). Enabling professional development: What have we learned? In A. Lieberman & L. Miller (Eds.), *Staff development for education in the '90s: New demands, new realities, new perspectives* (2nd ed.; pp. 61–82). New York: Teachers College Press.

McLaughlin, M. W. (1993). What matters most in teachers' workplace context? In

J. W. Little & M. W. McLaughlin (Eds.), *Teachers' work* (pp. 79–103). New York: Teachers College Press.

McLaughlin, M. W. (1998). Listening and learning from the field: Tales of policy implementation and situated practice. In A. Hargreaves, A. Lieberman, M. Fullan, & D. Hopkins (Eds.), *International handbook of educational change* (pp. 70–84). Boston: Kluwer Academic.

McLaughlin, M. W., & Marsh, D. D. (1978). Staff development and school change. *Teachers College Record, 80*, 69–94.

McLaughlin, M. W., & Oberman, I. (1996). *Teacher learning: New policies, new practices.* New York: Teachers College Press.

McLaughlin, M. W., Pfeifer, R. S., Swanson-Owens, D., & Yee, S. (1986). Why teachers won't teach. *Phi Delta Kappan, 67,* 420–426.

McLaughlin, M. W., & Talbert, J. E. (1990). The contexts in question: The secondary school workplace. In M. W. McLaughlin, J. E. Talbert, & N. Bascia (Eds.), *The contexts of teaching in secondary schools: Teachers' realities* (pp. 1–14). New York: Teachers College Press.

McLaughlin, M. W., & Yee, S. M. (1988). School as a place to have a career. In A. Lieberman (Ed.), *Building a professional culture in schools* (pp. 23–44). New York: Teachers College Press.

Metz, M. H. (1993). Teachers' ultimate dependence on their students. In J. W. Little & M. W. McLaughlin (Eds.), *Teachers' work* (pp. 104–136). New York: Teachers College Press.

Miles, M. B. (1978). *On "networking."* Unpublished manuscript. (ERIC Document Reproduction Service No. ED 181 874)

Mullis, I. V. A., Dossey, J. A., Foertsch, M. A., Jones, L. R., & Gentile, C. A. (1991, November). *Trends in academic progress* (Report No. 21-T-01). Washington, DC: U.S. Department of Education, Office of Educational Research and Improvement, National Center for Education Statistics.

Mullis, I. V. A., Dossey, J. A., Owen, E. H., & Phillips, G. W. (1991, June). *The state of mathematics achievement: Executive summary: NAEP's 1990 assessment of the nation and the trial assessment of the states* (Report No. 21-ST-03). Washington, DC: U.S. Department of Education, Office of Educational Research and Improvement, National Center for Education Statistics.

Murnane, R. J., & Levy, F. (1996). *Teaching the new basic skills.* New York: Free Press.

Murphy, J. (1990). The educational reform movement of the 1980s: A comprehensive analysis. In J. Murphy (Ed.), *The educational reform movement of the 1980s: Perspectives and cases* (pp. 3–56). Berkeley: McCutchan.

Murphy, J., & Adams, J. E., Jr. (1998). Reforming America's schools 1980–2000. *Journal of Educational Administration, 36,* 426–444.

National Commission on Excellence in Education. (1983). *A nation at risk: The imperative for educational reform.* Washington, DC: U. S. Department of Education.

National Commission on Teaching and America's Future. (1996). *What matters most: Teaching for America's future.* New York: Author.

National Council of Teachers of Mathematics. (1989). *Curriculum and evaluation standards for school mathematics.* Reston, VA: Author.

National Council of Teachers of Mathematics. (1991). *Professional standards for teaching mathematics.* Reston, VA: Author.

National Research Council. (1989). *Everybody counts: A report to the nation on the future of mathematics education.* Washington, DC: National Academy Press.

National Research Council. (1990). *Reshaping school mathematics: A philosophy and framework for curriculum.* Washington, DC: National Academy Press.

National Science Board. (1983). *Educating Americans for the 21st century.* Washington, DC: National Science Foundation.

Nias, J. (1998). Why teachers need their colleagues: A developmental perspective. In A. Hargreaves, A. Lieberman, M. Fullan, & D. Hopkins (Eds.), *International handbook of educational change* (pp. 1257–1271). Boston: Kluwer Academic.

Odden, A. (1991). New patterns of education policy implementation and challenges for the 1990s. In A. Odden (Ed.), *Education policy implementation* (pp. 297–327). Albany: State University of New York Press.

Odden, A. R., & Busch, C. (1998). *Financing schools for high performance.* San Francisco: Jossey-Bass.

Odden, A. R., & Marsh, D. D. (1987). *How state education reform can improve secondary schools* (Policy Paper No. PC87-12-14-SDE). Berkeley: University of California, Policy Analysis for California Education (PACE).

Palumbo, D. J., & Calista, D. J. (1990). Opening up the black box: Implementation and the policy process. In D. J. Palumbo & D. J. Calista (Eds.), *Implementation and the policy process: Opening up the black box* (pp. 3–18). New York: Greenwood Press.

Patton, M. Q. (1990). *Qualitative evaluation and research methods* (2nd ed.). Newbury Park, CA: Sage.

Paulson, S. K. (1985). A paradigm for the analysis of interorganizational networks. *Social Networks, 7,* 105–126.

Peterson, P. E. (1977). *Schools, groups, and networks: A political perspective.* Unpublished manuscript, University of Chicago. (ERIC Document Reproduction Service No. ED 181 876)

Peterson, P. E., Rabe, B. G., & Wong, K. K. (1986). *When federalism works.* Washington, DC: Brookings Institution.

Powell, A. G., Farrar, E., & Cohen, D. K. (1985). *The shopping mall high school: Winners and losers in the educational market place.* Boston: Houghton Mifflin.

Purkey, S. C., & Smith, M. S. (1983). Effective schools: A review. *Elementary School Journal, 83,* 427–452.

Rogers, E. M., & Kincaid, D. L. (1981). *Communication networks: Toward a new paradigm for research.* New York: Free Press.

Romberg, T. A. (1988). *Changes in school mathematics: Curricular changes, instructional changes, and indicators of changes* (CPRE Research Report Series RR-007). New Brunswick, NJ: Rutgers University, Center for Policy Research in Education.

Romberg, T. A. (1989). *Reform of school mathematics.* Memo prepared for the Center for Policy Research in Education, University of Wisconsin.

Rosenholtz, S. J. (1989). *Teachers' workplace.* New York: Longman.

Rosenholtz, S. J., & Kyle, S. J. (1984). Teacher isolation: Barriers to professionalism. *American Educator, 8*(4), 10–15.

Sabatier, P. A. (1986). Top-down and bottom-up approaches to implementation research: A critical analysis and suggested synthesis. *Journal of Public Policy, 6,* 21–48.

Salomon, G., & Perkins, D. N. (1998). Individual and social aspects of learning. In P. D. Pearson & A. Iran-Nejad (Eds.), *Review of research in education* (Vol. 23, pp. 1–24). Washington, DC: American Educational Research Association.

Sarason, S. B. (1990). *The predictable failure of educational reform.* San Francisco: Jossey-Bass.

Scherer, J. (1981). The working of nets: Executive summary and policy recommendations, Part IV. Rochester, MI: Oakland University. (ERIC Document Reproduction Service No. ED 227 186)

Secada, W. G., & Adajian, L. B. (1997). Mathematics teachers' change in the context of their professional communities. In E. Fennema & B. S. Nelson (Eds.), *Mathematics teachers in transition* (pp. 193–219). Mahwah, NJ: Erlbaum.

Sizer, T. R. (1984). *Horace's compromise: The dilemma of the American high school.* Boston: Houghton Mifflin.

Smith, J. R. (1991, August 21). *Memorandum to potential applicants for participation in the Middle Grades Mathematics Renaissance.* Sacramento: California State Department of Education.

Smith, M. S., & O'Day, J. (1991). Systemic school reform. In S. Fuhrman & B. Malen (Eds.), *The politics of curriculum and testing* (pp. 233–268). Philadelphia: Falmer Press.

Snyder, J., Bolin, F., & Zumwalt, K. (1992). Curriculum implementation. In P. W. Jackson (Ed.), *Handbook of research on curriculum implementation* (pp. 402–435). New York: Macmillan.

Stanley, D. (1989). *Design and implementation of the Math A course.* Berkeley: University of California, Professional Development Program (PDP).

Stocks, J., & Schofield, J. (1997). Educational reform and professional development. In E. Fennema & B. S. Nelson (Eds.), *Mathematics teachers in transition* (pp. 283–308). Mahwah, NJ: Erlbaum.

Truman, D. B. (1951). *The governmental process: Political interests and public opinion.* New York: Knopf.

Twentieth Century Fund. (1983). *Making the grade.* New York: Author.

U.S. Department of Education. (1991). *American 2000: An education strategy.* Washington, DC: U.S. Government Printing Office.

Walker, D. F. (1990). *Fundamentals of curriculum.* San Diego: Harcourt Brace Jovanovich.

Weatherley, R., & Lipsky, M. (1977). Street-level bureaucrats and institutional innovation: Implementing special-education reform. *Harvard Educational Review, 47,* 171–197.

Wildavsky, A. (1979). *Speaking truth to power: The art and craft of policy analysis.* Boston: Little, Brown.

Winter, S. (1990). Integrating implementation research. In D. J. Palumbo & D. J.

Calista (Eds.), *Implementation and the policy process: Opening up the black box* (pp. 19–38). New York: Greenwood Press.

Wisconsin Center for Education Research. (1992). Collaboration breaks mathematics teacher isolation and builds professionalism. *WCER Highlights, 4,* 1–2. (University of Wisconsin–Madison, School of Education)

Yin, R. K. (1989). *Case study research: Design and methods* (rev. ed.). Newbury Park, CA: Sage.

Index

About the Author

JACOB E. ADAMS, JR. (Ph.D., Stanford University) is an associate professor of education and public policy at Peabody College, Vanderbilt University, and a research fellow with the Peabody Center for Education Policy. He also serves as chairman of the board of directors of the Kentucky Institute for Education Research. Professor Adams's research focuses on the policy context of education, with particular attention to ways in which finance, implementation, and accountability policies shape school capacity. Prior to his academic career, Dr. Adams worked for federal, state, and local governmental officials and served as associate director of Policy Analysis for California Education (PACE), a state education policy research center located jointly at the University of California–Berkeley and Stanford University.